LIFE IN THE FACE OF DEATH

McMaster New Testament Studies

The McMaster New Testament Studies series, edited by Richard N. Longe-necker, is designed to address particular themes in the New Testament that are of concern to Christians today. Written in a style easily accessible to ministers, students, and laypeople by contributors who are proven experts in their fields of study, the volumes in this series reflect the best of current biblical scholarship while also speaking directly to the pastoral needs of people in the church today.

Life in the Face of Death

*The Resurrection Message
of the New Testament*

Edited by

Richard N. Longenecker

WILLIAM B. EERDMANS PUBLISHING COMPANY
GRAND RAPIDS, MICHIGAN / CAMBRIDGE, U.K.

CONTENTS

03 02 01 00 99 98   7 6 5 4 3 2 1

ISBN 0-8028-4474-X

Contents

CONTENTS

Contributors

RICHARD BAUCKHAM   Professor of New Testament Studies, School of Divinity, St. Mary's College, University of St. Andrews, St. Andrews, Scotland, UK

PETER G. BOLT   Lecturer, Biblical Studies, Moore Theological College, Sydney, Australia

JOEL B. GREEN   Associate Dean of the School of Theology and Professor of New Testament Interpretation, Asbury Theological Seminary, Wilmore, Kentucky, USA

DONALD A. HAGNER   George Eldon Ladd Professor of New Testament, Fuller Theological Seminary, Pasadena, California, USA

G. WALTER HANSEN   Associate Professor of New Testament and Director of Global Research Institute, Fuller Theological Seminary, Pasadena, California, USA

MURRAY J. HARRIS   Professor Emeritus of New Testament Exegesis and Theology, Trinity Evangelical Divinity School, Deerfield, Illinois, USA

WILLIAM L. LANE   Paul T. Walls Professor of Wesleyan and Biblical Studies, Department of Religion, Seattle Pacific University, Seattle, Washington, USA

ANDREW T. LINCOLN   Senior Professor of New Testament, Wycliffe College, University of Toronto, Toronto, Ontario, Canada

CONTRIBUTORS

RICHARD N. LONGENECKER   Distinguished Professor of New Testament, McMaster Divinity College, McMaster University, Hamilton, Ontario, Canada

ALLISON A. TRITES   Payzant Distinguished Professor of Biblical Studies, Acadia Divinity College, Acadia University, Wolfville, Nova Scotia, Canada

EDWIN YAMAUCHI   Professor, History Department, Miami University, Miami, Ohio, USA

Preface

THIS IS the third volume in the McMaster New Testament Studies series, sponsored by McMaster Divinity College, Hamilton, Ontario, Canada. The series is designed to address particular themes in the New Testament that are (or should be) of crucial concern to Christians today. The plan is to prepare and publish annual symposium volumes, with the contributors being selected because of their proven expertise in the areas assigned and their known ability to write intelligibly for readers who are not necessarily academics. Each article included in the symposium volumes, therefore, will evidence first-class biblical scholarship but will also be written in a manner capable of capturing the interest of intelligent laypeople, theological students, and ministers. In purpose, the articles will be both scholarly and pastoral. In format, they will be styled to reflect the best of contemporary, constructive scholarship, but in a way that is able to be understood by and speaks to the needs of alert and intelligent people in the church today.

This third symposium volume in the MNTS series focuses on the resurrection message of the New Testament, asking, in particular, regarding the significance of that message for the living of life, the facing of death, and the longing for the future after death. It is a subject that lies at the heart of the Christian gospel and that resonates with most of the deepest concerns of the human consciousness. It is also a subject that has often been treated exegetically, theologically, and pastorally. We believe, however, that it needs firmer rootage in the biblical materials and better personal application than it usually receives in either scholarly writings or the popular press. So we have prepared this third MNTS volume with the hope that it will prove to be of help to many earnest Christians who seek to think and live in a more Christian fashion, and thereby have a positive impact on the church at large.

Unabashedly, the authors of this volume have taken certain critical stances and used a variety of interpretive methods in their respective treatments. The only criterion they have followed in so doing is that of greatest compatibility with the material being studied. It is expected that their academic expertise will be evident in what they write. More than that, however, it is hoped that through their efforts the resurrection message of the New Testament will be more truly and ably presented than is usually the case. And what is prayed for is that by such a truer and abler presentation, Christians will be strengthened and encouraged in their respective ministries, pilgrimages, and witness as they continue to live out their lives in the face of their most bitter foe, death.

Our heartfelt thanks are expressed to Dr. William H. Brackney, Principal and Dean of McMaster Divinity College, and to the faculty, administration, and boards of the college, for their encouragement and support of the entire project. We also express our deep appreciation to the family of Herbert Henry Bingham, B.A., B.Th., D.D., a noted Canadian Baptist minister and administrator of the previous generation, which has generously funded the third annual "H. H. Bingham Colloquium in New Testament" at McMaster Divinity College, held during June 16-17, 1997. It was at that colloquium that the authors of the present volume presented their papers and received criticism from one another, from the editor, and from others in attendance, before then reworking and polishing their papers, as necessary, prior to final editing and the normal publication process. Most heartily, however, we thank those who have written articles for this volume, for they have taken time out of busy academic schedules to write in a more popular fashion — in many cases, distilling from their academic publications material of pertinence for the Christian church generally. We also thank Dr. Allan W. Martens, my able assistant, and Dr. Daniel C. Harlow, Editor of Biblical Studies at Eerdmans, for their expert editorial work on the volume. And we thank Bill Eerdmans and the Wm. B. Eerdmans Publishing Company for their continued support of the series.

THE EDITOR

CHAPTER 1

Introduction

RICHARD N. LONGENECKER

LIFE IS for living! But there is also a dark side to life: the mocking specter of death that permeates every facet of human activity and invades every corner of our human consciousness. Death is a stark and haunting reality that is very much a part of the personal story of us all.

Death is, in fact, the great enigma of life. Why, with all of life's potential and promise, all of life's preparations, all of life's accomplishments, must everything end in death? Why this termination of our human existence? It is also the ultimate frustration. For despite humanity's cleverness, we are all powerless before its inevitability. We may postpone it through advances in medical science, assuage its physical pains through drugs, relieve its emotional trauma through palliative care, rationalize its purpose, or even deny its existence. But we cannot escape it!

Many view death as "the fundamental crime" that makes life ultimately futile. Shakespeare in *Macbeth* captured the despair that most people must have felt in seventeenth century England:

> Out, out brief candle!
> Life's but a walking shadow, a poor player, that struts and frets his
> hour upon the stage, and then is heard no more. It is a tale told by an
> idiot, full of sound and fury, signifying nothing.
> (Act 5, Scene 5)

And such a view continues to epitomize the attitude of many people today — with some going on to modernize it by speaking out against the stupidity and cruelty of achieving an irrelevant old age in a sharply changed world.

1

1. Two Common Responses

Death as an Ultimate Good

It can be argued, of course, that life without death would lack meaning and significance — that is, that nothing of positive value (i.e., "life") can be appreciated without seeing it in relation to its negative (i.e., "death"). The gods of the Greek pantheon are a case in point. Though quantitatively greater than humans in their powers, virtues, and vices, they were qualitatively different from mortal men and women *only* in the fact that they were immortal. They were destined to live forever and so were not subject to "fate," whereas all humans die. But this meant, as Laszlo Versényi points out:

> Since they face nothing ultimate — literally the last thing — nothing ultimately serious and irremediable ever happens to them. Since it is not their fate to die, life itself loses its urgency; no issue, no single moment of it is of fateful importance. Life itself is simply not fatal to them. In contrast to men, for all their passing sorrows and afflictions, the gods live without true seriousness. (*Man's Measure*, 32-33)

Indeed, the reality and inevitability of death often give new meaning and significance to one's life. This is the testimony of countless people who have brushed up against death in some personal manner — whether through war, accident, illness, or some other calamity. It is, in fact, a truth of great importance for any theory of ethics or human endeavor. "Nothing," as Boswell once caustically observed, "so focuses the mind as the spectre of death."

Yet though philosophically viable, such an axiom provides little comfort when one actually encounters death directly. For though explainable as necessary for the betterment of the human race generally, the heavy mantle of the inevitability of death still weighs humanity down with fear and dread. Death still remains for each of us our greatest terror and our most bitter foe.

Death as Religion's Trump Card

It is also often said that death is religion's "trump card," for people fear death and religion capitalizes on that fear by claiming to provide answers.

But death is not the invention of religion. Rather, death is religion's greatest challenge. For every religion and every religious philosophy "worth its salt" — or, at least, with any hope of acceptance — must necessarily offer some explanation for death's universal tyranny, some program for alleviating death's effects, and some hope for death's final eradication, thereby providing people with a way of living out their lives in the presence of this ultimate and most vexing human problem.

2. Seven Classical and Distinctive Approaches

Seven rather classical and distinctive approaches to human death have been offered by the world's major religions and religious philosophies. These seven may be identified as follows — leaving the development of the New Testament's resurrection message to the authors of the present volume.

Hinduism — The Way of Negation

In the *Vedas* (Sanskrit for "knowledge"), the oldest writings of Hinduism, little attention is paid to death as such. The authors of these psalms, incantations, hymns, and formulas of worship were mostly interested in life and so speak only vaguely about death and an afterlife. The *Vedas* have no developed concept of the soul and fear most what is referred to as "re-death" or "the second death" — that is, as Krishna called it, "the terrible wheel of death and rebirth."

The *Upanishads* (Sanskrit for "sitting down beside" or "secret session"), which is a philosophical collection of teachings on the *Vedas* that dates from the seventh century B.C., however, view life far more negatively than do the *Vedas* themselves. The *Upanishads* give prominence to *Atman*, the eternal "soul," which is the inmost being of every person and the inmost essence of all that exists. This inmost "soul" has no personal characteristics and so is both birthless and deathless. And it is Hinduism as defined by the *Upanishads* that is most practiced in India today and is the best known form of Hinduism worldwide.

In Hinduism, as interpreted by the *Upanishads*, death has no reality at all, for the soul has neither a beginning nor an end. What appears to be born and subsequently to die is not real, but only an illusion — with such an

3

illusion being the creation of, and so totally subject to, the contingent world. It is only because people have misunderstood their true natures and that of the world about them that they believe in such concepts as "birth" and "death." But they can deliver themselves from this ignorance by the acquisition of the true knowledge that comes about by the spiritual discipline of *Yoga*.

For Hinduism, then, the endless cycle of the reincarnation of the soul is the basic human problem, not death. Physical death is only the end of one's illusory self. The endless cycle of reincarnation, however, goes on and on until finally the full acquisition of knowledge comes about. And that knowledge is defined primarily in terms of negation: the recognition of the illusory character of everything that appears to exist, and so the denial of the seemingly phenomenal stuff that makes up everything pertaining to people and the world.

Buddhism — The Way of Acceptance

Buddhism and Hinduism in their "purer" forms have much in common. In fact, Buddhism is often thought of as a non-orthodox expression of Hinduism, since both lay stress on the path of true enlightenment for understanding and overcoming death. Yet Gautama Buddha (ca. 563-483 B.C.) rejected the authority of the *Vedas* and opposed the *Upanishads* in their assertion that death is illusory. Rather, Buddha insisted that both suffering and death are real and so cannot be dealt with simply by negation.

No facet of a person's life, according to Buddhist teaching, is free from the forces of natural causation in the world or can escape final oblivion. This includes suffering and death, which are inextricable features of human existence. The problem for humans is not the illusory nature of suffering and death. Rather, it is the fact that human beings try to be permanent entities in an impermanent world — that humans fail, through a lack of knowledge, to accept their own situation. In resisting impermanence and change, people suffer; and in denying death, they only delude themselves.

For Buddhism, death is an unavoidable fact of human existence that must be fatalistically accepted. Death causes anguish only when one tries to elude it — either by explaining it away or by attempting to retreat into the confines of some eternal soul supposedly untouched by it. Rather, the supreme spiritual achievement of Buddhists is *Anatman* (or *Anatta*), where one enters into a state of "non-self" by means of contemplation. In fact, one of the methods practiced by Buddhist monks for overcoming a fear of death, for being free from a revulsion to change and decay, and for suppressing unwarranted desires for permanence or changelessness is to contemplate over a long period of time the situation of a human corpse in its various stages of decomposition. For by such a method one can be trained to accept that both death and life are ultimately nothing, and thereby be brought into a state of "non-self."

Confucianism — The Way of Resignation

The Chinese philosopher Confucius (ca. 551-479 B.C.) devoted far less attention to the subject of death than did the writers of the *Vedas* or the *Upanishads*, or than did his contemporary Gautama Buddha. Confucius advocated a social, ethical, and political system of teaching that focused entirely on living here and now both ethically and well. He was generally unconcerned about speculations about death and was agnostic regarding any afterlife. For him and for the purer forms of Confucianism after him, the most that can be said about death is: "Where there is life there must be death, and where there is a beginning there must be an end. Such is the natural course" (quoting the Confucian scholar Yang Hsiung, who lived ca. 53 B.C.–A.D. 18, from his *Fa Yen*).

But Confucianism has become intermingled down through the centuries with Taoism, Buddhism, and a variety of popular views of death and the afterlife. As a result, many Confucianists today believe in the continued existence of an indestructible soul and in a Chinese version of reincarnation — that is, that at death the human substance returns to the natural processes from which it originally came, there to reenter the cosmic cycles of production and dissolution. So the prevalent attitude toward death within popular Confucianism is that of acceptance and resignation (so paralleling modern humanism), though with a bit of Chinese-style reincarnation thrown in as well.

Platonism — The Release of an Inherently Immortal Soul

The most prevalent non-Christian view of death in the Western world had its origin in the teachings of the Greek philosopher Plato (ca. 427-347 B.C.).

In the Orphic cult, which claimed to stem from the legendary Thracian poet and musician Orpheus, the celebrated pun was *sōma sēma,* "the body is a tomb." Out of this conceptual background, Plato developed his doctrine of the inherent immortality of the human soul and his view of death.

In his earlier *Apology,* which depicts Socrates' defense at his trial, Plato is rather reserved and ambiguous regarding death. For while he presents Socrates as believing that he had "great reason to hope that death is a good," the reasons given for such a hope seem somewhat tentative: "Either death is a state of nothingness and utter unconsciousness, or, as we are told, there is a change and migration of the soul from this world to another place" (*Apology* 40C). Furthermore, Socrates' final words in the *Apology* leave matters quite unresolved regarding the relative merits of life versus death, and vice versa: "The hour of departure has arrived, and we go our ways — I to die, and you to live. Which is better only God knows" (ibid. 42A). In his later *Phaedo,* however, which purports to be a conversation between Socrates and his friends on the day of Socrates' execution, Plato is more definite: "When death attacks a man, his mortal part dies but his immortal part retreats before death, and goes away safe and indestructible" (*Phaedo* 106E).

In the *Phaedo* Plato says that Socrates' reasons for believing that the soul is immortal were based chiefly on his view of the nature of knowledge: (1) that knowledge is composed of ideas, and ideas can neither come from things nor consist in things; (2) that ideas are changeless and eternal, without themselves coming into existence or passing away; and (3) that since ideas reside in the soul and not in anything material, it must follow that the soul is also changeless and eternal (*Phaedo* 99D–107A). Yet Plato concludes the *Phaedo* by having Socrates relate a "tale" to his friends regarding the destiny of the soul after its release from the body, which story concludes with these words: "A man of sense will not insist that these things are exactly as I have described them. But I think that he will believe that something of the kind is true of the soul and her habitations, seeing that she is shown to be immortal, and that it is worth his while to stake everything on this belief" (ibid. 114D).

In Greek philosophical thought as influenced by Plato, there is, therefore, a basic anthropological dualism: the body is corporeal and mortal, with physical death inevitable; but the soul is noncorporeal and immortal, with what makes up the soul being the true essence of a person. The relation of the soul to the body is comparable to that of a grain of wheat in its husk, an oyster in its shell, or a ghost in a machine — or, stated more crudely in today's parlance, comparable to an angel in a slot machine. The body imprisons the soul during one's human existence (so the pun *sōma sēma*, "the body is a tomb"), with the result that as long as the soul remains imprisoned in the body, true wisdom cannot be fully acquired. At death, however, the soul is released from its imprisonment. So while physical death was never taken lightly by the Greeks, sorrow over a person's death was mitigated by the thought of the true person being released from his or her material confinement. At times, in fact, death was welcomed and suicide condoned, particularly when circumstances were considered terribly adverse and situations impossible.

Judaism — Death a Fearsome and Tyrannical Foe, Yet Hope in God

In the Hebrew Scriptures death is viewed as a fearsome and tyrannical foe. Yet there is also expressed in those same writings a hope in God for the future. In the main, that hope is focused on God's faithfulness to his people, the nation Israel: its continuation, protection, increase, prosperity, and influence.

Such a hope for the welfare of the people of Israel corporately is exemplified in God's promise given to Abraham in Gen 12:3:

> I will make you into a great nation,
>   and I will bless you;
> I will make your name great,
>   and you will be a blessing.
> I will bless those who bless you,
>   and whoever curses you I will curse;
> and all people on earth
>   will be blessed through you.

And where that promise is repeated, the future hope is always expressed in terms of the welfare of the nation — as, for example, in Gen 13:16, "I will make your offspring like the dust of the earth, so that if anyone could count the dust, then your offspring could be counted"; and in Gen 15:5, "Look up at the heavens and count the stars, if, indeed, you can count them. So shall your offspring be."

The standard view of death in the Hebrew Scriptures is that it is ordained by God as the inevitable, final event in every person's life. While God looks tenderly on the death of his faithful ones (cf. Ps 116:15) — and while he somehow keeps covenant with his people even after their deaths (cf. Pss 16:10; 49:15; 73:23-26) — death, nonetheless, ends all human experiences and a person's relationship with the ongoing life of the nation.

Associated with this view of death is a concept of the place of the dead, which in the Hebrew Scriptures is called Sheol and roughly corresponds to the Greek idea of Hades. The etymology of the term is disputed. Some argue that "Sheol" derives from a Hebrew noun meaning "hollow place"; others, from a Hebrew verb that means "to be desolate"; and still others from an Assyrian verb that means "to sink." More likely, it comes from the Hebrew verb "to ask" *(šāʾal)* and connotes a place where only questions and uncertainty abound. Existence in Sheol was viewed as shadowy and subpersonal, with its inhabitants called "shades" *(rĕpāʾîm)*. They were called "shades" not because they were thought of as ghosts or spirits, but because they existed as nonpersonal entities who had only the semblance of their former selves — being bereft of all personality and strength.

The emphasis in the thought of ancient Israel was on the unity of the human personality, with the material and immaterial aspects of human personality being so intertwined that neither was able to exist or function apart from the other. The dead in Sheol, therefore, were thought of as vague entities that merely existed in a monotonous underworld, without the powers associated with human life and apart from communion with God. So the consciousness expressed in Ps 115:17-18:

> It is not the dead who praise the LORD,
>   those who go down to silence;
> it is we [the living] who extol the LORD,
>   both now and forevermore.

And so the various laments of God's people recorded in the Hebrew Scriptures, as, for example, that of Job 10:20-22:

> Are not my few days almost over?
>   Turn away from me so I can have a moment's joy

before I go to the place of no return,
  to the land of gloom and deep shadow,
to the land of deepest night,
  of deep shadow and disorder,
  where even the light is like darkness.

Likewise, that of Psalm 88, as the writer cries out in verses 3-5 and 10-12:

For my soul is full of trouble
  and my life draws near to Sheol.
I am counted among those who go down to the pit;
  I am like a person without strength.
I am set apart with the dead,
  like the slain who lie in the grave,
whom you remember no more,
  who are cut off from your care.
. . . .
Do you show your wonders to the dead?
  Do the shades rise up and praise you?
Is your love declared in the grave,
  your faithfulness in Abaddon [the "Place of Destruction"]?
Are your wonders known in the place of darkness,
  or your righteous deeds in the land of oblivion?

The hope of the faithful in Israel was not that they would never die
or somehow escape Sheol. Death and Sheol were as much a part of every
person's experience as birth and family. Nor did they think of what would
later be called "immortality" or "resurrection." These concepts may have
had some rootage in what they said and felt about covenantal relationship
with God, but they did not come to expression in Israelite thought until
later. Rather, the thought of the righteous with regard to death and dying
in ancient Israel was simple and realistic: "I am about to die," said Joseph
to his brothers (Gen 50:23); "I am about to go the way of all the earth,"
said David on his death bed to his son Solomon (1 Kgs 2:2). Death and
Sheol were as undeniable and unavoidable as that.

The hope of the righteous in the religion of Israel was simply (1) for
a long life, (2) for a good death, (3) for the continuance of one's ideals in
one's posterity, and (4) for the continued welfare of the nation — all, some-

how, as ordained by God and under his blessing. So the counsel of the author of *Sirach*, which was written during the first quarter of the second century B.C.:

> Fear not death, it is your destiny. Remember that the former and the latter share it with you. This is the portion of all flesh from God, and how can you withstand the decree of the Most High! Be it for a thousand years, for a hundred, or for ten that you live, in Sheol there are no reproaches concerning life. (41:3-4; cf. *Sirach* 17:22-23; *Tobit* 3:10; 13:2)

Sometime during the fifth through the second centuries B.C., however, there began to arise within Judaism a number of developments in the conceptualization of the dead and of Sheol. Some of these developments came about as Jews were forced by circumstances to rethink issues having to do with theodicy (i.e., the vindication of God's justice in the face of national calamities and personal catastrophes). Other developments probably were due to the impact of particular Greek ideas regarding persons and their experiences after death on Jewish thought. Still others may be explained as Jewish responses to widespread Greek attempts to gain an encyclopedic knowledge — which, among Jewish thinkers, encouraged new analyses of previously held beliefs and various attempts to work out in a more intellectualized manner Judaism's traditional piety.

The influence of Greek ideas on Israel's religion can be seen in such matters as (1) representations of the dead as disembodied "spirits" or "souls" with enhanced personal qualities, as found in such writings as *1 Enoch*, the *Testament/Assumption of Moses*, and *2 Enoch*, (2) portrayals of Sheol as divided into various compartments where the dead carry on relatively full personal existence apart from their bodies, as in *1 Enoch* 22:1-14 and *4 Ezra* 7:75-101, and (3) the advocacy of views similar to a Platonic doctrine of immortality, as in *Wisdom of Solomon, 4 Maccabees,* and *2 Enoch*. The impact of the Greek proclivity to intellectualize and systematize knowledge — coupled with the external calamities that befell the Jewish people at that time — caused many Jews to rethink their views of the afterlife in a manner that was consistent with both a Jewish anthropology generally and certain passages in the Hebrew Scriptures that seemed to suggest something more positive for the faithful after death. So there arose within Second Temple Judaism a doctrine of resurrection that applied not only to the nation but also to pious individuals within Israel and that involved not the "soul" alone but the whole person. Immortality and resurrection doctrines, in fact, were subjects of frequent debate within Israel during the Second Temple period, with, it seems, a resurrection doctrine (in somewhat differing forms) gaining the ascendancy and becoming standard in the rabbinic writings of the Talmud.

For most Jews today, thoughts of the afterlife have to do primarily with God's preservation and prospering of the nation Israel, though hopes are also directed among more orthodox and conservative Jews to the resurrection of faithful individuals. Yet throughout Jewish history there have always been those who accepted the Platonic idea that the human soul is immortal, and so cannot be affected by physical death. Jewish funeral practices, however, point back to the older understanding that God does not save the individual from death, but rather preserves and prospers the nation of Israel regardless of the death of its present leaders and people. Furthermore, the respect paid to the body of a deceased person through ritual cleansing (as well as the general Jewish repugnance of embalming or performing autopsies) witnesses to the inseparability of the body and the soul, both in death and in a future resurrection life sometime after death.

Naturalistic/Religious Humanism — Death a Natural Phenomenon, with Being Remembered the Greatest Hope and Immortality Ascribed Only to the Human Race and Human Ideals

The Renaissance of the fourteenth through the sixteenth centuries reached back behind the so-called Dark Ages of the fifth to the fifteenth centuries, when perspectives on life and the world had become solidified and rather encrusted, to recapture much of what was deemed worthy in the classical period of Greek philosophy. The focus in the Renaissance was on humanity alone, apart from any supernatural context or conditioning. So in the naturalistic humanism that developed, death was viewed as a perfectly natural phenomenon — a feature inextricably linked with human nature itself, and therefore to be accepted as a purely natural occurrence. Though death is often a traumatic experience for the family and friends of the deceased, it is, nonetheless, a datum of nature that must not be denied or overly sentimentalized, but should simply be accepted.

Some Renaissance thinkers also wanted to hold on to some form of personal immortality, in line with Greek dualistic anthropology. So while they spoke of death as a perfectly natural phenomenon, they also wanted to believe that in some way the essential personhood of the individual was not affected by it — that is, that the vital features of personhood were somehow inherent in one's immortal soul, which was somehow detachable from a person's physical makeup. But most Renaissance thinkers viewed death as the end of personhood and thought of "immortality" only in collective terms as having to do with human ideals. And this is true of most forms of naturalistic humanism and so-called religious humanism today, with death being understood as bringing to an end the personhood, uniqueness, and irreplaceability of an individual and immortality attributed only to a person's ideals as passed on to his or her posterity.

Death in naturalistic or religious humanism is considered a perfectly natural occurrence. It is an event to be accepted as calmly as possible, simply because it is an occurrence that is inevitable and unavoidable. Still, being human, most naturalistic or religious humanists, despite their "courageous" stance philosophically, have found it difficult in practice to accept the inevitability of their own deaths in such a passive fashion. For most humanists, as for most people of the Western world generally, personal oblivion is a terribly repugnant concept. They seem deeply angry about the prospect of personal oblivion. So their credo is: "If I cannot be personally immortal, then I want at least to be remembered!"

The chief hope for a naturalistic or religious humanist, therefore, is being remembered for one's person and achievements. Thus memorial services, plaques, and monuments are popular. Likewise, a naturalistic or religious humanist is vitally interested in the preservation of the human race and the continuance of a person's ideals in one's posterity. But for the person himself or herself, death ends it all.

Christianity — Death the Final Enemy, but a Defeated Foe — With Life Now Being Experienced Partially "in Christ" and "with Christ," and in the Future to Be Experienced Fully at Christ's Coming (Parousia) and the Believer's Personal Resurrection

Christianity's vision of life, death, and the afterlife shares much with Judaism — whether it be the religion of ancient Israel, Second Temple Judaism ("Early Judaism"), Rabbinic Judaism, or Orthodox, Reform, or

Conservative Judaism today. Historically, the Christian religion arose within the cradle of Judaism, and it has profited greatly from its parentage.

Common to Judaism and Christianity are the foundational convictions (1) that God has created and redeemed his people for life and fellowship with himself, (2) that death is ordained by God, and (3) that God looks tenderly on the death of his faithful ones (cf. Ps 116:15). Also common to Judaism and Christianity are the convictions (4) that God, who is the covenant-keeping God, somehow keeps covenant with his people even after their deaths (cf. Pss 16:10; 49:15; 73:23-26; also Rom 8:38-39: "I am convinced that neither death nor life . . . will be able to separate us from the love of God that is in Christ Jesus our Lord"), and (5) that at death God's people somehow enter into a corporate relationship with God and with one another, which relationship has also been ordained by God — in Judaism, having been members of God's people Israel, now at death "gathered to one's fathers"; in Christianity, having been "in Christ" and "with Christ," now at death being "with Christ" more intimately. Perhaps it should also be noted that common to Second Temple Judaism and Christianity, as well, are debates regarding such matters as (1) the existence and nature of an "intermediate state," and (2) relations between the concepts of "resurrection" and "immortality" — with similar variations of belief being evident within both groups.

Nonetheless, while sharing much with Judaism, Christianity's focus on Jesus of Nazareth and its distinctive resurrection message make it different from Judaism. Thus it takes a somewhat different approach toward death, and it expresses itself differently regarding how God's people are to live their lives presently in the face of death and what lies beyond death for the believer in the afterlife. But these are matters that are the subjects of the chapters to follow, and so must be left for the authors of those chapters to develop.

3. An Amalgam of Views Today

We live today amidst an amalgam of all of the above responses and traditions. So it is not surprising to find many of these views reflected in contemporary thought and competing for people's allegiance today. In general, it may be said that five attitudes toward death are commonly taken by people today, with much overlapping being accepted between them.

13

Death Is an Illusion

One attitude is that death is an illusion, which can be treated as nonexistent by the dispelling of ignorance through a system of teaching that trains the mind to view it as being only illusory. This attitude stems from Eastern religious philosophy, particularly Hinduism, and is prominent in the West where influences from the East have been experienced. It is also the main tenet of so-called Christian Science. In this view, (1) physical death is denied, (2) the training of the mind to renounce the reality of everything material is emphasized, and (3) the human "spirit" or "soul" is viewed at "death" as returning to the world of the spiritual (whether that spiritual world is understood in personal or impersonal terms) and/or as reincarnated into another seemingly corporeal existence, with that further reincarnation being only another step toward a final, eternal, noncorporeal, and nonpersonal existence.

Death Is a Perfectly Natural Phenomenon

Another attitude taken is that death is a perfectly natural phenomenon, which is to be accepted with as much tranquillity as possible. This attitude stems from a number of sources: from Buddhism or Confucianism (its Eastern heritage); from Stoicism or the Epicureans (its Classical heritage); and/or from naturalistic or religious humanism (its Western heritage). In this view, (1) resignation in the face of the natural and inevitable is stressed, (2) training the mind to accept death as only part of the world process of change and decay — and so, not to think of death in personal terms — is advocated, (3) making the most of our human lives, both personally and on behalf of others, is strongly urged — with the hope that thereby one will be remembered, even though faced with the sure prospect of personal oblivion, and (4) working for the continuance and well-being of the human race generally, as well as for the continuance and development of one's own ideals in the lives of one's posterity in particular, are taught as humanity's only hope.

Death Is the Release of One's Immortal Soul

A third attitude toward death often taken by people today is that death is the release of one's immortal soul from the debilitating effects of imprisonment within a physical body and a material world. This attitude stems primarily from Greek philosophy, particularly Platonism — though it may also carry with it nuances drawn from Hinduism, Buddhism, or the more popular forms of Confucianism. In this view, the following mixture of responses to death usually ensues: (1) sorrowful resignation with regard to the "departure" of a person at death, (2) a welcoming of death as the liberator of the real person, and (3) comfort in thinking of the deceased person as now living a happier "soulish" existence in some spiritual realm apart from the physical world — with often, though not always, (4) an expectation that at some future time, whether at death or some distant period of time, those departed souls will be reincarnated into new bodies.

Death Ends Human Existence, Yet There Is Hope in God

A fourth attitude is that death brings to an end the existence of the whole person, both physically and spiritually; yet that death is ordained by God and under his providence, and so there is hope both corporately and individually for God's people. This hope is usually expressed in some form of resurrection language. This is an attitude that stems from Judaism, with its roots in Scripture and with developments taking place during the periods of Second Temple Judaism and Talmudic Judaism. With such a stance, there result the following attitudes: (1) a mixture of grief, sadness, even anger, though also acceptance over the termination of human life at death, (2) hope in God for continued corporate preservation and prosperity, with a belief that the deceased's personal ideals will have a part in influencing for good that future corporate life, and (3) hope in God for the restoration of God's faithful ones somehow in the future, with that restoration at times visualized in some form of personal resurrection.

Death Is the Last Enemy, But the Resurrection of Christ Provides Life

A fifth attitude toward death is to be found in the documents collectively called the New Testament, as well as in the Christian writings that build on those documents. To a great extent, as has been noted, Christianity shares much of the Jewish vision regarding life, death, and the afterlife. A distinctively Christian understanding of such matters, however, goes even beyond that contained in the Hebrew Scriptures and developed by Jewish thinkers throughout the centuries. In the pages that follow, therefore, that distinctly Christian understanding — with its focus on the resurrection of Jesus Christ from the dead and its concomitant teaching regarding the resurrection of believers in Christ — will be spelled out, with attention given principally to the data of the New Testament itself.

What we find throughout the world today, then, is an amalgam of these five attitudes toward life, death, and the afterlife. There still remain, of course, distinctive stances on these matters among the more staunch adherents of the various religious and philosophical systems of thought. Yet among people generally — and particularly in the West — there has been a considerable shifting of views and blending of perspectives. The plethora of positions advanced, in fact, has only increased the confusion among many people as to what to think about death, and so increased the confusion as to how one should (or, even can) live in the context of its presence.

4. A Focus on Life in the Face of Death

But while there are vastly different attitudes toward death — and while, regardless of how one understands it, death remains a sobering reality that permeates every facet of human existence and invades every corner of our human consciousness — death is far from being the whole of the human story. Rather, life is for living. So the focus of human thought and action is to be on life.

Life may appear in some tyrannical circumstances and sordid situations to be "a walking shadow, a poor player, that struts and frets his hour upon the stage, and then is heard no more . . . a tale told by an idiot, full of sound and fury, signifying nothing" (to quote again Macbeth's soliloquy). Likewise, it may be thought of in that way by certain jaded individuals. But it was never meant to be that way by God, its creator! And the great human cry is that it ought not to be that way in any person's experience! In fact, every human being whose spirit has not been broken by some form of tyranny or some experience of debauchery is convinced that life is for living — even though all thoughtful people also know that life must always be lived out in the context of the reality of death.

Christians have a special interest in life — both in their own lives and in the lives of others, both humanly and spiritually. They have this special interest in life because through Christ they have come into living relation with God, who is life's creator, redeemer, sustainer, and eventual re-creator. What Christians believe they have in "the Word made flesh" and the words of Holy Scripture is a message from God that speaks both aptly and directly to our human situation and that offers a new perspective on life, death, and the afterlife. And this new perspective, Christians believe, is to be found most distinctly in the resurrection message of the New Testament.

What follows in the pages of this volume, therefore, are attempts (1) to position the New Testament's resurrection message in the religious, cultural, and sociological contexts of the ancient Near East, the Greco-Roman world, and Second Temple Judaism (chapters 2-4), (2) to focus on the portrayals of Jesus' resurrection and the resurrection message in both the Synoptic Gospels and the Fourth Gospel (chapters 5-6), (3) to explicate the nature, development, and significance of Paul's message on the resurrection of believers (chapters 7-9), and (4) to highlight three New Testament "case studies" of the impact of the resurrection message as drawn from the experiences of the early church (chapters 10-12).

Selected Bibliography

Aldwinckle, Russell. *Death in the Secular City. Life after Death in Contemporary Theology and Philosophy.* Grand Rapids: Eerdmans, 1974.

Bailey, L. R., Sr. *Biblical Perspectives on Death.* Philadelphia: Fortress, 1979.

Becker, Ernst. *The Denial of Death.* London: Collier Macmillan, 1973.

Boros, Ladislaus. "Has Life a Meaning?" In *Immortality and Resurrection,* edited by Pierre Benoit and Roland Murphy. New York: Herder, 1970 (also *Concilium* 60 [1970] 11-20).

―――――. *The Mystery of Death.* New York: Herder & Herder, 1965; New York: Seabury, 1973.

Bowker, John. *The Meanings of Death.* Cambridge: Cambridge University Press, 1991.

Carse, J. "Death." In *Abingdon Dictionary of Living Religions,* edited by Keith Crim. Nashville: Abingdon, 1981, 208-12.

Fosdick, Harry Emerson. *The Assurance of Immortality.* New York: Macmillan, 1917.

Gervais, Karen Grandstrand. *Redefining Death.* New Haven, Conn.: Yale University Press, 1986.

Hick, John H. *Death and Eternal Life.* New York: Harper & Row, 1976.

Hock, Frederick H., ed. *Death and Eastern Thought: Understanding Death in Eastern Religions and Philosophies.* Nashville: Abingdon, 1974.

Hocking, William E. *Thoughts on Death and Life.* New York: Harper, 1917.

Kübler-Ross, Elisabeth. *On Death and Dying.* New York: Macmillan, 1969.

Pelikan, Jaroslav. *The Shape of Death: Life, Death, and Immortality in the Early Fathers.* New York: Abingdon, 1961.

Rahner, Karl. *On the Theology of Death.* New York: Seabury, 1973.

Riemer, Jack, ed. *Jewish Reflections on Death.* New York: Schocken, 1975.

Versényi, Laszlo. *Man's Measure. A Study of the Greek Image of Man from Homer to Sophocles.* Albany: State University of New York Press, 1974.

I. Background Perspectives

CHAPTER 2

Life, Death, and the Afterlife in the Ancient Near East

EDWIN YAMAUCHI

Issues of life, death, and the afterlife were of vital concern in the ancient Near East. Striking similarities existed between many of the religions of this time and region. Yet there were also profound differences. Of major importance for the subject of this volume are the views and approaches that were prevalent in ancient Egypt, Mesopotamia, Ugarit, Persia, and Israel. The following discussions will concentrate on the myths, ritual texts, and funeral practices of each of these areas, but will deal little with tombs.

1. Egypt

From Egypt we have an abundance of hieroglyphic texts written on walls, coffins, and papyrus that deal with the subjects of death and the afterlife. The most important periods of Egyptian history are: (1) the Old Kingdom (Dynasties III-VI, ca. 2700-2200 B.C.), the age of the pyramids; (2) the Middle Kingdom (Dynasties XI-XII, ca. 2134-1786 B.C.), when the capital was shifted south to Thebes; and (3) the New Kingdom or Empire (Dynasties XVIII-XX, ca. 1550-1069 B.C.), when Egypt was at its height.

Death

The Egyptian word for death *(mwt)* contains a pictograph of a man falling

21

on his knees with blood streaming from his head. Death was personified in the magical texts as a fearsome being. A euphemism for the dead was "Westerners," since the west was where the realm of the dead was placed. All of the tombs in Egypt were placed on the west bank of the Nile, with the exception of a few at Amarna. The ideal age for the Egyptians was 110 years (cf. Gen 50:26). The reality, however, was quite otherwise. For, as P. B. Adamson estimates, "the best-cared for section of the Egyptian population (members of the pharaonic household) during a prosperous period (ca. 1580-950 B.C.) only had a life expectation of c. 39.8 years" ("Human Diseases and Deaths in the Ancient Near East," *Welt des Orients* 13 [1982] 11).

Osiris

The most important god concerned with the cult of the dead was Osiris. Though there are allusions to Osiris from as early as the Fifth Dynasty, our most complete version of the myth of his death and dismemberment by Seth — and of his twofold resuscitation by Isis — is to be found in Plutarch, who wrote in the second century A.D. (cf. J. Gwyn Griffiths, *Plutarch's De Iside et Osiride* [Cardiff: University of Wales Press, 1970]). His account seems to accord with scattered statements made in various Egyptian texts.

According to the myth, Seth tricked his brother Osiris into climbing inside a beautiful chest, which he then tossed into the Mediterranean Sea, thereby killing Osiris. The chest eventually washed up on the shore at Byblos in Phoenicia, where Isis, the sister and wife of Osiris, discovered it after a long search. She brought it back to Egypt and revived Osiris by magic. But then Seth cut Osiris up into fourteen parts and scattered his parts widely. Isis was able to collect all the parts except his penis, which had been swallowed by a fish. Isis fashioned a substitute penis and had intercourse with the reconstructed Osiris. She bore Horus, who continued the conflict with Seth.

Osiris himself became king of the underworld. And after the New Kingdom even ordinary people aspired to be identified with Osiris, for he had triumphed over death. Regarding his resuscitation, however, Roland de Vaux has aptly observed:

What is meant by Osiris being "raised to life"? Simply that, thanks to the ministrations of Isis, he is able to lead a life beyond the tomb which is an almost perfect replica of earthly existence. But he will never again come among the living and will reign only over the dead. . . . This revived god is in reality a "mummy" god. (*The Bible and the Ancient Near East* [Garden City, N.Y.: Doubleday, 1971] 236)

Magical Texts

In order to achieve immortality the Egyptians relied on magical texts, such as the Pyramid Texts of the Old Kingdom, the Coffin Texts of the Middle Kingdom, and the Book of the Dead in the New Kingdom.

The first of the Pyramid Texts appeared on the walls of the pyramid of Unas in the Fifth Dynasty. The magical inscriptions describe the ascent of the king to the sky and his admission into the company of the gods. The Pharaoh is likened to the stars: "You shall reach the sky as Orion, your soul shall be as effective as Sothis [Sirius], . . . for you belong to the stars who surround Reʿ, who are before the Morning Star" (R. O. Faulkner, *The Ancient Egyptian Pyramid Texts* [Oxford: Clarendon, 1969] 135). Utterances 273-74 of these Pyramid Texts seem to reflect a cannibalistic eating of corpses — a practice that is attested in the Predynastic Era (cf. M. A. Murray, "Burial Customs and Beliefs in the Hereafter in Predynastic Egypt," *Journal of Egyptian Archaeology* 42 [1956] 86-96). For here we read:

> He has broken the backbones
> And has taken the hearts of the gods;
> He has eaten the Red Crown,
> He has swallowed the Green One.
> The King feeds on the lungs of the Wise Ones,
> And is satisfied with living on hearts and their magic.
>
> (Faulkner, *Ancient Egyptian Pyramid Texts*, 82)

There is no evidence of the sacrifice of retainers in Egypt itself. But there is a spectacular example of such a practice from Kerma, an Egyptianized settlement that dates from the seventeenth century B.C. in Nubia, south of Egypt. Here, in huge tumuli or grave mounds, up to four hundred followers, many of them women, were buried alive with their chieftains (cf. B. Trigger, *Nubia* [Boulder, Colo.: Westview, 1976] 93).

During the First Intermediate Period (ca. 2200-2040 B.C., between the

Old Kingdom and the Middle Kingdom) a decentralization of power took place, with the result that the promise of immortality, which had been the prerogative of the Pharaoh and his family alone, was now claimed by others. According to L. H. Lesko, "By the time of the Coffin Texts, the hereafter had been democratized, and any goal, including the solar voyage, was considered attainable by all" ("Death and the Afterlife in Ancient Egyptian Thought," in *Civilizations of the Ancient Near East,* ed. J. M. Sasson [New York: Scribner's, 1995] 3:1768). The most prominent god in these texts is the air god Shu, whose aid was needed to make the ascent to the next world.

In the New Kingdom, long papyrus scrolls called in Egyptian *pert em hru* (i.e., "Manifested in the Light"), which are popularly known as the Book of the Dead, were included in the burials. The most celebrated copy is the seventy-eight-foot-long Papyrus of Ani in the British Museum (see Budge, *Book of the Dead*). The Book of the Dead contains about two hundred different spells. Though the spells are not set out in any systematic arrangement, they deal with four topics: (1) the protection of the body in the tomb; (2) the journey to the afterworld; (3) the judgment of the gods; and (4) existence in the next world. Vignettes illustrate various aspects of the texts.

In the famous judgment scene in the Papyrus of Ani, the heart of Ani is weighed in a balance against *ma'at,* the "feather of truth." The guardian of the balance is Anubis, a jackal god who was in charge of wrapping mummies. The registrar is Thoth, the god of wisdom. Ani had to appear before forty-two different gods. As he passed the various tests given by each of the gods, he avoided being devoured by the monster Amemit, who was part hippopotamus and part crocodile. Instead, he received offerings, was directed into the presence of Osiris, and was given an allotment in a kind of Elysian Fields. There were, however, still dangers to be avoided, for magical spells were included in the Book of the Dead to protect Ani from crocodiles and serpents.

A revealing section of the Book of the Dead is chapter 125, the so-called "Negative Confession," where the deceased swears that he has not been guilty of a series of sins or cultic derelictions:

I have not done that which the gods abominate.
I have not defamed a slave to his superior.
I have not made (anyone) sick.
I have not made (anyone) weep.

I have not killed.
I have given no order to a killer.
I have not caused anyone suffering.
I have not cut down on the food-(income) in the temples.
I have not damaged the bread of the gods.
I have not taken the loaves of the blessed (dead).
I have not had sexual relations with a boy.
I have not defiled myself.

(Pritchard, *Ancient Near Eastern Texts*, 34)

The Realm of the Dead

We have a number of guides to the topography of the underworld, which is called *Amduat* or "That Which is in Duat" (cf. E. A. Wallis Budge, *The Egyptian Heaven and Hell* [1925; reprint, La Salle, Ill.: Open Court, 1974]; D. Mueller, "An Early Egyptian Guide to the Hereafter," *Journal of Egyptian Archaeology* 58 [1972] 99-125; A. Piankoff, *The Wandering of the Soul* [Princeton: Princeton University Press, 1974]). The dead had to know every place and obstacle in the underworld in order to traverse safely the dangerous terrain.

One problem with the subterranean world was that of having to walk upside down. Spells were included in the Coffin Texts to preclude this difficulty (cf. Zandee, *Death as an Enemy*, 9). In order to reach the "Lands of the Blessed" (that is, *Sekhet-Aaru*, "Field of Reeds," or *Sekhet-hetepet*, "Field of Peace") the dead had to cross a stream with the aid of a ferryman who is called *mȝ.f ḥȝ.f*, or "he who looks to his rear." The *Sekhet-Aaru* was divided into seven sections, each of which had a gate. Entrance through each of the seven gates was gained by a knowledge of their respective names.

Mummification

The extremely dry climate of Egypt helped to preserve bodies that were thrown into the desert. Gradually more formal processes of embalming were developed. Our best information about embalming comes from the Greek historian Herodotus (*History* 2.86-89), who visited Egypt in the fifth century B.C.

The process of embalming took from thirty to two hundred days. The viscera were removed and placed into four canopic jars, named after the sons of Horus: (1) *Imesty* (human shape) for the liver; (2) *Hapy* (ape) for the lungs; (3) *Duamutef* (jackal) for the stomach; and (4) *Qebekhsenuef* (hawk) for the intestines. The heart was removed, wrapped in linen, and placed back in the cavity. The brain was extracted by a sharp utensil through the nostrils. The Egyptians considered the brain merely stuffing for the head! The body was then packed with dry natron (sodium bicarbonate), a naturally desiccating agent found in Wadi Natrun. After the cavities had been packed with linen padding, the body was covered with oil and spices. Then it was wound in yards of linen, between which numerous amulets were inserted (cf. J. J. Davis, *The Mummies of Egypt* [Winona Lake, Ind.: BMH Books, 1972]; D. A. Rosalie, ed., *Manchester Museum Mummy Project* [Manchester: Manchester University Press, 1979]; J. E. Harris and E. F. Wente, *An X-Ray Atlas of the Royal Mummies* [Chicago: University of Chicago Press, 1980]).

Not only were humans mummified, but a great number of sacred animals were mummified as well. The Apis bulls were buried in huge sarcophagi in the Serapeum at Saqqara. Excavations in the 1960s and 1970s in that area have uncovered a sacred animal necropolis containing four million mummified ibises and five hundred baboons (both of which were sacred to Thoth), five hundred thousand hawks (representing Horus), and a score of cows (representing Isis) (cf. J. D. Ray, "The World of North Saqqara," *World Archaeology* 10 [1978] 151).

The Opening of the Mouth

The most important ritual was the "Opening of the Mouth" ceremony, which was performed initially on the day of burial and then repeated at the annual mortuary feast (R. B. Finnestad, "The Meaning and Purpose of *Opening the Mouth* in Mortuary Contexts," *Numen* 25 [1978] 118-34). It required a dozen participants, including a priest who touched with a cere-monial adze the eyes, ears, nostrils, and mouth of the mummy, and also the eyes, ears, nostrils, and mouth of the statue representing the deceased. Chapter 23 of the Book of the Dead reads:

> The god Ptah shall open my mouth, and the god of my town shall unfasten the swathings, the swathings which are over my mouth. There-

upon shall come Thoth, who is equipped with words of power in great abundance, and shall unlock the fetters, even the fetters of the god Set which are over my mouth. (Budge, *Book of the Dead,* 433-34)

A gruesome aspect of the sacrifice involved in this ceremony was the cutting off of the leg of a live calf. A sumptuous funerary meal was then served, which included a leg of a bull, bread, beer, and wine.

Aspects of a Person

The Egyptians did not believe in a bodily resurrection from the dead. Nonetheless, separate aspects of a person's personality — or, as some have interpreted them, separate modes of a person — were believed to remain active after death, even though the person's corpse remained in the tomb. The Egyptian term *ba,* which has often been translated "soul," represents a complex concept. According to L. V. Žabkar:

> This Ba comes into existence at or after death, is corporeal in nature, performs physical activities as eating, drinking, and copulating, and has wide-ranging freedom of movement through the realms of the after-life. Moreover, this Ba is not a part of the deceased but is in effect . . . the deceased himself in the fullness of his being, physical as well as psychic. (*Study of the Ba Concept,* 162)

The *ba* was depicted as a human-headed bird who moved about freely or hovered over the corpse. One celebrated writing from the Middle Kingdom (from ca. 2000 B.C.) is "The Dispute of a Man with His Ba" (cf. H. Goedicke, *The Report about the Dispute of a Man with His Ba* [Baltimore: Johns Hopkins University Press, 1970]). This man was so weary with life that he not only contemplated suicide but also doubted the efficacy of funerary arrangements.

The *ka,* moreover, was a man's double. The creator god Khnum fashioned both the child and his *ka* at the same time. Often Egyptians were buried with a *ka*-statue. It was believed that the *ka* ate the funerary provisions. Other aspects of a person in Egyptian thought included the *akh* ("spirit" or "transfigured spirit"), the *shut* ("shadow"), and the *ren* ("name"). Wallis Budge concludes:

The whole man consisted of a natural body, a Spirit-body, a heart, a double, a Heart-soul, a shadow, a Spirit-soul, and a name. All these were, however, bound together inseparably, and the welfare of any single one of them concerned the welfare of all. (*Book of the Dead*, 81)

Provisions for the Dead

In Egyptian thought the dead did everything people did while alive — plowing, reaping, eating, drinking, and making love. Nourishment could be provided by an offering of food and drink, and so royal families and wealthy nobles left endowments for priests to make daily offerings of bread and beer to the dead. Food and drink could also, however, be provided magically by paintings. So in some Middle Kingdom tombs elaborate paintings of daily life — including the slaughtering of cattle and the baking of bread — were included. Passersby were entreated to say "a thousand bread, a thousand beer, a thousand oxen" on behalf of the deceased. On the other hand, the Book of the Dead provided spells to keep the deceased from eating filth and drinking polluted water in the underworld.

Shawabtis/Ushabtis

Small statues called either *shawabtis* or *ushabtis* ("answerers") were also placed with the deceased in their tombs to work on behalf of the deceased in the afterlife. Chapter 5 of the Book of the Dead is entitled "The Chapter of Not Allowing the Deceased to do Work in the Underworld," and chapter 6 is called "The Chapter of Making *Ushabti* Figures do Work for a Man in the Underworld." Spells on the statues commanded: "O *Shawabti*, if the deceased is called upon to do work in the next world, answer 'Here I am!' Plough the fields, fill the canals with water, and carry the sand of the east to the west" (cf. B. Brier, *Ancient Egyptian Magic* [New York: Morrow, 1980] 170). In the tomb of Tutankhamon, for example, were discovered 413 *ushabtis* of alabaster, limestone, and wood. Taharqa, a Pharaoh of the Twenty Fifth Dynasty, had over a thousand stone *ushabtis* buried with him.

Letters to the Dead

A number of interesting "Letters to the Dead" have been discovered (cf. S. R. Keller, *Egyptian Letters to the Dead in Relation to the Old Testament and Other Near Eastern Sources* [Ann Arbor: University Microfilms, 1991]). Some of them were written on papyri, but most were inscribed on bowls (cf. E. Yamauchi, "Magic Bowls: Cyrus H. Gordon and the Ubiquity of Magic in the Pre-Modern World," *Biblical Archaeologist* 59 [1996] 51-55). In these letters the living plead with the dead to intervene in various family crises. A widower, for example, writes to his wife, who had died three years earlier, to remind her how well he had treated her and to affirm that he had not had relations with her three sisters, who were still living in the house. Why, he asks plaintively, was she causing him trouble? (Cf. A. H. Gardiner and K. Sethe, *Egyptian Letters to the Dead Mainly from the Old and Middle Kingdoms* [London: Egypt Exploration Society, 1928] 9.)

2. Mesopotamia

Mesopotamia, the area of the Euphrates and Tigris Rivers, is today in Iraq. The Sumerians flourished in lower Mesopotamia in the third millennium B.C. During the early second millennium B.C., the Amorites from the west established the Old Babylonian and Old Assyrian dynasties. After the destruction of Babylon by the Hittites in 1595 B.C., the Kassites from the Zagros Mountains occupied Mesopotamia. In the first millennium B.C., first the Assyrians and then the Neo-Babylonians established far-flung empires, which swallowed up Israel and Judah (cf. A. Hoerth, G. Mattingly, and E. Yamauchi, eds., *Peoples of the Old Testament World* [Grand Rapids: Baker, 1994]). We have an abundance of cuneiform texts written in Sumerian and Akkadian, the latter being a Semitic language used by both the Assyrians and the Babylonians.

Death and Burial

Though the gods were immortal, some of them — such as Apsu, Tiamat, and Kingu — were killed in the course of the primeval conflict that is related in the *Epic of Creation*. Death *(mûtu)* was the lot of all humans, with the rare exception of such heroes as Utnapishtim and his companions, who were the survivors of the Flood. In death, the body *(pagru)* became a corpse *(shalamtu)* and the person gave up his breath *(zaqîqu)* and became a ghost *(eţemmu)* (cf. J. Bottéro, *Mesopotamia: Writing, Reasoning, and the Gods* [Chicago: University of Chicago Press, 1992]; see esp. chap. 15, "The Mythology of Death").

From the Early Dynastic Period of Sumer (ca. 2700 B.C.), Leonard Woolley discovered graves at the site of Ur that contained sacrifices of a king's retinue that accompanied him at his death. He also discovered a great death pit:

> In it lay the bodies of six men-servants and sixty-eight women; the men lay along the side by the door, the bodies of the women were disposed in regular rows across the floor, every one lying on her side with legs slightly bent. (C. L. Woolley, *Ur of the Chaldees* [New York: Norton, 1965] 58)

In addition to burial in cemeteries, the dead were sometimes buried underneath their own houses in a special section called the "wing of the house" *(shiddi eţem kimti)*. The oldest son, who was called the "caretaker" *(paqid)*, had the responsibility of maintaining such duties toward his parents as pronouncing their names and providing them with food and drink. Fresh water would be poured into a pipe that led down into the tomb.

A banquet for departed ancestors, called a *kispu*, would be held, usually at the end of the lunar month. At Mari we have evidence of a *kispu* that was celebrated by a royal family in honor of former kings. An Old Babylonian *kispu* text reads: "Come (dead ancestors), eat this, drink this, and bless Ammisaduqa son of Ammiditana, the king of Babylon."

The Descent of Inanna/Ishtar

There is a famous myth of the Sumerian goddess Inanna, or her Akkadian counterpart Ishtar, which is called in Sumerian "The Descent of Inanna to the Nether World" and in Akkadian "The Descent of Ishtar to the Nether World" (cf. Pritchard, *Ancient Near Eastern Texts*, 107-9). It is one of our most important documents for an understanding of Mesopotamian concepts of the afterlife (cf. E. Yamauchi, "Descent of Ishtar," in *The Biblical*

World, ed. C. Pfeiffer [Grand Rapids: Baker, 1966] 196-200; T. Jacobsen, *The Treasures of Darkness: A History of Mesopotamian Religion* [New Haven: Yale University Press, 1976] 55-63).

The Sumerian goddess Inanna (Akkadian Ishtar) was the most important goddess in the Mesopotamian pantheon. She was the goddess of love and the goddess of war. The consort of the goddess, the Sumerian Dumuzi (Akkadian Tammuz), was originally a king of Uruk who was deified as the consort of the city's protectress, Inanna.

Inanna's sister, Ereshkigal, was the Queen of the underworld and the goddess of death. A myth entitled "Nergal and Ereshkigal" relates how Nergal was summoned to the underworld because he failed to pay proper respect to Ereshkigal's messenger Namtar, the god of pestilence (cf. Pritchard, *Ancient Near Eastern* Texts, 103-4). Nergal, however, posted his own forces at the various gates and overpowered Ereshkigal. He spared her and accepted her proposal to rule the underworld with her.

Inanna, who was the Queen of Heaven, wished to seize control of Ereshkigal's kingdom as well. So she descended there. In her descent the goddess was led through seven gates. At each gate one of her seven objects of clothing or adornment was removed until she was stark naked. Evidently the rules of the underworld permitted no one to approach Ereshkigal's presence except in that condition. Inanna threatened the gatekeeper, warning him:

> If thou openest not the gate so that I cannot enter,
> I will smash the door, I will shatter the bolt,
> I will raise up the dead, eating the living,
> So that the dead will outnumber the living. (ibid., 107)

According to the Sumerian text, Inanna was killed before the Anunnaki, the seven infernal judges, just as Ereshkigal fastened her eye on her. Her corpse was then hung on a nail. The Akkadian text, however, speaks of Namtar attacking Ishtar with his sixty maladies. And with the death of the goddess, all reproduction ceased among man and beast.

Anticipating possible dire consequences, Inanna had left instructions with her servants to seek help from the gods in case she did not, in due course, return. In the Sumerian account, the god Enki created two sexless creatures to whom he entrusted "the food of life" and "the water of life." The creatures succeeded in reviving Inanna by sprinkling her with their elements of life. Once brought back to life again, however, the goddess's troubles were not yet over. For she then needed to get a substitute to take her place in the underworld.

Inanna was accompanied in her search for a suitable substitute by a company of ghoulish demons, who were very eager to do their duty. In fact, they almost dragged off Ninshubur, Inanna's faithful minister, before she interceded for him. She found out, however, that her husband Dumuzi, instead of mourning her absence, had "dressed himself in a noble garment and seated himself nobly on (his) seat." In a fury, Inanna "fastened the eye on him, the eye of death," and said: "As for him, carry him off!"

Because the end of the myth is missing in both the Sumerian and the Akkadian versions, earlier scholars thought that Inanna/Ishtar had descended to the underworld to resurrect Dumuzi/Tammuz. We now know from other texts that it was the goddess herself who sent her husband there (see E. Yamauchi, "Tammuz and the Bible," *Journal of Biblical Literature* 81 [1965] 283-90). One of these other texts also indicates that Dumuzi/Tammuz had his sister Geshtinanna take his place in the underworld for half of each year.

The last twelve lines of the Akkadian "Descent of Ishtar to the Nether World" have sometimes been viewed as indicating the resurrection of Tammuz. This is not, however, a case of resurrection, but rather a depiction of the ascent of Tammuz's spirit to smell the burning incense and partake of the offerings made for the dead (cf. E. Yamauchi, "Additional Notes on Tammuz," *Journal of Semitic Studies* 11 [1966] 10-15). Mourning for the departed Tammuz seems also to have been practiced in Israel, as well as in Mesopotamia — as is evident in Ezek 8:14, which relates how the prophet found some women of Jerusalem weeping for Tammuz.

The Gilgamesh Epic

The most celebrated Mesopotamian epic is that of Gilgamesh, the king of Uruk, who reigned about 2600 b.c. (cf. Pritchard, *Ancient Near Eastern Texts*, 72-98; Heidel, *Gilgamesh Epic*). Because Gilgamesh was oppressing his people, the gods sent a wild creature named Enkidu to overpower him. But Gilgamesh and Enkidu became fast friends and embarked on a number of adventures together. When, however, the two heroes rejected the advances of the goddess Ishtar, she killed Enkidu. Thus Gilgamesh was confronted with the fact of death.

The passage in which Gilgamesh mourns his friend Enkidu before the divine tavern keeper Siduri is one of the most poignant in ancient literature:

> My friend, whom I love dearly,
> Who with me underwent all hardships,
> Enkidu, whom I love dearly,
> Who with me underwent all hardships,
> Has gone to the fate of mankind.
> Day and night I wept over him,
> I would not give him up for burial —
> (saying) "my friend perhaps will rise up to me at my cry!"
> Seven days and seven nights
> Until a worm dropped out at me from his nose.
> Since his death, I have not found life.
> I kept roaming like a hunter in the open country.
>
> (T. Abusch, "Gilgamesh's Request and Siduri's Denial,"
> in *The Tablet and the Scroll,* ed. M. E. Cohen,
> D. C. Snell, and D. B. Weisberg
> [Bethesda, Md.: CDL Press, 1993] 2)

Tablet XI of the Gilgamesh Epic tells of Gilgamesh's encounter with Utnapishtim, the Babylonian "Noah," who survived the Flood. Utnapishtim challenges Gilgamesh to try to remain awake for six days and seven nights — but, of course, Gilgamesh fails. Gilgamesh is then directed by Utnapishtim to seize a plant growing underwater in the Apsu (the personification of waters) called "An Oldster Man Becomes a Child," which had the power to rejuvenate. But, alas, a snake later steals the plant from the hero.

The Abode of the Dead

The underworld was called "The Great City" (*Irkallu*) or "The Great Below" (*Kigallu*) — even, at times, "Earth" (*Erṣetu*). It was also called "The Land of No Return" (*Erṣit la tari*). It seems that the Mesopotamians conceived of the Underworld as consisting of three levels: (1) the lowest was the court of the *Anunnaki*, the gods of the underworld, (2) the middle belonged to

Apsû, the personification of waters, and (3) the upper level under the surface of the earth was the "residence of the spirits of men."

The entrance to the underworld was in the west, where the sun descended. The sun god *Shamash* traveled under the earth and then reappeared in the east each day. The *Ḫubur* was the sea or river that the dead had to cross with the aid of a ferryman, who was called *Ḫumut-tabal*, or "Bring fast!"

The Gilgamesh Epic describes the underworld as follows:

> The abode of Irkalla,
> To the house which none leave who have entered it,
> On the road from which there is no way back,
> To the house wherein the dwellers are bereft of light,
> Where dust is their fare and clay their food.
> They are clothed like birds, with wings for garments,
> And see no light, residing in darkness.
>
> (Pritchard, *Ancient Near Eastern Texts*, 87)

Nonetheless, those with large families, those who had fallen in battle, and those who had led good lives had a somewhat better situation in the underworld than others (cf. Heidel, *Gilgamesh Epic*, 191-92).

Ghosts and Demons

In Mesopotamian thought the deceased could affect the living. They could be called up to foretell the future by necromancers, who were called *mushêlu eṭemmi* or "those who make the phantoms reascend" (cf. I. L. Finkel, "Necromancy in Ancient Mesopotamia," *Archiv für Orientforschung* 29-30 [1983-84] 1-17).

To be left unburied was the worst fate possible, since the *eṭemmu* would become a restless ghost. According to Middle Assyrian law (#53), such would be the punishment meted out to a woman who had an abortion: "If a woman has had a miscarriage by her own act, when they have prosecuted her (and) convicted her, they shall impale her on stakes without burying her" (Pritchard, *Ancient Near Eastern Texts*, 185). Such also was the action of the Assyrian king Esarhaddon against his enemies: "The corpses of their warriors unburied I gave to the wolf to eat" (R. C. Thompson, *The Prisms of Esarhaddon and Ashurbanipal* [London: Oxford University Press, 1931] 23). In the folklore of Mesopotamia, the ghosts of those who were denied funerary offerings — as well as malformed fetuses, still-born children, suicides, women who died in childbirth, or youths who died unmarried — were especially feared (cf. M. Bayliss, "The Cult of the Dead Kin in Assyria and Babylonia," *Iraq* 35 [1973] 116).

After descending to the underworld, the spirit of Enkidu at one point ascends like a "wind-puff" for a meeting with Gilgamesh. In that meeting Gilgamesh asks his friend about the nature of the underworld and Enkidu answers:

> "Him whose corpse was cast out upon the steppe hast thou seen?"
> "I have seen: His spirit finds no rest in the nether world."
> "Him whose spirit has no one to tend (it) hast thou seen?"
> "Lees of the pot, crumbs of bread, offals of the street he eats."
> (Pritchard, *Ancient Near Eastern* Texts, 99)

Especially significant were the "male incubus" *(lilû)* who attacked women sexually at night and the "female succubus" *(lilitu)* who did the same against men. The latter also specialized in killing babies (cf. J. A. Scurlock, "Baby-snatching Demons, Restless Souls and the Dangers of Childbirth," *Incognita* 2 [1991] 137-85). The *lilitu* were the spirits of women who had died before marrying or having children. Many magical texts were written to protect families against such ghosts and demons (cf. G. Castellino, "Rituals and Prayers against 'Appearing Ghosts,'" *Orientalia* 24 [1955] 316-32; E. Yamauchi, "Magic or Miracle? Demons, Diseases and Exorcisms," in *The Miracles of Jesus,* Gospel Perspectives 6, ed. D. Wenham and C. Blomberg [Sheffield: JSOT Press, 1986] 99-101).

Substitute figures of ghosts were made and tossed into the river. At the traditional time when Tammuz was said to have descended back into the underworld, in the month called by his name (i.e., June-July), a haunting spirit could be sent down with Tammuz (cf. J. A. Scurlock, "Magic Uses of Ancient Mesopotamian Festivals of the Dead," in *Ancient Magic and Ritual Power,* ed. M. Meyer and P. Mirecki [Leiden: Brill, 1995] 93-107). *Lilit(h)* continued to be the object of magical spells down through the Middle Ages (cf. J. Trachtenberg, *Jewish Magic and Superstition* [Philadelphia: Jewish Publication Society, 1961] 36-37; E. Yamauchi, *Mandaic Incantation Texts* [New Haven: American Oriental Society, 1967] 22-34).

3. Ugarit

The ancient city of Ugarit, which flourished in the Late Bronze Age (1500-1200 B.C.), was located on the Syrian coast across from Cyprus at a site called Ras Shamra. The site has yielded important religious texts, which were written in a unique alphabetic cuneiform. These have shed valuable light on the Canaanite culture of Syria-Palestine — a culture that was both absorbed and combated by the Israelites. As in early Hebrew texts, the alphabet of the Ugaritic texts represents only consonants, which can be vocalized by a comparison with other Semitic dialects. The Ugaritic texts also provide striking verbal comparisons to the parallelism of Hebrew poetry.

The Dead

At Ugarit it was believed that when a man died, his "soul" *(npsh;* cf. the Hebrew word *nepeš)* went out of his nose like a gust of wind or a whiff of smoke. Excavations at Ras Shamra have revealed that the dead were buried in vaults under their houses, the vaults being provided with funnels to supply the dead with water.

The Conflict between Mot and Baal

The Ugaritic god Mot was the personification of death, who was thought of as an insatiable abyss who swallowed up not only mortals but even the god Baal. He is described as "the darling of the gods" *(mdd ilm),* which may be a euphemism. In some passages Mot seems to personify ripe grain that was sown into the fields. Baruch Margalit has aptly observed: "Mot is not only a giant serpent who devours animal life. He is also the god of brown and barren earth, the enemy of green-growth symbolized by Baal" (*Matter of "Life" and "Death,"* 102).

The mourning rites over the death of Baal included many actions mentioned in the Old Testament as well — such as sitting on the ground, placing dirt on the head, lacerating the skin, and cutting the hair. Baal's funeral wake involved the sacrifice of seventy buffalo, seventy oxen, and many other animals to provide nourishment for him on his way down to the realm of Mot. In the Netherworld, Baal was accorded a privileged place in a kind of Elysian Fields. Anath, Baal's sister, avenges his death by killing Mot, and then she dismembers him. Baal, however, comes back from the underworld, reinstating the fertility of the earth. But Mot also lives again. Margalit analyzes the message of the myth as follows:

> In sum: there is no question that for the Ugaritic poet and his tradition Death is mightier than Life. Life, like Baal, exists intermittently, as sporadic intervals in an eternity of non-existence. Life/Baal, like the seasons, is perpetual only insofar as it is recurrent; or, metaphorically (in the case of Baal), "resurrected." ("Death and Dying in the Ugaritic Epics," in Alster, *Death in Mesopotamia*, 249)

The Myth of Aqhat

In the myth of Aqhat, the goddess Anat covets the bow of Aqhat, son of Danel. She tempts him with a promise of "life" *(hym)* and "immortality" (*bl-mt*, literally "non-death"). But he does not believe her, and responds:

> Do not beguile me, O Virgin!
> For to a hero thy lies are loathsome!
> As for man, what does he get as his destiny?
> What does man get as his fate?
> White glaze is poured [on] the head,
> Plaster on top of my pate.
> I'll die the death of everyone.
> Yea, I shall surely die!
> (C. H. Gordon, "Poetic Legends and Myths from Ugarit,"
> *Berytus* 25 [1977] 16; cf. M. D. Coogan, *Stories from Ancient Canaan* [Philadelphia: Westminster, 1978] 37)

Thereupon Anat has Aqhat killed. The elaborate ritual undertaken to mourn Aqhat's death is described. And later Aqhat's sister Pughat takes revenge on the killer Yutpan (cf. S. B. Parker, "Death and Devotion: The Composition and Theme of *AQHT*," in *Love and Death in the Ancient Near East*, ed. J. H. Marks and R. M. Good [Guilford, Conn.: Four Quarters, 1982] 71-83).

The Abode of the Dead

We do not have Ugaritic texts that describe the underworld as we have in the Babylonian texts. There are no extant references to rivers, a ferryman, gates, or judgment. The Netherworld is referred to simply as "earth" *(arṣ),* which is located in a deep, underground region, like a vast cave. It was also called the "city" *(qrt)* of Mot. Its entrance was seen as being located in the region of two hills at the edge of the earth, to the north of Ugarit. Its inhabitants are called "those who went down into the earth" *(yrdm arṣ).* In some texts the dead are also called "gods" *(ilm),* that is, "divine beings" (cf. M. C. Astour, "The Nether World and Its Denizens at Ugarit," in Alster, *Death in Mesopotamia,* 227-38). The ruler over the dead was the sun goddess Shapash. One can compare her role with the Babylonian sun god Shamash, who also traversed the underworld at night from west to east in a subterranean tunnel, taking with him offerings for the dead.

The Rapiuma and the Royal Mortuary Ritual

The Ugaritic texts speak of *rp'um* or *rapiuma,* a word that is cognate with the Hebrew *rĕpā'îm.* The *rĕpā'îm* are regarded in some Old Testament passages as pre-Israelite inhabitants of Canaan (as in Gen 15:20), while in other passages they are depicted as spirits of the dead (as in Isa 26:14). The word is derived either from the Semitic root *rp',* meaning "to heal," or from the root *rph,* which means "to become slack." In Ugaritic the word refers to ancestors who reside in the underworld (cf. J. F. Healey, "The Ugaritic Dead: Some Live Issues," *Ugarit-Forschungen* 18 [1986] 27-32).

An important funerary text *(KTU* 1.161) summons the presence of the deceased, including the "heroes of the underworld" *(rapi'i arṣi).* The liturgy prescribes libations and offerings that are to be offered especially to the "divine ancestor" *(ilib)* to secure blessings on the reigning king Ammurapi (cf. D. Tsumura, "The Interpretation of the Ugaritic Funerary Text KTU 1.161," in *Official Cult and Popular Religion in the Ancient Near East,* ed. E. Matsushima [Heidelberg: Winter, 1993] 40-55).

Marzeaḥ Feasts

According to Marvin Pope, the Ugaritic *mrz ̒* or *marzeaḥ* was a feast for departed ancestors that corresponds to the Mesopotamian *kispu*. The *rapiuma* were invited to the *marzeaḥ*. One Ugaritic text speaks about the god El, who in the *marzeaḥ* became exceedingly intoxicated:

> El sacrificed in his house,
> Provided game in the midst of his palace.
> He invited the gods to mess.
> The gods ate and drank,
> Drank wine to satiety,
> Must to inebriation.
>
> (M. H. Pope, "The Cult of the Dead at Ugarit,"
> in G. Young, ed., *Ugarit in Retrospect*
> [Winona Lake, Ind.: Eisenbrauns, 1981] 177)

Other scholars, however, such as Theodore Lewis, are not convinced of Pope's thesis (see Lewis, *Cults of the Dead*). For in most Ugaritic texts the word *marzeaḥ* is used to designate an organization that involved drinking, but without any funerary associations. Thus Brian Schmidt writes: "In conclusion, the association of the Ugaritic *marzeaḥ* with mortuary matters has yet to be established" (*Israel's Beneficent Dead*, 66).

A similar Hebrew word occurs twice in the Old Testament. In Jer 16:5 the prophet is commanded not to enter a *bêt marzeaḥ* (NIV: "house where there is a funeral meal"), which may be parallel with the *bêt mišteh*, or "house of drinking," in Jer 16:8. On the other hand, in Amos 6:7 *marzeaḥ* seems to refer only to a luxurious banquet (NIV: "feasting") without any funerary association.

4. Persia

Ancient Persia (modern Iran) developed an enormous empire under such Achaemenian kings as Cyrus, Darius, and Xerxes (ca. 550-330 b.c.), before it was conquered by Alexander the Great. After a brief occupation by the Seleucids, a national Parthian (or Arsacid) Dynasty developed from ca. 250

B.C. to A.D. 225. The Sassanid Dynasty (A.D. 225-640) adopted Zoroastrianism as the state religion.

The dates of the great Persian prophet Zoroaster have been placed somewhere between 1000 to 600 B.C. The only certain texts that can be ascribed to Zoroaster himself are called the *Gathas*. The *Avesta* may have circulated orally earlier, but was probably not written down until the sixth century A.D. Many of the important cosmological and eschatological Pahlavi texts, such as the *Bundahishn,* were not composed until the ninth century A.D. — after the Zoroastrians (modern Parsis) fled the Muslim conquest of Iran to settle in Bombay, India (cf. E. Yamauchi, "Religions of the World: Persia," in *The International Standard Bible Encyclopedia,* rev. ed., ed. G. W. Bromiley [Grand Rapids: Eerdmans, 1988] 4:123-29; idem, *Persia and the Bible,* 395-410).

Death

Man has a "body" *(tan)* that is composed, in addition to the obvious corporeal features, of four invisible aspects: (1) "life" or "vitality" *(jan);* (2) "soul" *(urvan);* (3) "light" *(bod);* and (4) "spirit" *(frawahr* or *fravashi).* The Old Persian word for man is *martiya* (cf. the modern Persian word *mard*), which signified one who is mortal. The pre-Zoroastrian traditions held that the "soul" lingered for three days before departing to a subterranean kingdom of the dead ruled by Yima, the first man to die.

When death comes, Zoroastrians try to dispose of the polluting corpse within a day, if possible. The body is washed in *gomez,* the urine of a bull or cow. According to Parsi custom the dead person should be seen by a dog, which was an animal revered by Zoroastrians. To bury a man or a dog in the earth was to be guilty of defiling the earth. Nor should one defile water or fire with the dead. This is the rationale for the practice of exposing the dead to vultures.

The exposure of the dead was a custom attested by Herodotus for the Magi, the priests of the Medes and Persians. The exposure of the dead was not followed by the Achaemenids and is not found in the oldest parts of the *Avesta*. Parsis in Bombay still dispose of their dead in *dakhmas* or "Towers of Silence." There the corpse is stripped by vultures within a half hour. The sun-bleached bones are eventually cast into a pit.

The Bridge of the Separator

Zoroaster spoke of the judgment of individuals at "The Bridge of the Separator" (the *chinvato peretu*), which he anticipated crossing with his followers. The Avestan *Vendidad* set the beginning of this bridge leading over Hell to Paradise on the heights of Mt. Alburz in northern Iran. The later *Bundahishn* gives an elaborate account of the nature of the bridge. If the soul is righteous, the bridge becomes broad. But if the soul is wicked, the bridge stands on its edge and shrinks to a razor's edge, causing sinners to plummet into Hell (cf. M. Boyce, ed., *Textual Sources for the Study of Zoroastrianism* [Manchester: Manchester University Press, 1984] 82-85, for vivid Pahlavi passages describing the latter action).

Each man's deeds are weighed carefully on scales of hair's-breadth precision before the gods Mithra, Sraosha, and Rashnu. If his good deeds outweigh his evil deeds, he will be saved. Three days after his death he will meet his own personified "conscience" *(daena)*. According to the Pahlavi *Denkard,* this encounter will be with a beautiful female figure if he has been righteous, but with a hideous hag if he has been wicked.

Heaven

The dwelling place of the righteous is described in the *Gathas* as the "House of Ahura Mazda." There are numerous descriptions of this paradisical realm as being "a realm without heat or cold, snow or rain; without cares or suffering, tears or pain; a realm without darkness, sickness, old age, or death; a realm where labor and want are equally unknown." According to some texts the soul ascends through three stages (or seven stages) — such as the region of the stars, the moon, and the sun — to the Paradise of Infinite Lights.

The word "paradise" stems from the Median word *paradiza* (Old Persian: *paridaida*), which literally meant "beyond the wall" and hence an "enclosure" or "park." It was taken into Hebrew as *pardes* and rendered into Greek as *paradeisos*. The Septuagint translators of the Hebrew Bible used the latter word in Gen 3:8-10 for the Garden of Eden (cf. Yamauchi, *Persia and the Bible*, 332-34).

Hell and Hamestagan

The fate of the wicked in Hell is described by Zoroaster as follows: "Long-lasting darkness, ill food, and wailing — to such an existence shall your conscience lead you by your own deeds, O wicked ones." Hell is also called the "House of Worst Purpose." Pahlavi texts, however, also assigned an intermediate state called *Hamestagan* between earth and the sphere of the stars, which was for those whose good deeds and wicked deeds exactly balanced. There they suffered only the pains of heat and cold.

Resurrection and the Fiery Trial

There is no certain affirmation of belief in a resurrection by Zoroaster in the *Gathas*. The concept appears relatively sparsely in the *Avesta*. The fullest account of a resurrection appears in the Pahlavi *Bundahishn*. In that ninth-century A.D. writing, after Gayomart, the primeval just Man, and the first human pair are raised, then the rest of humanity arise with the coming of the final "savior" *(saoshyant)* to be subject to the fiery judgment.

Zoroaster spoke of a judgment by molten metal, apparently referring to an ordeal in which molten metal was poured on an accused person. As developed in the *Bundahishn*, the "Final Restoration" *(Frashkert)* will be introduced by a fiery ordeal:

> Then the divine Airyaman and Fire will melt all the metal in the hills and mountains and will cause all souls, both righteous and wicked, to rise on the spot where they died to go through an ordeal by fire and molten metal for their purification.

The sins of the damned will be burnt away by the ordeal and the wicked will be purged. Adults will be restored as men and women of forty and children as youths of fifteen.

5. Israel

The Hebrews believed that people had a *nepeš*, which is translated "soul." They were also imbued with a "spirit" (Hebrew *rûaḥ*). For the Hebrews, however, a person was a holistic creature, rather than a trichotomous individual — that is, with separable elements of "body," "soul," and "spirit," as in the Greek sense.

Death and Burial

The word *mût,* "to die," and its derivatives occur more than a thousand times in the Old Testament. "Death" *(mawet)* came into the world as a punishment for human sin (Gen 3:2). Every person in Old Testament times suffered death, with the apparent exceptions of Enoch (Gen 5:24) and Elijah (2 Kgs 2:3-12).

Inhumation or burial in tombs was the normal practice. Because of Egyptian influence, however, Jacob was embalmed (Gen 50:2). The bodies of Saul and his sons were cremated by the people of Jabesh Gilead because their bodies had been mutilated by the Philistines (1 Sam 31:12). Even criminals were to be buried (Deut 21:22-23). To be left unburied and eaten by dogs was the terrible fate of Jeroboam I and Jezebel (1 Kgs 14:11; 21:23; cf. 2 Kgs 9:35).

Sheol

The most common word in the Old Testament for the place of the dead is Sheol *(šĕ'ôl),* which occurs sixty-five times, all but fifteen being in poetical passages. Its etymology is disputed, but it may come from the verb *šā'al,* "to ask." It is rendered uniformly in the Septuagint as Hades, the Greek term for the underworld and its god. The dead descend to Sheol, which was located below the earth (Ps 139:8).

Since in some passages Sheol parallels "grave" *(qeber),* R. Laird Harris has attempted to deny that Sheol means more than this ("The Meaning of the Word Sheol as Shown by Parallels in Poetic Texts," *Journal of the Evangelical Theological Society* 4 [1961] 129-35). But in view of the similarities that exist between the Hebrew idea of Sheol and concepts from Mesopotamia, few scholars today find this position persuasive.

The synonym *bôr,* usually translated "pit," occurs sixty-five times in the Old Testament. *Abaddon* (NIV: "destruction") is found only in Ps 88:11; Job 26:6; 28:22; 31:12; and Prov 15:11 (cf. Tromp, *Primitive Conceptions of*

Death; S. Jellicoe, "Hebrew-Greek Equivalents for the Nether World, Its Milieu and Inhabitants, in the Old Testament," *Textus* 8 [1973] 1-19).

The abode of the dead was viewed by the Hebrews as being dusty (Job 17:16; 21:26). As D. R. Hillers notes, "Especially common is the idea that death is a return to the dirt, a conception that encompasses the whole fleeting life of man" ("Dust: Some Aspects of Old Testament Imagery," in *Love and Death in the Ancient Near East,* ed. J. H. Marks and R. M. Good [Guilford, Conn.: Four Quarters, 1982] 107). It is also dark (Ps 143:3; Lam. 3:6) — so dark that Job 10:22 declares that even its light is darkness. It is silent (Ps. 94:17; 115:17). Its inhabitants are not able to praise God (Ps. 30:9; 88:10; 115:17; Isa 38:18).

The *rĕpā'îm* were the "spirits of the departed," as in the taunt against the king of Babylon (Isa 14:9-11):

The grave [Hebrew *šĕ'ôl*] below is all astir
to meet you at your coming;
it rouses the spirits of the departed to greet you —
all those who were leaders in the world;
it makes them rise from their thrones —
all those who were kings over the nations.
They will all respond,
they will say to you,
"You also have become weak, as we are;
you have become like us."

A Mortuary Cult in Israel?

References in the Old Testament to a mortuary cult and the veneration of ancestors are relatively rare. Such practices were condemned in Israel. Deut 26:14, in fact, has the pious Israelite say, "I have not eaten any of the sacred portion while I was in mourning, nor have I removed any of it while I was unclean, nor have I offered any of it to the dead." R. de Vaux comments:

These funeral rites have sometimes been explained as evidence for a cult of the dead. Sometimes the argument is that the deceased person was feared, and that the living therefore wanted to protect themselves from him, or to secure his good will; at other times, it is argued that the living

44

attributed a kind of divinity to the dead. There is no foundation for either opinion in the Old Testament. (*Ancient Israel: Its Life and Institutions* [1961; reprint, Grand Rapids: Eerdmans, 1997] 61)

Other scholars, however, read the explicit condemnation of such practices as the tip of an iceberg, which, they believe, points to practices similar to those of the Canaanites and the Mesopotamians (cf. H. C. Brichto, "Kin, Cult, Land and Afterlife — A Biblical Complex," *Hebrew Union College Annual* 44 [1973] 1-52). Paolo Xella, for example, asserts: "The Hebrew Bible's explicit condemnations of popular Canaanite rites betray the extent to which the daily life of the faithful of YHWH was permeated by these very traditions" ("Death and the Afterlife in Canaanite and Hebrew Thought," in *Civilizations of the Ancient Near East*, ed. J. M. Sasson [New York: Scribner's, 1995] 3:2067). Likewise, using archaeological evidence, the Ugaritic texts, and reading between the lines, Elizabeth Bloch-Smith has argued for a widespread mortuary cult in Israel, which existed up until Hezekiah's reforms in the eighth century and the reforms of Josiah in the seventh century (*Judahite Burial Practices and Beliefs about the Dead* [Sheffield: JSOT Press, 1992]; cf. also M. Smith and E. M. Bloch-Smith, "Death and Afterlife in Ugarit and Israel," *Journal of the American Oriental Society* 108 [1988] 277-84).

Necromancy

There are numerous prohibitions in the Old Testament against various means of divination — in particular, against necromancy, which used mediums to call up the spirits of the dead (cf. Lev 19:26; 20:6, 27; Deut 18:10-11; 1 Sam 28:3, 9; Isa 8:19; 19:3). The detailed case of necromancy in Saul's use of the witch of En-Dor to raise the spirit of Samuel (1 Sam 28:3-25) is exceptional. It is worth noting that Samuel was recognizable and that he was aware of events taking place on the earth (cf. B. B. Schmidt, "The 'Witch' of En-Dor, 1 Samuel 28, and Ancient Near Eastern Necromancy," in *Ancient Magic and Ritual Power*, ed. M. Meyer and P. Mirecki [Leiden: Brill, 1995] 111-29).

Immortality

Although many passages in the Old Testament betray a pessimistic, even fatalistic, view of death, there are also passages that speak of a hope in Yahweh's help and presence beyond death — in particular, Ps 16:9-11; 49:10-15; 73:23-28; and Job 19:25-27. Robert Martin-Achard concluded that the emphasis of these passages is on a fellowship with God that transcends death, though they do not yet sing of a "victory over Sheol" or envisage a resurrection (*From Death to Life*, chap. 3). And K. Spronk has gone further to argue that these passages, which speak of God's power extending beyond the grave, are indications of an Israelite belief in a beatific afterlife (*Beatific Afterlife in Ancient Israel and the Ancient Near East* [Kevelaer: Butzon and Bercker, 1986] 72-81).

On the basis of cognate Ugaritic texts, Mitchell Dahood has proposed some controversial interpretations of the Psalms, discovering more passages that promise immortality and even resurrection — as, for example, Ps 17:15, which he renders, "At my vindication I will gaze upon your face; at the resurrection I will be saturated with your being" (*Psalms I: 1–50* [Garden City, N.Y.: Doubleday, 1966] 93, 99). Dahood's proposals, however, have been criticized by Bruce Vawter (cf. "Intimations of Immortality and the Old Testament," *Journal of Biblical Literature* 91 [1972] 158-71).

Resurrection

In Isa 25:8 the hope is expressed that God "will swallow up death forever." Most scholars, however, agree that the clearest references in the Old Testament to the resurrection of individuals are to be found in two passages. The first is Isa 26:19: "But your dead will live; their bodies will rise. You who dwell in the dust, wake up and shout for joy. Your dew is like the dew of the morning; the earth will give birth to her dead." The second, Dan 12:2: "Multitudes who sleep in the dust of the earth will awake: some to everlasting life; others to shame and everlasting contempt" (cf. G. F. Hasel, "Resurrection in the Theology of Old Testament Apocalyptic," *Zeitschrift für die alttestamentliche Wissenschaft* 92 [1980] 267-84).

In the period between the Old and New Testaments, there was a growing emphasis on the resurrection of the dead. The Pharisees even held that those who denied the resurrection had no share in the world to come (cf. Mishnah *Sanhedrin* 10:1; Acts 23:6-7; 24:14-15). The Sadducees, on the other hand, who recognized only the Torah (the Pentateuch), denied the resurrection (cf. Matt 22:23; Mark 12:26), and, according to Josephus, denied even an afterlife. Jews like Philo, who were influenced by Plato, spoke of the preexistence and the immortality of the soul. (On these developments, see G. W. E. Nickelsburg, Jr., *Resurrection, Immortality, and Eternal Life in Intertestamental Judaism* [Cambridge: Harvard University Press, 1972].)

Until recently we had no clear evidence for what the Qumran community, which is commonly identified with the Essenes, believed about the afterlife. A recently published text, "The Messiah of Heaven and Earth (4Q521)," has the first definitive reference to belief in a resurrection among the Qumran convenanters: "then he (the Messiah) will heal the sick, resurrect the dead (*'z yrp' hllym wmtym yhyh*)" (cf. R. H. Eisenman and M. Wise, *The Dead Sea Scrolls Uncovered* [Rockport, Mass.: Element, 1992] 21, 23; M. Wise, M. Abegg, Jr., and E. Cook, *The Dead Sea Scrolls: A New Translation* [San Francisco: Harper & Row, 1996] 421).

Zoroastrian Influence on Judaism?

Many scholars have maintained that Zoroastrianism influenced Judaism in its development of such beliefs as a final judgment, resurrection, a fiery trial, heaven, and hell — as well as in its development of apocalypticism generally. Bernhard Lang, for example, who holds that Ezekiel 37 expresses a belief in a resurrection, asserts: "Indeed, the concept of bodily resurrection was borrowed from the ancient Iranians. It first appears in the teachings of the Iranian prophet Zoroaster" ("Afterlife: Ancient Israel's Changing Vision of the World Beyond," *Bible Review* 4 [1988] 19; cf. idem, "Life After Death in the Prophetic Promise," in *Congress Volume: Jerusalem 1986,* ed. J. A. Emerton [Leiden: Brill, 1988] 154-55). The foremost champion of Persian priority is Mary Boyce, who maintains that the Achaemenid period was the age in which Zoroastrianism exerted its greatest influence on the Jews (see her *Zoroastrians*).

At first glance, this may seem a plausible scenario, since the Jews in exile came under the control of the Persians after the conquest of Babylon by Cyrus in 539. On closer examination, however, this widely held thesis evidences a number of real problems. One major problem is that the details about Persian eschatology are drawn almost entirely from the *Bundahishn,* which is a ninth-century A.D. Pahlavi writing. We are, in fact, lacking any religious texts from the crucial Parthian era (250 B.C. to A.D. 225). A second problem is that there is no convincing evidence that Cyrus was a Zoroastrian. For though Boyce claims that he was, the evidence for such a claim is lacking (cf. Yamauchi, *Persia and the Bible,* 422-24). And third, as we have noted earlier, many scholars of Zoroastrianism, contrary to Boyce's interpretation, do not credit Zoroaster himself with a belief in a resurrection. Franz König, for example, concludes that the earliest attestation of Zoroastrian belief in a resurrection cannot be dated before the fourth century B.C. (cf. *Zarathustras Jenseitsvorstellungen und das Alte Testament* [Vienna: Herder, 1964]).

Whether a fourth-century B.C. date would be prior or posterior to Daniel depends on one's view of the date of the composition of Daniel. Along with other scholars such as Donald J. Wiseman, Kenneth A. Kitchen, Alan R. Millard, and T. C. Mitchell, I have maintained the traditional Neo-Babylonian/Persian date of Daniel. I have pointed out that the abundant evidence of contacts between the Greek world and Near Eastern world prior to Alexander negates the use of Greek words in Daniel as an argument for a late date (see my *Greece and Babylon* [Grand Rapids: Baker, 1967]). Most scholars, however, adhere to a Maccabean date (ca. 165 B.C.) for Daniel's composition — as, for example, John J. Collins (cf. his *Daniel* [Minneapolis: Fortress, 1993]), though he has, at least, abandoned the argument of the Greek words.

There are, of course, numerous Persian loan words in the biblical Aramaic of Daniel (cf. F. Rosenthal, *A Grammar of Biblical Aramaic* [Wiesbaden: Harrassowitz, 1961] 58-59). Yet all of these terms — with the exception of *raz,* "mystery" — are nonreligious terms, as has been pointed out by James Barr ("The Question of Religious Influence: The Case of Zoroastrianism, Judaism, and Christianity," *Journal of the American Academy of Religion* 53 [1985] 201-33).

There are also fundamental differences in how the Jews and the Persians conceived of the resurrection. The Jewish dead, who are buried, rise from the dust of the earth, whereas the Persian dead, who are exposed, must be recreated from the elements. Furthermore, in Zoroastrianism the resurrection is linked with the Fiery Ordeal and the Renewal, whereas in Judaism resurrection hope means life beyond the grave with Yahweh. The case for a reliance of Judaism on Zoroastrianism, therefore, is highly speculative at best (cf. my *Persia and the Bible,* 458-66). It is, therefore, best to hold that belief in a resurrection was an inner-Jewish development and to abandon the appeal to a retrojection from very late Persian sources.

Conclusion

Hebrew concepts of death and the afterlife were quite dissimilar from those of the Egyptians. On the other hand, there are a number of striking similarities between certain expressions of the Hebrews and those of the people of Mesopotamia and Ugarit. Unlike the Egyptians and Mesopotamians, the Hebrews had no reference to a river or a ferryman in the realm of the dead. Though the Negative Confession lists several ethical and ritual standards, the Egyptians relied mostly on magic to secure a happy afterlife. The Anunnaki, or "judges" of Mesopotamia, did not offer moral judgment, but simply determined the fates of the dead — which seems to have depended primarily on their status in life. Though the god Baal experienced seasonal "resurrection," there was no such hope for humans (cf. H. W. F. Saggs, "Some Ancient Semitic Conceptions of the Afterlife," *Faith and Thought* 3 [1958] 165, 173).

Unique to the Hebrews' understanding, however, was faith in a single, all-powerful God, who had no need of sustenance such as was provided in the sacrifices to pagan deities (cf. E. Yamauchi, "Anthropomorphism in Ancient Religions," *Bibliotheca Sacra* 125 [1968] 29-44). He was a God who punished evildoers, though they might prosper in this life, and rewarded his followers, though they might suffer here. As some of the Old Testament passages indicate, the Hebrews came over time to believe that God was a God who would maintain fellowship with them beyond the grave, who would vanquish death, and who would raise the dead.

Selected Bibliography

Alster, Bendt, ed. *Death in Mesopotamia.* Copenhagen: Akademisk Forlag, 1980.

Boyce, Mary. *Zoroastrians.* London: Routledge, 1979.

Budge, E. A. Wallis. *The Book of the Dead.* Reprint. New Hyde Park, N.Y.: University Books, 1960.

Heidel, Alexander. *The Gilgamesh Epic and Old Testament Parallels.* Chicago: University of Chicago Press, 1949.

Lewis, Theodore J. *Cults of the Dead in Ancient Israel and Ugarit.* Atlanta: Scholars Press, 1989.

Margalit, Baruch. *A Matter of "Life" and "Death."* Kevelaer: Butzon and Bercker, 1980.

Martin-Achard, Robert. *From Death to Life.* Edinburgh: Oliver and Boyd, 1960.

Pope, Marvin H. "The Cult of the Dead at Ugarit." In *Ugarit in Retrospect,* edited by G. Young. Winona Lake, Ind.: Eisenbrauns, 1981, 159-79.

Pritchard, James B. *Ancient Near Eastern Texts Relating to the Old Testament.* Rev. ed. Princeton: Princeton University Press, 1955.

Schmidt, Brian B. *Israel's Beneficent Dead.* Tübingen: Mohr-Siebeck, 1994.

Scurlock, Jo Ann. "Death and the Afterlife in Ancient Mesopotamian Thought." In *Civilizations of the Ancient Near East,* edited by J. M. Sasson. New York: Charles Scribner's Sons, 1995, 4:1883-93.

Tromp, Nicholas J. *Primitive Conceptions of Death and the Nether World in the Old Testament.* Rome: Pontifical Biblical Institute, 1969.

Yamauchi, Edwin. *Persia and the Bible.* Grand Rapids: Baker, 1990.

Zaehner, R. C. *The Dawn and Twilight of Zoroastrianism.* New York: G. P. Putnam's Sons, 1961.

Žabkar, L. V. *A Study of the Ba Concept in Ancient Egyptian Texts.* Chicago: University of Chicago Press, 1968.

Zandee, Jan. *Death as an Enemy according to Ancient Egyptian Conceptions.* 1960. Reprint, New York: Arno Press, 1977.

CHAPTER 3

Life, Death, and the Afterlife in the Greco-Roman World

PETER G. BOLT

DEATH WAS a grim reality in the first-century Greco-Roman world. In all sorts of ways, its shadow hung heavily over every aspect of human life and endeavor. The gospel of Jesus Christ, however, brought a message of life from the dead that had the potential to make an enormous impact on the lives of all who heard it. People today often fail to appreciate just how radical this message was in the first century — and continues to be today. That is usually because we have failed to appreciate — or, perhaps, have become immune to — the fact that this resurrection message was originally, and continues to be today, spoken to those for whom death was, and is, an everyday reality.

1. Life under the Shadow of Death

Life was brief, and death was always a sobering reality in the thought and activities of ancient people. Indeed, the inhabitants of the Greco-Roman world lived constantly under the shadow of death.

The Brevity of Life

Accurate statistics for the first century A.D. are unavailable. Average life expectancies, however, can be estimated. Deriving statistical information from ancient tombstones is fraught with difficulties, with results rightly classed as being only "highly approximate" (Wiedemann, *Adults and Children,* 14-15). Nonetheless, Roman tombs suggest an average life expectancy of about twenty-two years for men and twenty years for women, with Egyptian tombs yielding a figure of about thirty years average for both (Horsley, *New Documents,* vol. 3, text 11). Other estimates, based on comparative population studies, posit that most people of the Greco-Roman world had an average life expectancy of somewhere around twenty to twenty-five years; that only 40 percent of the population reached that age; and that only 50 percent of children made it to their tenth birthday (cf. Wiedemann, *Adults and Children,* 15).

Life hung so much in the balance that Seneca "the Younger," the eclectic Roman philosopher, writing sometime between A.D. 63-65 — the closing years of his life — recommended living only one day at a time:

> Let us go to our sleep with joy and gladness; let us say: "I have lived; the course which Fortune set for me is finished" [quoting the first-century B.C. Roman poet Vergil, *Aeneid* 4.653]. And if God is pleased to add another day, we should welcome it with glad hearts. . . . When a man has said: "I have lived!," every morning he arises he receives a bonus. (*Epistolae ad Lucilium* 12 ["On Old Age"] 8-10)

Death an Ever-Present Reality

Not only was life short in the first-century Greco-Roman world, but death was an ever-present reality. In another letter to Lucilius, Seneca wrote: "Most men ebb and flow in wretchedness between the fear of death and the hardships of life" (*Epistolae* 4 ["On the Terrors of Death"] 5). Such thoughts were by no means original. Euripides, the Athenian poet of the fifth century B.C., had written: "Know that death is a debt we all must pay" (*Alcestis* 419). And Horace, the Roman poet, writing about 23 B.C., agreed: "Pallid death with impartial steps knocks at the doors of poor men's hovels and of king's palaces" (*Odes* 1.4.13).

Seneca's reiteration of these ancient observations shows that nothing much had changed in the first century. People were well aware that death threatened everyone alike, regardless of age or station in life, and that it threatened from all quarters. Seneca's letters, again, witness eloquently to such realizations:

Death should be looked in the face by young and old alike. We are not summoned according to our rating on the censor's list. (*Epistolae* 12 ["On Old Age"] 8-10)

No man has ever been so far advanced by Fortune that she did not threaten him as greatly as she had previously indulged him. Do not trust her seeming calm; in a moment the sea is moved to its depths. Reflect that a highway man or an enemy may cut your throat; and, though he is not your master, every slave wields the power of life and death over you. (*Epistolae* 4 ["On the Terrors of Death"] 8)

2. Three Factors Contributing to the Precariousness of Life

Many matters made first-century life precarious. Three key factors in particular, however, can be isolated and need here to be highlighted.

Roman Power

Roman political propaganda proclaimed that Augustus (63 B.C.–A.D. 14), the first Roman emperor, brought life to a world that was teetering on the brink of destruction. Augustus, in fact, was hailed as "the beginning of good news," "the beginning of the breath of life," and "the end of regrets for having been born" (Price, *Rituals and Power*, 55). And this rhetoric, when transferred to Augustus' successors, served to propagate the view that the emperor was "the source of all good things" (*Papyrus Oxyrhynchus* 1021.5-13, which was written on November 17, A.D. 54, the date of Nero's accession).

The fact that Rome had put an end to inter-city strife was viewed by many as an escape from certain death. Aelius Aristides, a Greek rhetorician of the second century A.D., wrote in praise of Roman leadership vis-à-vis the city of Rome and its neighbors:

As a consequence of their mutual discord and unrest, the cities were already as it were on the refuse heap; but then they received a common leadership and suddenly came alive again. (*Eulogy of Rome*, 155-57)

Such a viewpoint regarded the emperor as the source of life for all. For, as Seneca "the Younger" stated it:

As long as [the emperor] is alive, your dear ones are alive — you have lost nothing. Your eyes ought to be not only dry, but even happy. In him you have all things; he takes the place of all. (*De Consolatione Ad Polybium* 7.4)

And when Seneca composed a soliloquy for Nero, he stressed the tremendous power that the young emperor had inherited from those before him:

Have I of all mortals found favour with heaven and been chosen to serve on earth as vicar of the gods? I am the arbiter of life and death for the nations? (*De Clementia* [addressed to the emperor Nero] 1.1.2)

But Roman imperial power was a two-edged sword — with both the power to save life and the power to kill. Quoting Seneca again:

To give safety to many and to recall them to life from the very brink of death and to earn the civic crown through clemency — that is happiness. . . . This is divine power, to save life in mobs and states; but to kill many and indiscriminately is the power of conflagration and collapse. (*De Clementia* 1.26.5; cf. Ps-Seneca, *Octavia* 438-44)

And, sadly, in Rome's hands imperial power was wielded in both directions.

Despite Seneca's best efforts of advice, Nero's cruelties filled Rome with ghosts (cf. Pliny the Elder, *Historia Naturalis* 30.5). Nero, however, was not the first to spill blood for Rome's cause. The victories won by Augustus undoubtedly brought the world certain advantages. Yet despite the advantages won by her domination of the ancient world, Rome was also the cause of much violence, exploitation, and oppression. The power of Rome was irresistible, and her mastery of both land and sea was achieved at great human cost.

As acknowledged by Augustus himself, the *Pax Romana* was a "peace secured by victory" (*Res Gestae Divi Augusti* [Augustus' official biography] 13) — that is, a "peace" founded on military might, destruction, and violence. As Tacitus, the Roman historian of the late first and early second centuries A.D., put it in his history of the Julian dynasty after Augustus: "After [Augustus] there had been undoubtedly peace, but peace with bloodshed" (*Annales* 1.10.4).

Rome's avarice was insatiable and her plunder unceasing. Propertius, a Roman poet who wrote during the last half of the first century B.C., early complained about Rome's belligerent policies: "Now o'er such wide seas are we tempest tossed; we seek out a foe and pile fresh war on war" (*Elegies* 3.5.10-12). And Petronius, the aristocratic companion of Nero, wrote in his satirical, rather cynical novel: "The conquering Roman now held the whole world, sea and land and the course of sun and moon. But he was not satisfied. Now the waters were stirred and troubled by his loaded ships" (*Satyricon* 119.1-3).

When Britain was finally conquered in A.D. 43 and the island "at the world's end" brought under Roman sway, Tacitus, in a biography of his father-in-law Julius Agricola, has the Briton Calgacus reflect on the Roman conquerors and say:

> These deadly Romans, whose arrogance you cannot escape by obedience and self-restraint. Robbers of the world, now that earth fails their all-devastating hands, they probe even the sea. . . . To plunder, butcher, steal, these things they misname empire: they make a desolation and they call it peace. (*De Vita et Moribus Julii Agricolae* 30.3-5; 31.2)

Thus, despite the imperial rhetoric, to live under Rome's rule was to live under the shadow of death.

Malevolent Magic

Being powerless before an irresistible political regime often encourages the growth of magical practices. It is, therefore, not surprising that magic was a dark constant at all levels of first-century Greco-Roman society.

Malevolent magic, which through the use of lead curse tablets deposited in graves was used to procure advantage in politics, law, business, sport, and love, had been a feature of ancient life for centuries. Although not officially sanctioned, it was still operative in the first century. Laws enacted in A.D. 17 seem to have made the practice of magical arts a capital offense. Two years later, however, when the popular Roman general Germanicus died unexpectedly on October 9, A.D. 19, curse tablets were discovered in the floor of his house (Tacitus, *Annales* 2.69; cf. 3.13; Suetonius, *Lives of the Caesars* 4.3). In A.D. 26 Claudia Pulchra faced charges that included the use of curse tablets against the emperor Tiberius (Tacitus, *Annales* 4.52), as did Servilia later under Nero (ibid. 16.31). In the seventies, Pliny testified that "there is no one who is not afraid of curses and binding spells" (*Historia Naturalis* 28.4.19). And by the second century A.D., malevolent magical practices were sufficiently well-known for the rhetorician and sophist Apuleius to expect it to ring true for his readers when he told of a man being killed by malevolent magic (*Metamorphoses* [or, *The Golden Ass*] 9.29, 31) — perhaps through curse tablets (cf. ibid. 3.17).

In a world in which life was brief and brutal, the threat of malevolent magic wielded incredible power over people's lives. The curses of such magic aimed to bring about all kinds of suffering on their intended victims. Often, in fact, they sought to bring about another person's death — sometimes explicitly, sometimes through the cursing of bodily parts crucial to a person's survival.

Prevading Illness

Without the restraints of modern medicine and modern health measures, illness regularly invaded the fabric of ordinary life in the ancient world, bringing with it the threat of death. This was particularly tragic with respect to the death of a child.

Illness Generally

Illness brought about incredible suffering. The Hippocratic case studies, for example, speak repeatedly of the distress and misery that accompanied the progress of disease: great pain in various parts of the body, violent and continuous headaches, ulcerated throats and suppurating ears, vomiting and diarrhea, speech disturbances and deafness, paralysis, boils and abscesses, difficulty breathing, convulsions, delirium, rigor, coma, bleeding from various orifices, and so on — and all with no analgesics, antibiotics, or other benefits of modern medicine. In the forty-two cases in which the length of an illness is specifically mentioned in the Hippocratic case studies, those who died (approximately 60 percent) endured the disease for anywhere from 2 to 120 days, with their suffering lasting on average 19.4 days; those who survived had to endure the disease for anywhere from 3 to 120 days, with an average of 34.8 days of illness.

But it was not just illness generally that cast a shadow over human life in antiquity. The fact of the brevity of life made illness even harder to bear. This was recognized long before the first century in the *Prayer of Kantuzilis for Relief from his Suffering:*

> Life is bound up with death, and death is bound up with life. Man cannot live for ever; the days of his life are numbered. Were man to live for ever, it would not concern him greatly even if he had to endure grievous sickness. (J. B. Pritchard, *Ancient Near Eastern Texts Relating to the Old Testament,* 3rd ed. [Princeton: Princeton University Press, 1955], 400-401)

Living under the shadow of death brought additional suffering for family members who had to watch their loved ones die slowly because of a long illness, knowing that they were powerless to provide any real help.

The Death of a Child

The death of a child was particularly tragic. The mortality rate amongst children in the Roman empire was extremely high (cf. Wiedemann, *Adults and Children,* 11-17). This does not mean, however, that people became hardened to the death of children (contra Wiedemann, ibid. 16-17).

Certain statements from antiquity, it is true, suggest an attitude of indifference toward the death of children. Most notable is that of the Stoic philosopher Marcus Aurelius, who often repeated the saying said to be from Epictetus: "When you kiss your child, you should say: 'Perhaps it will be dead in the morning.'" Because death had to be accepted as an event as natural as the harvesting of corn, Marcus Aurelius would not pray that his sick child would not die, but prayed instead: "May I have no fear of losing him." Plutarch also, having been initiated into the mysteries of Dionysos and believing in the immortality of the soul, commended his wife for responding in a similar manner when their two-year-old daughter died while he was away (*Consolatio ad Uxorem* 608B-609D).

Such statements, however, are best regarded as philosophical responses that attempted to cope in a purely intellectual fashion with parental grief, rather than as indicating any general parental impassibility in antiquity about the death of children. For the philosophical approach was not the only response. Plutarch's advice to his wife, in fact, reveals that weeping was a more characteristic response, even if such a response was considered unseemly to the philosopher (ibid. 610B–C). Furthermore, the evidence derived from grave stones, as unrepresentative as it may be, suggests that the loss of a child was regarded by many as a grievous tragedy (cf. Garland, *Greek Way of Death,* xi; contra Wiedemann, *Adults and Children,* 42). Thus, just as childhood death was a common feature of ancient life, so too was parental grief.

The death of a child represented the death of a family's hopes for the future. As one tombstone reads: "Here Philippus laid his twelve-year-old son, Nicoteles, his great hope" (*Anthologia Graeca* 7.453) — a sentiment echoed in a later Jewish Hellenistic writing that depicts an old man's grief regarding the death of his son: "I have become childless, O King [Solomon], and without hope I keep watch at the grave of my son" (*Testament of Solomon* 20:20). Indeed, part of these "hopes" concerned the parents' own future, for the loss of a child was mourned as the loss of a natural harvest (cf. *Anthologia Graeca* 7.467), which left the parents with no one to care for them in their old age or to bury them properly. But such a rationale hardly exhausts the sense of tragedy in the frequently occurring sentiment that something seems awry in parents burying their children, rather than vice versa (*Anthologia Graeca* 7.261, 361, 466; cf. also 468, 638).

The ancient tombstones testify to feelings of tragedy not only on behalf of the parents but also on behalf of the child itself. A first- or second-century A.D. inscription on the tombstone of a seven-year-old complains: "I did not know what it is to enjoy the life of a man"; another: "What great hopes would there have been if the fates had allowed it" (cf. Wiedemann, *Adults and Children,* 41-42). Dying young, therefore, was also a tragedy because it meant that bitter fate had cheated a person of life before having reached his or her allotted span.

Such a consciousness of tragedy was frequently expressed in terms of dying unmarried. Sometimes the death of an unmarried person was accepted philosophically. Usually, however, a profound sense of parental grief is patent on the tombstones of such a person. For neither their position nor their possessions could prevent death from snatching people's children away from them before the proper time — as witness, for example, the inscription on the tomb of a son who died at fifteen years and twenty-four days, which laments: "Neither your grandfather's high office helped thee, nor the riches of thy father!" (*Anthologia Graeca* 7.602).

Malevolent magic exploited such parental emotions. Curses were directed against particular families, and so spells had to be purchased in order to protect against child-killing *daimons* (i.e., "ghosts of the dead"). Magical practices added to concerns about the death of a child. For in popular perception, those who died before their allotted span of life were believed to be barred from full entry into the underworld (cf. the Roman comic dramatist Plautus, *Mostellaria* 499-500), and so to have a special propensity for becoming ghosts. Such ghosts were considered potent agents of magic. They were frequently summoned to perform a magician's bidding.

Furthermore, it was widely believed that witches would kill small children in order to use them for their spells (cf. Cicero, *In Vatinium* 6.14; Horace, *Epodes* 5; Petronius, *Satyricon* 63.8). This, of course, added to parental fears, as reflected in a first-century A.D. epitaph of a slave-boy who was not yet four years old:

> The cruel hand of a witch has snatched me away,
>> while she remains on earth to harm people with her skills.
> Parents: Watch carefully over your children!
>> (*Carmina Latina Epigraphica,* ed. F. Buecheler, 987)

And given the supposed magical powers of such youthful victims, they may also have been liable to postmortem mutilation. The elder Pliny spoke of the practice of "tearing to pieces for sinful practices the limbs of still-born babies" (*Historia Naturalis* 28.20.70). Some of the magical spells, in fact, actually made use of parts of human bodies in their rituals — as, for example, the eye from a corpse of one who had been violently killed (*Papyri Graeci Magicae,* ed. K. Preisendanz and A. Henrichs, I.247-48), or "a young boy's heart" (ibid. IV.296-466; IV.2645ff.; cf. Ps-Phocylides 101-3, 149-50; Apuleius, *Metamorphoses* 2.20-30; 3.17).

It would hardly be a comforting prospect for a parent to know that a beloved child could be mutilated in the grave. Nor was there any comfort in knowing that one's child was entering into some in-between existence in which he or she could be manipulated for all kinds of nefarious purposes. Indeed, particularly for children, life was short, and death cast a dark shadow across it all.

3. Staving Off Death

One way to cope with death, of course, was to attempt to stave it off as long as possible. Homer had declared that "there is no escaping disease sent by Zeus" (*Odyssey* 9.410). Nevertheless, many people sought such an escape.

When a person was ill, there were three sources from which help could be sought. There were the physicians, who in the first century A.D. were still the disciples of Hippocrates, "that prince of medicine" (Pliny, *Historia Naturalis* 7.51.171; cf. Apuleius, *Florida* 19). There were the gods, some of whom, such as Asklepios, were especially known for their healing abilities. And there were the magicians.

There may have been some kind of loose protocol through which a sufferer passed, turning first to the physicians, then to the gods, and then to the magicians (cf. Thucydides, *History of the Peloponnesian War* 2.47; Hippocrates, *De Morbo Sacro* 4; see also *Sirach* 38:1-15; *Papyrus Oxyrhynchus* 1381) — each time seeking "salvation" or healing in the face of death. But could these "agencies" deliver?

The Physicians

A person of the first century who was ill had only one question in mind: Will I live or die? Although the physicians attempted to provide what assistance they could to alleviate a person's affliction, apparently the greater part of their role consisted in discerning the signs of the course of the illness that would enable them to predict the answer to this question (cf. Hippocrates, *Prognostics*, chaps. 1, 20, 24, and 25). But no matter how skilled the physicians were in predicting whether a patient would live or die, ultimately they were powerless in the face of death. They knew that they could only help in certain situations, and their reputations depended on their being able to discern aright those cases where they could help. As a later Hippocratic disciple rather sophistically argued: Since medicine was the art of cure, the physician should only deal with the curable. If a patient died, the doctor should not have been dealing with that case — for, by definition, it did not belong to his art! (cf. Hippocrates, *De Arte* 3 and 8).

The Gods

When the physicians could not help, it was time to call on the gods. Through oracles, the gods could assist with the all-important diagnostic question of whether a patient would live or die. But they were often able to do more. Asklepios, for example, was a good second option for help, for, as a second-century A.D. papyrus puts it, "he often saves people after all medical efforts have failed to liberate them from the diseases binding them, if only they turn to him in worship, however briefly" (*Papyrus Oxyrhynchus* 1381).

Nonetheless, despite various acts of "salvation" from particular diseases, if it was a person's time to die, not even the gods could save that person (cf. Homer, *Odyssey* 3.236ff.). The reaction was often fatalistic: "Why sigh we for our dead sons, when not even the gods have power to protect their children from death?" (*Anthologia Graeca* 7.8). The gods simply abandoned the dying (cf. Euripides, *Hippolytus*, 1473-74; idem, *Alcestis*, 22). Traditional Greek religion, in fact, did not provide any help for the problem of death and dying. It assumed that to be human is to be mortal and that immortality belonged only to the gods, so help had to be sought from other sources.

The Magicians

If, in the face of death, the gods and the physicians either could not or would not help, then that left only the magicians. As Plutarch, the late first-to early second-century A.D. essayist, author, and priest of the god Apollo, said: "People with chronic diseases, when they have despaired of ordinary remedies and customary regimens, turn to expiations and amulets and dreams" (*De Facie in Orbe Lunae* 920B).

The magicians were thought able to provide some assistance in predicting the outcome of an illness. Often they used some such "prognostic of life and death" as "Democritus' Sphere," which the late fifth- to early fourth-century B.C. philosopher Democritus devised in applying Leucippus' atomistic theory to an understanding of the human soul. It consisted of numbers set out on two registers and was used as follows:

> Find out what day of the month the sick one took to bed. Add his name from birth to the day of the month and divide by thirty. Look up on the

"sphere" the quotient: if the number is on the upper register, the person will live; but if it is on the lower register, he will die. (*Papyri Graeci Magicae*, ed. K. Preisendanz and A. Henrichs, XII.351-64)

People, however, wanted more than merely prognostic advice. They hoped to "drag out their life with food and drink and magic spells, trying to keep death out of the way" (Euripides, *The Suppliant Women*, 1109ff.). The magicians were considered especially useful if there was a suspicion that an affliction had been caused by magic. If Pliny the Elder was right that in the seventies of the first century "there [was] no one who [was] not afraid of curses and binding spells" (*Historia Naturalis* 28.4.19), then it follows that probably "everyone" — or, at least, most people — used amulets to protect themselves against the diseases inflicted by malevolent magic. "Magic," as Kotansky and Spier conclude, "enticed the workaday person with a means of escaping a creation fraught with uncertainty and anxiety, a world that in the end could not itself provide a promise of health in its present society nor safety in the life to come" ("The 'Horned Hunter,'" 329).

But did magic promise any greater chance of success than the physicians or the gods? It may well have done so. For the magicians provided people with charms that were supposed to ward off all sorts of calamities, illnesses, and death — or, as was claimed, a "stele that is useful for all things; it even delivers from death" (cf. *Papyri Graeci Magicae*, ed. K. Preisendanz and A. Henrichs, IV.1167-1226). They also claimed the ability to "raise the dead," though it is not exactly clear what such a promise entailed. Sometimes, it seems, "raising the dead" referred to the reanimation of a corpse for the sake of asking it questions (cf. Apuleius, *Metamorphoses*, 2.28-30; *Papyri Graeci Magicae* IV.1990ff.; 2140-44; also the necromancy in Homer, *Odyssey*, 11). More often, as in a number of extant spells, it meant the "raising" of a ghost to be used as an assistant for magical purposes (cf. Mark 6:14-16).

Yet sometimes a magician's charm appears to have been asking for something more: the actual resurrection of a dead body (*egersis sōmatos nekrou*). Thus the incantation of one magician of about A.D. 346:

I conjure you, spirit coming in air, enter, inspire, empower, resurrect (*diaegeiron*) by the power of the eternal god, this body; and let it walk about this place, for I am he who acts with the power of Thayth. (*Papyri Graeci Magicae*, ed. K. Preisendanz and A. Henrichs, XIII. 278-83)

What was desired here? The term *diaegeiron* may indicate that it was simply a reanimation of the *daimon* (ghost) corpse. And since what was being asked for was that the raised body walk around the room, all that may have been desired was a magical performance rather than the restoration of a person to life (cf. the magical "gimmicks" in *Papyri Graeci Magicae,* ed. K. Preisendanz and A. Henrichs, VII.167-85; XIb.1-5).

One of the late Aramaic bowl texts provides another ambiguous example (cf. *Amulets and Magic Bowls,* Bowl 4). Admitting that the meaning of the two spells in lines 1-3 and 8 of Bowl 4 is obscure, J. Naveh and S. Shaked, the editors of *Amulets and Magic Bowls,* suggest that they may be spells protecting a tomb. But since the spell of lines 1-3 reads "to make his body alive," it could be that this first spell of Bowl 4 purposed to bring back to life again one who had died. Yet neither of these spells, which are both later than the first century, gives any indication about how it was to be used or any hint about its efficacy. The spells may only mean that ancient magicians (1) were well aware of the great tragedy of death, (2) were not content merely to provide spells to stave it off, and (3) wanted to offer charms that would somehow bring someone back from the dead.

4. When Death Is Inevitable

Death for those of the first-century Greco-Roman world was a harsh and obvious fact of life that was implacable, and therefore inevitable. As Homer once said: "Hades, I ween, is not to be soothed, neither overcome, wherefore he is most hated by mortals of all gods" (*Iliad* 9.158-59). Nothing, in fact, could be said in favor of this great enemy, for real life was firmly above the ground — or, again, as the classical Greek poet once said: "I would rather be a paid servant in a poor man's house and be above ground than king of kings among the dead" (*Odyssey* 11.487).

For obvious reasons, probably the majority of people in the first-century Greco-Roman world regarded death negatively. Literary and inscriptional testimony from the ancient world unite in frequently lamenting that death means the end of human life. That nothing much had changed during the following century is suggested by Lucian, a second-century A.D. Greek satirist, who commented when mocking the funeral practices of his day: "People think death the greatest of misfortunes" (*De Morte Peregrini* 24).

On the other hand, there were also those who looked on death more positively. Sophocles, a tragic poet of Athens in the fifth century B.C., was one who argued that the pain of life made death a welcome relief and that desire for a long life was folly:

> Never to have been born at all:
> None can conceive a loftier thought!
> And the second-best is this: Once born,
> Quickly to return to the dust.

> (*Oedipus Coloneus* 1218ff.)

Likewise Euripides, who with Aeschylus and Sophocles was regarded as a member of the great triad of fifth-century B.C. Greek tragic writers, in what amounts to a reversal of the Homeric emphasis on life above the ground, agreed: "Birth should be lamented; death rejoiced over" (*Cresphontes*, fragment 449). Or, as Aristophanes, the comic playwright, put the matter: "Everyone says that so-and-so is a happy fellow *(makaritēs);* he's passed away, gone to sleep. He's a fortunate fellow *(eudaimōn)* because he no longer feels any pain" (*Tagēnestai* = fragment in *Stobaeus,* ed. Kock, 121.18). Pliny's *Natural History* reveals that such sentiments were current in the first century when he writes, "Nature has granted man no better gift than the shortness of life" (*Historia Naturalis* 7.50) and when he calls sudden death "life's supreme happiness" (ibid. 7.53).

The Greek tragic poets may have hinted at the possibility of life beyond death in positing the potential for reunion with a deceased loved one. The suggestion is contained in a remark by Euripides: "For death is sweetest so, With dear dead to lie low" (*The Suppliant Women* 1000-8). Nonetheless, if there was any life beyond the grave, it remained even for Euripides a mysterious unknown: "The life of man is all suffering, and there is no rest from pain and trouble. There may be something better than this life; but whatever it be, it is hidden in mists of darkness" (*Hippolytus* 189).

As people lived under the shadow of implacable death, their helplessness bred the kind of resignation that could only "comfort" the bereaved with the comfortless statement contained in a second-century papyrus writing: "Truly, there is nothing anyone can do in the face of such things" (*Papyrus Oxyrhynchus* 115; cf. Mark 5:35). For what kind of hope did they have to cling to?

5. Hope?

Although Philo, the hellenized Jew, may have felt that hope was the "one thing which is naturally capable of consoling human life" (*In Flaccum* 20.176), Greeks and Romans generally did not regard hope as at all trustworthy (cf. Walsh, "Spes Romana, Spes Christiana"; see also 1 Thess 4:13; Eph 2:12). Most people of the Greco-Roman world seem to have viewed humanity as being perennially tormented by two grim tyrants: Hope and Fear (cf. Lucian, *Alexander* 8; *Charon* 15; *Demonax* 20). The fifth-century B.C. tragedians despised hope as the very thing that prevented human beings from appreciating their own mortality (cf. Aeschylus, *Prometheus Vinctus* 250, 253; Sophocles, *Ajax* 473ff.; see also Plato, *Gorgias* 523D). And Seneca, the first-century Roman philosopher, agreed:

> "Cease to hope and you will cease to fear" [citing Hecaton, the Stoic philosopher from Rhodes of about 100 B.C.]. Just as the same chain fastens the prisoner and the soldier who guards him, so hope and fear, dissimilar as they are, keep step together; fear follows hope. . . . The present alone can make no man wretched.
>
> (*Epistolae ad Lucilium* 5 ["The Philosopher's Mean"] 7-9)

Hope was suspect because it could so easily be revealed as false and empty, and therefore vain.

This did not mean, however, that there were no hopes on offer. The imperial rhetoric attempted to focus people's hopes on the emperors, who kept the "Augustan Hope" alive — to use a phrase inscribed on a coin that was struck in A.D. 41, the year of Claudius' accession (cf. Smallwood, *Documents*, 98). But the darker side of Rome's power meant that such earthly hopes could easily turn sour. What could the emperors do about death itself, especially since their belligerent *Pax Romana* was part of the problem? Furthermore, people generally tended to place their hopes in their children. But it is here, perhaps most acutely, that hope proved to be so vain, for death continued to sweep children away long before their time.

6. The Prospect of an Afterlife

Was there no source whence one might seek hope for life beyond the grave? Socrates in the fifth century B.C. is reported to have said that philosophers ought to study "nothing but dying and being dead" (Plato, *Phaedo* 64A), and it was the philosophers who elaborated Tragedy's hints of a positive afterlife.

Developmental schemas, of course, cannot be pressed too rigorously. The evidence suggests that all kinds of views were probably mingled together in the first century, as at other periods. Nonetheless, broadly speaking, a three-stage development in the views of the afterlife can be discerned in Greek thought (cf. Burkert, *Greek Religion*, 190-215). The most ancient idea was that dead people retained some kind of shadowy existence in their tombs, and that they could be a positive force for those still alive if they were kept happy by offerings — or, if not, they could be an unhappy and malevolent force, being outraged and angry ghosts. In the Heroic age, which may be identified as a second stage of development, the idea of a collective dwelling of the dead, which was the domain of Hades, emerged. This domain was usually located underground. With this stage there appear a few brief hints that a greater blessedness awaits the rare heroic figure — such as the Elysian plain for Menelaus (as in Homer's *Odyssey* 4.565) or the Islands of the Blessed for the heroes who fought at Thebes and Troy (as in Hesiod's *Opera et Dies* 166).

It was during a third stage in the development of thought that the more explicit concepts regarding life after death came to the fore. It was the philosophers who had been influenced by "Orphism," which was believed to have stemmed from the legendary Thracian poet and musician Orpheus, who provided a greater differentiation of the afterlife. And it was the mystery religions that served to democratize the idea of a happier existence beyond the grave. In addition, throughout these periods of development regarding an afterlife, it is possible to detect a growing shift toward the idea of an astral immortality; whereas the dead once resided in the underworld, as time went by, they were understood to be located in the astral regions.

7. Philosophical Views of Death

Although Lucian mocked those who thought that death was "the greatest of misfortunes" (*De Morte Peregrini* 24), Plato depicts Socrates as having been more agnostic, saying: "No one knows what death is, not even whether it is not for man the greatest among all goods" (Plato, *Apology* 29A). His logic led him to recognize death as one of two states: "A dead person is either the same as nothing, not having any kind of sensation of anything, or, death is the removal and relocation of the soul from here to another place" (*Apology* 40C). In the first century, these two views were advocated respectively by the Epicureans and Stoics, on the one hand, and the Platonists, on the other.

Death as Nothingness

As far back as Democritus (ca. 460-370 B.C.), who spoke of the soul as perishing along with the body, there were those who attempted to minimize the sting of death by proclaiming it to be only a natural event at the end of a person's life. The philosopher Epicurus (ca. 342-271 B.C.), for example, taught that the human body dissolved into its component parts and disintegrated at death, so that in the end death does not affect a person (*Ad Menoeceum* 124; cf. Plutarch, *Moralia* 1103D, 1105A; *Diogenes Laertius* 10.139). It was, therefore, sensible to enjoy life while it lasts — that is, to "eat, drink, and be merry, for tomorrow we die." And though this sentiment was ancient, cross-cultural, and long-lasting, it was particularly linked with Epicureanism. So there appeared on the wall of a second-century A.D. Epicurean meeting hall at Ephesus the statement that during life people were given release from concern about death (cf. Horsley, "Inscriptions of Ephesus," 152-53).

Epicureanism, with its denial of an afterlife, was still a force to be reckoned with in the first century. Epicureans were among the group of Athenians who brought Paul to the Areopagus to hear about his resurrection teaching (Acts 17:18-20). Although the Epicureans were roundly condemned in the Jewish world (cf. Josephus, *Antiquities* 10.11; *Mishnah Sanhedrin* 10:1; *Sipre Numbers* 112), they found bedfellows among the Sadducees, who did not share the afterlife expectations of their Pharisaic brethren (cf. Mark 12:18-27; Acts 23:6-11; *Sipre Numbers* 112).

PETER G. BOLT

At the end of the first century, Plutarch (ca. A.D. 46-120) still felt that Epicureanism was of sufficient strength to merit at least ten essays written in refutation. It was also a personal issue for him, for when consoling his wife on the death of their two-year-old daughter, he found it necessary to warn her against the Epicureans, who were saying "nothing is in any way evil or painful to 'what has undergone dissolution'" (*Consolatio ad Uxorem* 611D) — a teaching that he considered contrary to both "the traditional teaching" (ibid. 756B) and the Bacchic mysteries into which he and his wife had been initiated.

The Stoics urged people to detach themselves from life, possessions, and even their spouses and children, so as to be able to bid them farewell easily when it came time to die (Epictetus, *Enchiridion* 7). The virtuous man was absolutely brave because he did not regard pain and death as evils. He did not follow the maxim "eat, drink, and be merry" because pleasure was not regarded as a good. Yet though the Stoics lived differently than the Epicureans, they were also convinced that both body and mind dissolved at death.

A number of epitaphs from the first century B.C. and first century A.D. suggest that scepticism about immortality, which was engendered by both Epicureanism and Stoicism, echoed throughout the Roman world: "We are mortals, not immortals!" (*Corpus Inscriptionum Latinorum,* ed. T. Mommsen, 11.856); "When life ends, all things perish and turn to nothing!" (*Carmina Latina Epigraphica,* ed. F. Buecheler, 420); "We are and were nothing. Look, reader, how swiftly we mortals pass from nothing to nothing!" (*Carmina Latina Epigraphica* 1495); "I was not, I was; I am not, I don't care!" (a frequently recurring epitaph). These sentiments represent a self-conscious rejection of anything beyond the grave and an embrace of the resultant nothingness of life, albeit in two distinct forms.

Death as the Relocation of the Soul

Not everyone, however, seems to have been content with death being the end of life. The alternative was to propose, in a complete reversal of the Homeric emphasis, that death was just the beginning of true life. In the fifth century B.C. Euripides had allowed the possibility of something more, if only to set such an idea promptly aside (cf. his *Hippolytus* 189). But Antiphanes, the prolific comic writer of the fourth century B.C., was decidedly more positive:

We should not mourn overmuch for those who are dear to us. They are not dead; they have only gone before upon the road that all must travel. Some day we too shall come to the same way, to spend the rest of time in their society. (*Aphrodisius* = fragment in *Stobaeus*, ed. Kock, 124.27)

But it was those who had been influenced by Orphism who most extensively dealt with that postmortem possibility — whether through philosophical speculations or the practices of the mystery religions of the day.

Orphism

The words of a deceased Orphic initiate not only express the view that the pain of his life was over, but also hint that he had gone to another place: "I have flown out of the sorrowful, weary wheel" (cf. Harrison, *Prolegomena*, 589). Similarly, Pindar said that our bodies followed the strong call of death, but our "eternal image" *(eidōn aiōnos)* survives death, for that alone is of divine origin (fragment 131 = Plutarch, *Consolatio ad Apollonium* 120D). With such notions in mind, Socrates was tempted to agree with Euripides' question, "Who knows whether to live is to be dead, or to be dead to live?" (*Gorgias* 492E; cf. Heraclitus, in Clement of Alexandria, *Stromata* 3.3; Sextus Empiricus, *Outlines of Pyrrhonism* 3.230), before he went on to discuss the Pythagorean notion that the body *(sōma)* was a tomb *(sēma)* for the soul until death gave it sweet release.

Pythagoras and the Afterlife

Pythagorean notions of the soul being released from the body at death, with good souls flying to the upper realms and those attracted to the body being purged and/or reincarnated, or simply hovering around the bodily realms, can be traced from Pythagoras (*Diogenes Laertius* 8.31), through Plato's elaboration (*Phaedo* 108A–C; cf. idem, *Respublica* 517B; 114B–C) and on to Plutarch (*De Sera Numinis Vindicta* 564Aff.). Neopythagoreanism, in fact, was centered in Rome during the first century, having reached its zenith in the period from 60 B.C. to A.D. 70.

The death of Socrates had proven a great inspiration for such Pythagorean views. For Socrates affirmed that "when death comes to a man, then what is mortal about him, it appears, dies, but what is immortal and imperishable withdraws from death and goes its way unharmed and undestroyed" (Plato, *Phaedo* 106E). Hopefully, a good man's soul might then ascend to live "altogether apart from the body" in celestial bliss (ibid. 114B–C; cf. Plutarch, *De Sera Numinis Vindicta* 564A–B). This is "a great hope" (ibid. 114C), which, for the person who has filled his life with the proper pursuits, readies such a one for death (ibid. 63B–C). Less pure souls, however, enter the air, where they may hover around the earth as ghosts (*Phaedo* 81C–D) — or, after a time of purgation (cf. Plutarch, *De Sera Numinis Vindicta* 565Aff.), may return to yet another sphere of bodily existence (ibid. 565E–566A, 567F).

Fronto, a Roman rhetorician and orator of the second century A.D., expressed doubts about the helpfulness of a doctrine of the immortality of the soul when it came to the death of a child. For as Fronto said: "If the immortality of the soul should ever be proved, . . . it will not be an answer to the grief felt by parents" (Haines II, 226). The doctrine, however, certainly was enlisted for this purpose by its supporters. In the hands of Plutarch, in particular, it provided the major source of comfort for his wife when their little daughter died while he was away from home. Thus, as Plutarch reasoned, because she was only two, she had not grown accustomed to the body, and so was more likely to escape to the upper regions than to be reincarnated in the cycle of rebirth (*Consolatio ad Uxorem* 611E–F). Or, to enlist a saying from Menander that Plutarch uses elsewhere: "He whom the gods love dies young" (Plutarch, *Consolatio ad Apollonium* 119E).

If belief in the dissolution of the body led to a greater focus on the things of this life, belief in the transfer of the soul promoted just the opposite. Itemizing the three pleasures of life that later became associated with Epicurus, Socrates considered that the philosophical man did not care much for "the so-called pleasures, such as eating and drinking . . . [or] the pleasures of love" (Plato, *Phaedo* 64C). So by rising above the enjoyments of the body to the concerns of the soul, death could be faced without fear (ibid. 64Eff.; cf. Epicharmus, fragment 22 = Clement of Alexandria, *Stromata* 4.170).

8. Apotheosis

The doctrine of the immortality of the soul also provided an important, theoretical underpinning for belief in the apotheosis of the Roman emperors — that is, in their exaltation at death to divine rank or stature. This was a significant feature in the Roman construction of reality that was gaining momentum in the first century.

Mythical Translations

Because of their particular virtues, great people of the mythical past were viewed as having been transported to some blessed realm. The ancient myths told of these people as either disappearing or being translated to another place — either on or under the earth, or into the heavens. A person who was translated avoided death altogether, as can be seen in the contrast between the translation of Oedipus and the normal manner of dying:

> For without wailing or disease or pain,
> He passed away — an end most marvellous.
> (Sophocles, Oedipus Rex 1663-65)

Whereas in the stories from the past these great ones had been transported *bodily* to some blessed realm, by the first century their apotheosis or exaltation was not the avoidance of death. Rather, it was simply the transport of the soul to the heavenly realms after death.

Imperial Apotheosis

Imperial power had taken a new turn with the apotheosis of Julius Caesar and Augustus, when the mythology surrounding the deification of Romulus, the founder of Rome, was applied to these two great emperors (on the deification of Romulus, see the second-century B.C. Roman epic poet Ennius, *Annales* 65-66, 111-13; cf. also Cicero, *De Republica* 1.25, 2.17; Livy, *History of Rome* 1.15.6; Plutarch, *Camillus* 32.5, *Numa* 2, 3; *Romulus* 27-28). Julius Caesar had obviously died a purely human death (Suetonius, *Lives of the Caesars: Julius Caesar* 83.2). Nonetheless, his demise was presented like that of Romulus (Ovid, *Metamorphoses* 15.745; Appian, *Bella Civilia* 2.114; Livy, *History of Rome* 1.16; cf. Segal, "Heavenly Ascent," 1347). The comet that appeared at his death provided a basis for the theory that his soul had become a new star, and so he became the first human to be divinized since Romulus. Such notions, of course, did not pass without criticism. In the latter part of the first century B.C., for example, the Roman poet Propertius somewhat mockingly alluded to the apotheosis of Julius Caesar in speaking of his own trysts with his mistress: "One such night might make any man a god!" (2.15.40-43; cf. 2.5.1f.). But the Romulus myth continued to be pressed into service for the divinization of Augustus (Dio Cassius 56.46.1-2) — even, a couple decades later, for the deification of Gaius' sister Panthea, who died in A.D. 38 (Dio Cassius 59.11.3).

Claudius was the next emperor to be granted apotheosis when he died in A.D. 54. Although at a later period the exaltation of emperors to divine rank or stature would become so commonplace that it was emptied of any great significance, the apotheosis of Claudius suggests that this was not so in the mid-first century A.D., for his divinization was received with mockery and scorn. When Pliny the Younger reflected on the event, his comment was that "Nero deified Claudius only to make him a laughing stock" (Pliny, *Panegyricus* 11.1). Seneca "the Younger" (ca. 4 B.C.–A.D. 65), who was a contemporary to the decision, wrote a biting satire of Claudius' deification, the so-called *Apocolocyntosis,* in which the gods, climaxing with Augustus himself, express their disgust over Claudius being placed among them. An apotheosis assumed that the great man was being divinized because of his great virtue, and Claudius did not really fit this requirement.

Apotheosis of the Virtuous

Pythagorean philosophy, though not against the concept of apotheosis per se, stood opposed to any idea that apotheosis was the exclusive domain of the emperors. For Pythagorean doctrine suggested that if people cultivated virtuous souls — whether they were emperors or not — they could achieve immortality. Of course, this immortality was an immortality of the soul, with the body being left behind.

9. The Place of the Body

In the Homeric tradition, real life was bodily life, and the afterlife could not properly be called "life" at all. Normally, at death the "soul" flitted away from the body as its sinews were no longer able to hold the flesh and bones together (*Odyssey* 11.218ff.; cf. *Iliad* 23.97ff.) and went to the afterlife as a shadow, not a body (cf. *Iliad* 1.3-5; *Odyssey* 11). Even when a privileged few were granted immortality in the myths, it was a bodily existence in the regions of the blessed.

On the other hand, Orphic views derived the soul from the upper world and set it in opposition to the body. Coming from "the whole" *(to holon),* and being borne by the winds and entering the body while breathing (cf. Aristotle, *De Anima* 410^{b}28), the soul was linked with the air. At death the soul remained in the air, but the body returned to the earth (cf. Euripides, *The Suppliant Women* 531-536; *Inscriptiones Graeca,* ed. A. Kirchoff, vol. 1, 2.945.6).

It is a small step from the Orphic-Pythagorean notion that, on death, the pure soul soars aloft back to the divine, to the idea that a man of great virtue would join the gods in some special kind of sense through apotheosis (cf. Cicero, *De Republica* 2.17; *Sirach* 45:4-5, regarding Moses). Unlike the older translations, apotheosis involved not the body but only the soul. The funeral pyre was said to burn away the body so that the immortal part could ascend to the gods (cf. Apollodorus, *Bibliotheca* 2.7.7; Lucian, *De Morte Peregrini* 4, 6, 30, 33; *Anthologia Graeca* 16.185). Thus when the apotheosis of the emperors became standard, the heavenly ascent of the soul was symbolized in the funeral ritual by releasing an eagle from a cage on top of the pyre (Dio Cassius 35.4; Herodian 4.2; cf. Lucian, *De Morte Peregrini* 39). Down below, however, their bodies still burned. Heaven was the domain of souls, not bodies — which the virtuous person had spent a lifetime seeking to overcome.

Given such notions, it is not surprising that the idea of a body returning to life sat uncomfortably in first-century A.D. Greco-Roman thought. Pliny was aware of reports of people coming back from the dead, but he explained them as premature diagnoses of death (*Historia Naturalis* 7.51-52). He also knew of "cases of persons appearing after burial," but labeled them "prodigies" that fell beyond the scope of his inquiry (ibid. 7.52). Mythology provided several examples of resuscitations — that is, temporary restorations of the dead to life on this earth — which were followed by eventual death. And the eschatological myths of Plato (*Respublica* 10.614B) and Plutarch (*De Sera Numinis Vindicta* 563ff.) each had characters who underwent "resurrections" that enabled them to speak of their otherworldly journeys.

Temporary restorations to life, therefore, were not completely alien to the Greeks. Strictly speaking, however, these restorations were not "from the dead," for the person had not been buried and so had not entered the realm of the dead (only Alcestis and Eurydice were exceptions). When "resurrection" proper is mentioned in nonbiblical Greek literature, it is most commonly in a statement of its impossibility: the dead are not raised (cf. Homer, *Iliad* 24.551, 756, also 21.56; Aeschylus, *Eumenides* 647f.; also idem, *Agamemnon* 565ff., 1361; Sophocles, *El* 138-39; Euripides, *Helen* 1285-87; Herodotus, *History* 3.62.3f.; see also 2 Sam 12:22-23; Ps 88:10-12; and Aristotle, *De Anima* 1.3.406^{b}3-5).

This does not mean that people of the first-century Greco-Roman world were unaware of other possibilities. Since the time of Alexander, the Greeks had been fascinated by things Oriental — by the Magi, the Chaldeans, the Indians, and even the Jews. Plutarch was well aware that the Chaldeans expected a future new world in which "those who are resurrected require no food and cast no shadows" (*On Isis and Osiris* 370C). But his Pythagorean notions of the soul being captive in the body and real life being only that of the soul led him to regard such views as fabulous.

For Plutarch, it was only the pure souls above who "cast no shadows" — that is, those who have been liberated from the body (cf. *De Sera Numinis Vindicta* 564D) — not those resurrected to a new body in a renewed earthly situation. He saw no sense in taking the body to heaven. It was simply "against nature" to insist that the body has a role in the afterlife. Even the mythological bodily translations were abhorrent to him (cf. *Romulus* 28.4), for they "improbably ascribed divinity to the mortal features in human nature, as well as to the divine" (ibid. 28.6). Although Plutarch does not want to reject divinity arising from virtue, he is nonetheless adamant that "to mix heaven with earth is foolish." For it is only as the soul separates from the body that it "becomes altogether pure, fleshless *(asarkon)*." Thus Plutarch goes on to insist:

> We must, therefore, definitely not against nature send the bodies of good people up together into heaven, but implicitly believe that in accordance with nature their virtues and their souls, and divine justice, ascend from men to heroes, from heroes to demi-gods, and from demi-gods, after they have been made pure and holy, as in the final rites of initiation and have freed themselves from mortality and sense, to gods, not by civic law, but in very truth and according to right reason, thus achieving the fairest and most blessed consummation. (*Romulus* 28.7-8)

The phrase "by civic law" may be directed at the Roman practice of divinizing emperors by Senatorial decision. Plutarch's Pythagoreanism taught that all good souls will achieve this end — not by public law, but by the practice of virtue. But whatever he meant by his use of the phrase "by civic law," Plutarch clearly considered a bodily apotheosis to be completely misguided, for "to send bodies to heaven" is "against nature." And Celsus, the second-century opponent of Christianity, stood firmly in this tradition as he launched his vehement attacks against the doctrine of a *bodily* resurrection: "The soul may have everlasting life, but corpses, as Heraclitus said 'ought to be thrown away as worse than dung'" (Origen, *Contra Celsum* 5.14-15).

Excessive love of the body in this life causes a soul to be led away to the underworld "only with violence and difficulty" (Plato, *Phaedo* 108F). But a pure soul, such as that of Socrates, puts up no such resistance (ibid. 115C), being hopeful of something more beyond the grave (ibid. 63C; or, more tentatively, *Apology* 42A; cf. *Phaedo* 115A). The attitude of a pure soul should conform to the suggestion of a Pythagorean allegory:

> "Do not turn back on reaching the borders": that is, when about to die and seeing the border of life is near, bear it calmly and do not be disheartened. (quoted by Plutarch, *De Liberis Educandis* 12F)

In all likelihood, not many people of antiquity would have attained to such philosophical heights. Reaching the virtue necessary for apotheosis was made even more difficult if, as in the case of Claudius, a person's body was in some way marred. For then they bore the marks of divine disapproval on their very bodies. And this meant that the hope of apotheosis for the soul was of little comfort to the general population, whose lives were often ravaged by illness and its abiding effects. Most people, presumably, did not die without a struggle. For them, perhaps, the mysteries offered a better and far simpler alternative.

10. The Mysteries

The Orphic eschatology that lay behind Pythagorean-Platonic philosophy probably had its greatest impact on the rank-and-file of people in the first century A.D. through the mysteries. The first century was a time in which there appears to have been a general discontent with traditional religion and a resurgence of interest in the various mysteries. The influence of the Oriental mysteries — that is, those of Attis, Adonis, Osiris, and Mithras — largely postdated this period. But the much older Greek mysteries associated with Eleusis, Samothrace, and other islands of the Thracian sea, the general "Orphic" religiosity, and the Dionysiac mysteries were very popular and widespread. Whereas traditional religion connected immortality with the gods, and becoming divine could only be an aristocratic privilege, the mysteries made immortality accessible to the ordinary person.

These mysteries were a source of hope for people facing the pain of their own approaching death or the death of their children (cf. Plutarch, *Consolatio ad Uxorem* 611E), for they held out the promise of a better lot in the afterlife (cf. Plato, *Respublica* 364E–365A; see also *Papyri Graeci Magicae,* ed. K. Preisendanz and A. Henrichs, IV.475ff.; 502ff.; 645ff.). This was a great attraction for some of the Romans, who held that:

> Nothing is better than those mysteries. For by means of them we have been transformed from a rough and savage way of life to the state of humanity, and have been civilized. Just as they are called initiations, so in actual fact we have learned from them the fundamentals of life, and have grasped the basis not only for living with joy but also for dying with a better hope. (Marcus, in Cicero, *De Lege Manilia* 2.14.36)

The basis of this hope was not so much a belief as an action, for, like Orphism, it was based simply on being initiated (cf. Plato, *Respublica* 11.364C; Plutarch, *Quomodo Adolescens Poetas Audire Debeat* 21F = Sophocles fragment 753). The secrecy that surrounded the mysteries makes this initiation difficult to describe. Apparently, however, it consisted of a quasi-death enactment, which may actually have been life-threatening (cf. Apuleius, *Metamorphoses* 11.21), thereby bringing an initiate "to the very boundary between life and death" (ibid. 11.23; cf. *Papyri Graeci Magicae,* ed. K. Preisendanz and A. Henrichs, IV.719ff.).

This initiation held the promise of an afterlife in the regions of the blessed, as seen in Isis' promise to Lucius:

> You shall live blessed. You shall live glorious under my guidance; and when you have travelled your full length of time and you go down into death, there also, on that hidden side of earth, you shall dwell in the

Elysian Fields and frequently adore me for my favors. (Apuleius, *Metamorphoses* 11.6)

Initiates apparently obtained a "pass" to ensure that they were given their just deserts in the underworld. In a number of instances, gold leaves have been discovered in corpses' mouths, which, it seems, were to enable Persephone to identify initiates (cf. Harrison, *Prolegomena,* esp. 575ff.). Such discoveries indicate that Dionysos, who crossed so many boundaries himself, "aids in the crossing of what for the classical Greeks was the greatest of all divisions, the barrier of life and death and between the human and divine" (Segal, "Heavenly Ascent," 418-19).

Epilogue: The Christian Gospel of Resurrection

Into the first-century A.D. Greco-Roman world, languishing as it was under the shadow of death, came a new message of resurrection that would eventually take the Roman empire by storm. The gospel of Jesus Christ proclaimed him as the alternative to the emperor — the "Son of God" who promised life to the world, rather than the bloodshed of Rome. Likewise, by dealing with the *daimonic* or "ghostly" forces that had been previously manipulated for nefarious ends by the practitioners of magic, he promised to break the power of the dead over the living. Furthermore, and most important, as the one who had personally dealt with illness and death, he cast back the shadow of death from the world. For it was exactly the boundary between life and death and the barrier between the human and the divine that Jesus Christ crossed, both on his own behalf and on behalf of his followers.

Although he himself died, the movement he left in his wake proclaimed that he had escaped from death. This was no avoidance of death. Rather, it was an escape from the bowels of death, after having died and been buried. Neither was this a temporary release from the underworld. Rather, it became his permanent state of affairs when he had been exalted to heaven. Nor was this simply a reward for his own virtue. Since his death was a "ransom for many," his victory over death held the promise that he had defeated death on behalf of those who turned to him as well.

Christ's resurrection was no mere apotheosis of the soul, for it also involved his body. Apotheosis of the soul held promise only for the elite.

Those who were not among the great ones in terms of their achievements or their morality had little hope. And if they had some bodily disability, their chances were even more remote — as when the gods, during their mockery of the apotheosis of Claudius, who was lame in his right foot, declared: "Look at his body, born under the wrath of heaven" (Seneca, *Apocolocyntosis* 11; cf. 1).

On the other hand, the Christian proclamation of resurrection was filled with promise to all those in a broken world who could not raise themselves from the dust and whose virtue could not save them. They had a champion in Jesus Christ, who had gone on ahead of them and, in going ahead of them, had provided a ransom that guaranteed their future.

For many potential hearers of the gospel of Jesus Christ, the ability of human power to wreak havoc and to kill was a painful fact of their experience. They also knew what it was like for unseen forces to cause intense pain and suffering, and then, suddenly, to take life away. Human mortality was, indeed, a grim reality, and the shadow of death hung heavily across the nations.

The Christian gospel of resurrection, however, held out a strong and living hope to a dying world. It spoke of a coming kingdom, which was life and not death; of salvation, not corruption; and, for those who continued to live under the shadow of death, it presented the assurance that something had been done about human mortality: that a crucified man had defeated death, and that he had done so through resurrection.

Selected Bibliography

Bianchi, Ugo. *The Greek Mysteries.* Leiden: Brill, 1976.

Bolt, Peter G. "'Do You Not Care That We Are Perishing?' Jesus' Defeat of Death and Mark's Early Readers." Ph.D. diss., King's College, University of London, 1997.

Burkert, W. *Greek Religion: Archaic and Classical.* Translated by J. Raffan. Oxford: Blackwell, 1985.

Clark, Mark Edward. "Images and Concepts of Hope in the Early Imperial Cult." In *Society of Biblical Literature 1982 Seminar Papers,* edited by K. H. Richards. Chico, Calif.: Scholars Press, 1982, 39-44.

Garland, R. *The Greek Way of Death.* London: Duckworth, 1985.

Harrison, J. E. *Prolegomena to the Study of Greek Religion.* Cambridge: Cambridge University Press, 1903.

Horsley, G. H. R. "The Inscriptions of Ephesus and the New Testament." *Novum Testamentum* 34 (1992) 105-68.

————, ed. *New Documents Illustrating Early Christianity.* Vol. 3. Sydney: Macquarie University Ancient Documentary Research Centre, 1983.

Kotansky, R., and J. Spier. "The 'Horned Hunter' on a Lost Gnostic Gem." *Harvard Theological Review* 88 (1995) 315-37.

Naveh, Joseph, and Shaul Shaked. *Amulets and Magic Bowls: Aramaic Incantations of Late Antiquity.* Jerusalem: Magnes, 1985.

Price, S. R. F. *Rituals and Power: The Roman Imperial Cult in Asia Minor.* Cambridge: Cambridge University Press, 1984.

Segal, Alan F. "Heavenly Ascent in Hellenistic Judaism, Early Christianity and Their Environment." In *Aufstieg und Niedergang der römischen Welt,* vol. II.23.2, edited by W. Haase. Berlin: De Gruyter, 1980, 1333-94.

Smallwood, E. Mary. *Documents Illustrating the Principates of Gaius Claudius and Nero.* Cambridge: Cambridge University Press, 1967.

Walsh, P. G. "Spes Romana, Spes Christiana." *Prudentia* 6 (1974) 33-43.

Wengst, K. *Pax Romana and the Peace of Jesus Christ.* London: SCM, 1987.

Wiedemann, T. *Adults and Children in the Roman Empire.* London: Routledge, 1989.

CHAPTER 4

Life, Death, and the Afterlife
in Second Temple Judaism

RICHARD BAUCKHAM

HOPE FOR eternal life beyond death was a remarkable development in the faith and traditions of Second Temple Judaism. At the beginning of this period, in the late sixth century B.C.E., there may not have been any such belief at all. Only a small number of Jews, at most, were then likely to have believed in life after death. At the end of the period, however, in the late first or early second century C.E., belief in life after death had become dominant within Judaism.

1. The Situation in the Hebrew Scriptures and Early Judaism

Most Jews in the early days of Second Temple Judaism — and probably for several centuries afterwards — retained the old Israelite idea that the dead exist as "shades" (*rĕpā'îm*) in the underworld of Sheol (*šĕ'ôl*). Sheol was a kind of mythical version of the tomb, a place of darkness and silence, from which no one returns. This concept of "shades" in Sheol was not a belief in the survival of the human spirit at death — that is, a belief in the spiritual or mental part of a human being continuing to live when the body dies, as much of Greek thought after Plato believed. The shades were not immaterial beings, but shadowy, ghostly versions of living, bodily persons, who could hardly be said to be alive. They were the dead, in a silent, dark, joyless — indeed, deathly — existence, who were cut off from God, the source of all life. It is this view, which is not peculiar to Israel

80

but was common to many ancient peoples, that most of the Hebrew Scriptures take for granted.

There is, however, one Old Testament text that quite certainly refers to a desirable immortality for the righteous and to judgment after death for the wicked. That text is Dan 12:2-3, which reads:

> Many of those who sleep in the dust of the earth shall awake, some to everlasting life, and some to shame and everlasting contempt. Those who are wise shall shine like the brightness of the sky, and those who lead many to righteousness, like the stars forever and ever.

And the chapter in which this text is found concludes with God's promise to the prophet in 12:13:

> As for you, go your way and rest. You shall rise for your reward at the end of the days.

This passage, together with its addendum at the end of the chapter, stands in what is probably the latest book of the Old Testament (mid-second century B.C.E.).

A few scholars hold that Dan 12:2-3 (with v. 13) is the only reference to life after death in the Hebrew Scriptures. Others see hope for eternal life also in Isa 26:19 (cf. 25:7-8):

> Your dead shall live, their corpses shall rise. O dwellers in the dust, awake and sing for joy! For your dew is a radiant dew, and the earth will give birth to those long dead.

Likewise, some see such a hope in some verses in the Psalms, especially in 49:15 ("God will ransom my soul from the power of Sheol, for he will receive me") and 73:24 ("You guide me with your counsel, and afterward you will receive me with honor"). But these texts cannot be dated with any degree of certainty, and other possible references to life beyond death in the Old Testament are highly debatable. So it must be concluded that evidence for a belief in life after death in the Old Testament is, at best, minimal.

In the postbiblical period, however, belief in life after death, which only a very few Old Testament texts suggest, came to be the general belief

81

of Judaism. Ben Sira, writing at the beginning of the second century B.C.E., is probably the last Jewish writer of the Second Temple period of whom it can be confidently stated that he did not expect eternal life and judgment after death. (There are, of course, later writings that contain no reference to such a belief, but they cannot be shown to exclude it.) From the evidence of the literature of the period, therefore, it would seem that by the end of the Second Temple period (i.e., the late first or early second century C.E.) the vast majority of Jews believed in a desirable immortality for the righteous and in punishment after death for the wicked.

The one identifiable Jewish group who did not share this belief were the Sadducees. They were a small body of aristocratic families in Jerusalem who wielded a great deal of religious, political, and economic power, but they had little influence on the beliefs of other Jews. Since they have left no writings, it is not clear why they opposed the dominant trend. It is generally thought that they were theologically very conservative and so rejected belief in the resurrection because they could not find it in the Torah. Perhaps, as well, being wealthy and privileged people — who already enjoyed their rewards — they had less reason than others for hope beyond death.

Because both the Jewish historian Josephus and the New Testament writer Luke (in Acts 23:8) distinguish between the Sadducees, who did not believe in the resurrection, and the Pharisees, who did, it has often been thought that resurrection was a distinctively Pharisaic belief. But this is a misunderstanding. For while belief in the resurrection distinguished Pharisees from Sadducees, it did not distinguish Pharisees from most other Jews.

No doubt there were other Jews besides the Sadducees who were skeptical about rewards and punishments in the afterlife. Some would have been influenced by popular Epicurean philosophy, which promoted such a skepticism in the Mediterranean world generally. We have, of course, very little means of access to the beliefs of ordinary people, since even tomb inscriptions generally use conventional phrases that indicate very little about the beliefs of those interred. In addition, we need to remember that most of the Jewish writings we have from this period were preserved by Christians for religious use, and they were unlikely to preserve material that denied life after death. Yet the literature we do have rarely seems to be asserting or arguing belief in life after death against disbelief or denial. And the impression we get is that by the first century C.E. belief in eternal life and judgment after death was fairly general within Judaism.

2. Circumstances of the Origin of Belief in Life after Death

Belief in eternal life and judgment after death was a late development in the Jewish religion. It appears only in a few texts within the Hebrew Bible. But it became general and dominant in Jewish belief in the latter part of the Second Temple period. How did this happen?

There are two ways of answering this question. One is to inquire into the specific historical circumstances in which belief in life after death originated and gained widespread acceptance. In such an approach, the middle of the second century B.C.E. is pinpointed as the period of origin. This period, the Maccabean period, was a time of severe crisis for Jewish religion. It was the time when the Syrian king Antiochus IV Epiphanes, with some Jewish support, attempted to paganize the Jewish religion, and when many Jews fought and died for the sake of faithfulness to God's law. In this situation, the old problem of the flourishing of the wicked and the sufferings of the righteous arose with special force.

During the Maccabean period martyrs died without seeing any reward for their sacrifice, while pagan persecutors and Jewish apostates seemed to triumph. Even if, as faithful Jews hoped, God were to intervene to overthrow his enemies and establish the kingdom of his holy ones, the question would still be asked: What of the martyrs for whom this would come too late? Surely they should participate in the future glory of God's people, shouldn't they? In these circumstances the expectations that God would raise the dead, reward the righteous, and punish the wicked spoke with great relevance to the specific situation. It is not surprising that such expectations appear in the apocalypses written during this period (Dan 12:2-3, 13; *1 Enoch* 90:33), as well as in the rather later account of the Maccabean martyrs found in 2 Maccabees (7:9, 11, 22-23, 28-29; cf. 12:43-45; 14:36).

It is unlikely, however, that the Maccabean period was actually the historical point of origin for a belief in rewards and punishments after death. Isaiah 26:19, which very probably speaks of resurrection, is almost certainly older — as is also *1 Enoch* 22, which portrays the dead in Sheol waiting for their resurrection at the day of judgment. It seems that we are, in fact, too ill-informed by our sources to be able to know when and in what circumstances Jews began to believe in judgment after death and eternal life. The most we can say is that the circumstances of the Maccabean period may well have been important for the spread of a belief that already existed, but which was not widely held until this time.

Our ignorance on this matter, however, is not of crucial importance. For even if we knew the circumstances in which belief in life after death originated in the religion of Israel and early Judaism, we would not really have accounted for the importance that this belief acquired. Determination of the circumstances of its origin cannot explain why belief in life after death became and remained the general Jewish belief long after the particular circumstances in which it arose had passed.

3. Continuity of Belief in Life after Death with Old Testament Faith

A more profitable way of understanding how belief in life after death became general in Judaism is to inquire whether this belief is an intelligible development of the faith contained in the Hebrew Scriptures. Even though it is rarely expressed in them, could it nevertheless have been seen as an appropriate or even necessary consequence of belief in the God revealed in those Scriptures? Was this belief in continuity with central elements in Israel's tradition of faith?

The most important point to make here is that hope for a resurrection stands in strong continuity with the Old Testament's portrayal of God. Essential to this is God's sovereignty over life. All life comes from him. He gives it, and he takes it away. The conviction that God is the source of life and the sovereign power over life several times takes the form of the claim that God "kills and makes alive" (Deut 32:39; 1 Sam 2:6; 2 Kgs 5:7; cf. Tobit 13:2; Wisdom 16:13):

> YHWH kills and makes alive;
> he brings down to Sheol and raises up!
>
> (1 Sam 2:6)

These biblical texts are echoed in those postbiblical texts that see God as "the God who makes the dead live" (*Joseph and Aseneth* 20:7; cf. Pseudo-Philo, *Biblical Antiquities* 3:10). Deuteronomy 32:39, in fact, is quoted in *4 Maccabees* 18:19, where it forms the climax of a rehearsal of scriptural bases for expecting God to give the martyrs eternal life.

Such Old Testament texts in their contexts hardly refer to the resurrection of the dead. They mean that God is the living God of unlimited power, who can save his people out of the most serious threats to life, since life is his gift and he alone is able to grant it and withdraw it. He gives life to the living and rescues the living from dying. The question of new life for those who have died, however, had not yet arisen when these biblical texts were written. Nonetheless, it is clear that if a question of new life were to arise, the response would be in terms of the God of whom these texts speak as having the power to raise the dead. The texts, therefore, must be seen as possessing potential meaning, which later Jewish writers quite legitimately realized and utilized.

The thought of God as the source of life and as sovereign over life is not, of course, unconnected with the thought of God as Creator. The stories of the martyrs in 2 Maccabees are in this respect very illuminating. For the martyrs are confident that God will raise them to new life after death, and they base this faith on a thoroughly biblical understanding of God as "the Creator of the world who shaped the beginning of humankind and devised the origin of all things" (7:23) and as "the Lord of life and spirit" (14:46). The God who gave body and life in creation can be trusted to give them back, in new creation, to those who have given them up through faithfulness to his law to the point of death (7:11, 22-23; 14:46).

The hope of resurrection, however, did not, as has sometimes been argued, originate only in connection with the martyrs. The martyrs, indeed, are set forth as paradigmatic. They were those who so trusted God with their lives that they could give them up for him in the hope of receiving them back from him. Yet hope for a resurrection is based on more than just a response to martyrdom.

Hope for a resurrection life beyond death is, in fact, a radical version of Old Testament faith, found especially in the Psalms, that God will deliver from premature death those who are faithful to him and trust in him. In the Psalms death frequently appears as a power that threatens the psalmists. Premature death — that is, death from illness or from the attacks of one's enemies — is perceived as an evil from which God can be trusted to deliver his people. Usually the expectation is that God will save the psalmists from dying prematurely. But occasionally the psalmists seem to take the further step of hoping for final deliverance from death. The psalmists who wrote Pss 49:15 and 73:24 express the hope that God "will receive" them, language that probably echoes the stories of Enoch and Elijah being received or taken by God (Gen 5:24; 2 Kgs 2:3).

It is noteworthy that both Psalm 49 and Psalm 73 are preoccupied with the problem of the prosperity of the wicked. The psalmists discover hope in the reflection that the fate of those who trust in God must be different from that of those who trust in riches. God's justice and God's love are at stake in this. The breakthrough in these psalms is the conviction that even death cannot frustrate God's justice and God's love. If necessary, God's justice and love must triumph even beyond death.

What is new here is not these psalmists' belief that the righteous God will vindicate the righteous against their oppressors or their conviction that the loving God will not abandon his people to death. These are fundamental aspects of Old Testament faith. What is new in these psalms is that they give rise to a faith in life with God that extends even beyond death. Old Testament faith is being taken to a newly radical conclusion. Radical trust in God's justice and faithful love is what gives these psalmists their death-transcending hope. The same trust is implicit in the one undisputed reference to resurrection in the Hebrew Bible, that found in Dan 12:2-3, and it continues on in the extant writings of the postbiblical Jewish writers.

The Old Testament God — the Creator, the Source of life, and the Lord of life — undoubtedly *could* raise the dead. That he *would* do so only became clear once death was perceived as contradicting God's righteousness and God's love. The Old Testament God could be trusted to vindicate the righteous and to be faithful in his love for his own. If these purposes could be fully attained only beyond death, then he could be trusted to raise the dead. In this way it was precisely faith in the Old Testament God that led to the hope of resurrection as a virtually necessary implication.

It cannot be over-emphasized that when Jews came to believe in life after death the ground for their belief was God. They did not conclude, as philosophers in the Greek tradition did, that human nature is such that part of it — the real human person — is naturally immortal. It was not from reflection on what human nature is that Jews came to hope for eternal life, but from reflection on who God is: the sovereign Creator, the righteous Judge, and the faithful Father of his people.

4. Biblical Features of Postbiblical Belief in Life after Death

We have seen that, although belief in life after death was largely a development of the period after the composition of most of the Hebrew Scriptures, it was a development of the faith in God that is expressed in those Scriptures. This continuity with Old Testament theology also accounts for significant features of life after death as it was understood in Second Temple Judaism. It is these features that largely account for the distinctiveness of Jewish belief in life beyond death, as compared with the beliefs of other ancient cultural traditions such as the Greek tradition.

In the first place, we should note that this Jewish tradition takes death itself very seriously. There is hope for life after death not because death is a mere appearance or does not affect the real core of the person, but because God can and will raise the dead. Death is an evil that — when all the dead have been brought back from it — will itself be destroyed by God (Isa 25:7-8; Pseudo-Philo, *Biblical Antiquities* 3:10; *4 Ezra* 8:53).

Secondly, for the most part the Jewish tradition of belief in life after death maintains the holistic view of the human person that is found in the Hebrew Scriptures. In the Greek (Platonic) tradition, human beings consist of a physical and therefore mortal part (the body) and an immaterial and therefore immortal part (the spirit or the mind). At death the body dies, but the spirit is freed to live an immaterial existence forever. In the Jewish tradition, on the other hand, human beings are a psychosomatic whole. Their bodiliness is intrinsic to their created nature. This does not mean that nothing survives death. On the contrary, as we have seen, in the old Israelite tradition the shades of the dead are in Sheol. But this existence *in death* is not the eternal life *beyond death* for which later Judaism hopes. That can only be conceived as a fully embodied life.

The way in which the holistic view of the human person was maintained in Judaism varied. The older view simply thought of the dead returning to life. This could be pictured as the shades in Sheol being raised by God from the underworld to new life. As they had passed from bodily life to shadowy existence in death, so they will be brought back from that shadowy existence to bodily life. Or, alternatively, the return of the dead to life could be pictured as the rising of the corpses of the dead from their graves. These are alternative pictures, both reflecting a unitary view of the human person, which in its full bodily reality dies and is raised.

A later view, which by the end of the Second Temple period was beginning to overtake the holistic view, thought more dualistically of soul and body. At death these are separated: the soul or spirit goes to Sheol or "the chambers of the souls," while the body is laid in the tomb. At the resurrection, however, soul and body are reunited. This view is closer to the Greek one. But it is also decisively different from the Greek view, for the souls in Sheol are the souls of *the dead* who return to *life* only when soul and body are reunited. Both components of human nature die. Eternal life requires both together to live again.

The terms "soul" and "spirit" (of the dead) are, therefore, somewhat ambiguous in the Jewish writings of this period. In some texts they refer to the "shades" of the dead, in accordance with the old nondualistic view (e.g., *1 Enoch* 22:3-10). In others they refer to that part of the person that is separated from the body at death and reunited with the body in resurrection (e.g., *1 Enoch* 102:4).

A third feature of Jewish belief in life after death that reflects its continuity with the faith of the Hebrew Scriptures is the concern with God's righteousness and judgment. That God governs the world in righteousness, that he delivers and vindicates those who suffer injustice, and that he judges those who act unjustly, are pervasive themes in the Old Testament. The tensions that occur in faith in this God when the righteous suffer unjustly — and while their oppressors prosper and God does not appear to intervene — are recurrent in the Old Testament.

Just as Jewish eschatology believed that, for God to be God, his righteousness must finally prevail on the stage of world history, so it also held that individuals must face God's judgment after death. The righteousness that is not apparent in this life will come to light after this life. This is why Jewish eschatology (already in Dan 12:2) expects a dual destiny after death: vindication for the righteous and condemnation for the wicked. And this is why the expectation of resurrection so commonly appears in a context of judicial language about the final judgment and the perfected righteousness of God.

Fourthly, individual eschatology is not divorced from corporate eschatology. The fate of the individual after death is placed within the context of the final future of God's people in the world. This is a consequence of the way Jewish eschatology developed. It was first and foremost a hope for God's action, in salvation and judgment, in the world, for the coming of his kingdom over Israel and the nations. When hope for the future of individuals entered the picture, it was hope that they would rise to share in the fulfillment of God's promises for the redemption and restoration of Israel.

Hope for life after death, therefore, is not purely individualistic in the Jewish tradition. Certainly God values the individual — so much that he will not let the one he loves perish in death. But the individual belongs to a people, and finds his or her future in the future of that people and of the world. God's final purpose for individuals, for Israel, and for the world is one and is envisaged as coming about in one eschatological event (or complex of events).

A result of the inseparability of individual and corporate eschatology is that individuals do not enter into their final destiny immediately at death, but must wait for the general resurrection and the last judgment at the end of history. Sheol now becomes an intermediate state in which the dead await their future. From an early date (cf. *1 Enoch* 22) Sheol is envisaged as having distinct compartments for the righteous, who await vindication and glory at the last day, and for the wicked, who await condemnation. Both categories of the dead already know what awaits them at the last judgment, and so, although the righteous are not yet rewarded and the wicked are not yet punished, the former do already delight and the latter do already suffer in anticipation of their respective destinies (*4 Ezra* 7:75-101).

This seems to have been the most common view of the intermediate state in the Second Temple period. The view that the righteous already enjoy the delights of Paradise and the wicked already suffer the torments of Hell in the intermediate state before the resurrection at the end, however, can also be found in certain writings of Second Temple Judaism and was to become dominant after that period. This development is probably an example of the influence of non-Jewish religious traditions (of which we will say more in the next section), for such traditions always portrayed the souls of the dead as attaining their postmortem destiny immediately at death.

5. Divergent Views from a Dominant Belief

The features listed in the last section may be said to have characterized most Jewish belief in the afterlife during the later Second Temple period. Such beliefs, however, were not uniform, and on occasion they took forms that lacked one or more of these features. In most cases this was due to influences from non-Jewish, especially Greek, traditions of belief about the afterlife. Jewish life and culture in this period were far from isolated from the increasingly international culture of the Mediterranean world. Faithfulness to the God of Israel and his law did not prevent Jews from appropriating elements from other cultural traditions that did not violate their central beliefs. These cultural traditions included both sophisticated philosophical thought and rich mythological imagery related to the afterlife. It is not surprising, therefore, that Jewish beliefs about the afterlife were, in varying degrees and in different ways, influenced by these traditions.

Some instances where such influences led to expressions of Jewish belief that depart from the features listed in the last section can be mentioned here. For example, two Jewish writings of the late Second Temple period that borrow hellenistic philosophical ideas and language quite freely are 4 Maccabees and the Wisdom of Solomon. Both sound Greek in the way they speak of the righteous as not dying but only seeming to die (cf. Wisdom 3:1-4; 4 Maccabees 7:18-19; 16:25). Yet even in these writings the Greek idea of spiritual immortality is qualified by Jewish elements. For although according to 4 Maccabees the martyrs become immortal at death, this immortality was given to them and is not depicted as an inherent quality of the soul. Wisdom of Solomon even continues to place the future of the righteous in the context of a collective and cosmic eschatology (cf. Wisdom 3:7-8), which was a notion quite alien to Greek thinking.

The *Testament of Abraham,* a Jewish work that came (like Wisdom) from the Egyptian Diaspora, portrays the afterlife in images borrowed from Platonic and/or Egyptian descriptions. Here the judgment of individual souls and their assignment to their eternal destinies at death seem to have entirely taken the place of any expectation of resurrection and judgment at the end of history. Likewise, the Jewish historian Josephus expresses his own beliefs in thoroughly Greek ways. And he even — evidently for the benefit of his Gentile readers — reports the views of other Jews in much more Greek terms than they themselves would have used. So, for example, when he claims that the Pharisees believed in reincarnation (*Jewish War* 2.164), he should be seen as translating their expectation of bodily resurrection — a belief that non-Jews in the Greco-Roman world found very strange — into a form that was familiar to his Gentile readers.

Such examples show that Jews were quite willing to recognize a degree of commonalty between their own religious beliefs and those of other cultural traditions. What is generally impressive — across the wide range of Jewish writings that we have from this period — is the extent to which borrowings from non-Jewish sources were usually made consistent with, rather than at the expense of, the distinctively Jewish shape of Jewish expectations of life after death.

6. Images of the Afterlife in Second Temple Judaism

In attempting to specify in more detail how the future of the dead was envisaged in Second Temple Judaism, it is useful to focus on the images that were used by the writers. Since the eschatological future had not been experienced, it could not be the object of literal description. Rather, it could only be evoked by images. And though the images have conceptual content, it must always be remembered that it is in images rather than in concepts as such that the literature of our period generally portrays life after death. Some of these images became very stereotyped, and most recur in the New Testament.

Several images portray the dead coming back to life. The simplest is that the dead person who now lies in the grave will stand up (e.g., Isa 26:19; Dan 12:13; 2 Macc 12:44; *Psalms of Solomon* 3:12). Or it may be said that God will raise them up (e.g., 2 Macc 7:9, 14). This is the image evoked by the term "resurrection" (e.g., *Testament of Job* 4:9). A variation on this image is to imagine the dead as sleeping in the grave. In the future they will awake (Isa 26:19; Dan 12:2-3) or get up from sleep (*1 Enoch* 91:10; 92:3; *2 Baruch* 30:2). Or God will awaken them (Pseudo-Philo, *Biblical Antiquities* 3:10; 19:12, 13).

A different image sees God recreating the dead from their remains "as they were before" (*Sibylline Oracle* 4.181-82). This picture, with its reference to bones as the part of the body that remains after decay, is inspired by Ezekiel's famous vision of the valley of bones (Ezek 37:1-14) — which was originally a parable of the restoration of the nation, but was read in later Second Temple times as a picture of God restoring flesh to the skeletons of the dead and bringing them again to life in the resurrection (*4 Maccabees* 18:17; *4QPseudo-Ezekiel*).

Another powerful image of resurrection pictures the places of the dead — that is, the earth, the sea, Sheol, the chambers of the souls — as restoring what has been entrusted to them (e.g., *1 Enoch* 51:1; *4 Ezra* 4:41-43; 7:32; *2 Baruch* 21:23; 42:8; 50:2; Pseudo-Philo, *Biblical Antiquities* 3:10; 33:3). This legal image makes the point that the places where the dead go at death do not own the dead, as though they had a right to keep them for ever, but are merely entrusted with the dead for temporary safekeeping. When God, who so entrusted them, reclaims his deposit, the places of the dead must surrender them back to life.

All these images, with their various pictures of restoration from death to life, might seem in themselves to suggest mere resuscitation: a return to the same life as mortal people live in this life and in just the same bodily form. Indeed, some of the texts we have cited actually stress that the dead are restored just as they were before death (*Sibylline Oracle* 4.182; *2 Baruch* 50:2). However, the concern that these texts express in this way centers on the preservation of personal identity. For those who rise must be understood to be the same persons, in their distinctive embodied forms, who had died. As other images make clear, these texts are not denying that there will also be a highly significant transformation of the dead in a resurrection that is not just resuscitation to this life, but entry into eternal life.

2 Baruch 49:1–51:1 is unusual in explicitly reflecting on this issue, much as Paul does in 1 Cor 15:35. In answer to Baruch's question about the form in which the dead will live again, he is told that they will first be raised in precisely the form in which they died, so that they may be recognized and recognize each other as the same people who died. Then they will be transformed — the wicked into a worse condition than their present one, the righteous into glorious splendor appropriate to the eternal world in which they will then dwell.

Two common and closely related images show the righteous raised into heavenly glory. According to one, which has biblical precedent in Dan 12:3, they will shine like the stars (*1 Enoch* 104:2; *4 Ezra* 7:78, 125; *2 Baruch* 51:10; Pseudo-Philo, *Biblical Antiquities* 33:5; *4 Maccabees* 17:4-6). Because the sky and the heavenly bodies are bright and shining, Jewish tradition always imagined heavenly beings, such as God and the angels, as luminous and shining. Because the righteous dead will rise to share the incorruptible and undying life of the heavenly beings, they too will then be like the stars. So it amounts to the same thing when, according to the second of these two images, they are said to be like the angels (*1 Enoch* 104:4; *2 Baruch* 51:5, 10, 12). Whether they are sometimes said actually to become angels is somewhat doubtful (*1 Enoch* 51:4; Wisdom 5:5), but the meaning would not be significantly different.

This imagery might be thought to imply that the resurrected righteous will live in the heavens rather than on earth. Perhaps this is occasionally the picture (cf. *1 Enoch* 104:2; *2 Baruch* 51:10; *Testament of Moses* 10:9-10). More commonly, however, it is said that in the renewed cosmos the resurrected righteous will dwell on the transformed earth (*1 Enoch* 45:4-5; 51:5; *Sibylline Oracle* 4.187).

Sometimes Enoch and Elijah, whom God "took" to be with him in heaven (Gen 5:24; 2 Kgs 2:3), are understood as representative of life beyond death, as we have already noticed may well be the case in Pss 49:15 and 73:24. The image of an assumption to heaven is thereby evoked. In Wisdom 4:10-15, Enoch, though anonymous (as are all biblical figures in this work), is clearly recognizable and functions as a paradigm of those whom God loves and "takes" away from the wicked world. Their removal from the world, misunderstood by the ungodly, is therefore really a blessing to them. In *Testament of Job* 39:8–40:3, Job claims that not even his children's bones will be found in their graves, because they have been taken up into heaven. At the end of the story, three days after Job's death, he himself is taken up to heaven in a chariot (like Elijah) — but in his case it is his soul that ascends, while his body is laid in the tomb (52:1-12). This ascent to heaven at death does not seem to be an alternative to resurrection at the end of history, in which Job is promised he will participate (4:9).

We have alluded to the importance of light in the image of the resurrected righteous as shining like the stars. Reference to eternal light is frequent in references to the destiny of the righteous (cf. *1 Enoch* 58:3; 92:4; 108:12-13; *Psalms of Solomon* 3:12; *2 Enoch* 65:8; 1QS [Qumran *Community Rule*] 4:8). When they are said to wear garments of glory (*1 Enoch* 62:15-16) and to sit on thrones of glory (*1 Enoch* 108:12), it should be remembered that this glory is both the visible splendor of shining light and the honor that God will give them, in contrast to the dishonor that they have suffered in this life. The light in which the righteous will dwell contrasts with the darkness that is the fate of the wicked (e.g., *1 Enoch* 108:14).

We have treated here only the most common images that portray the resurrection of the dead and their transformation, in the case of the righteous, into incorruptible and immortal life. Many other images also occur that portray the circumstances and character of life in the age to come, such as descriptions of Paradise and the New Jerusalem and depictions of the punishments in Gehenna.

7. Conclusion

Some scholars lay great emphasis on the variety of Jewish beliefs about life after death in Second Temple Judaism. In my view, this emphasis is mistaken. Most of the texts are thoroughly consistent with each other, though not every aspect of the beliefs we have outlined is present in every text. This is only to be expected, since few of the texts set out to give a full account of human destiny after death. Moreover, to a large extent, as we have seen, the texts deal in images rather than concepts. Yet images that might not be fully consistent if taken entirely literally may nevertheless converge in the impression that they convey.

Although there are exceptions in certain respects, as we have noted, the writings that are extant from the period of Second Temple Judaism do seem to offer a dominant view that we may reasonably suppose was shared by most Jews of that time. And the fact that virtually all aspects of this view, which is generally common in most of these Jewish writings, are also to be found in the New Testament seems to confirm this conclusion. The first Christians did not derive their understanding of the afterlife from any specific Jewish group, such as the Pharisees or the Essenes, but shared the views that had become general in the Judaism of their day. Like other Jews, they recognized that this Jewish understanding of the afterlife — though only rarely explicit in the Hebrew Scriptures — was strongly rooted in Jewish convictions regarding the God of Israel as he is revealed in those Scriptures.

Selected Bibliography

NOTE: Most of the noncanonical Jewish literature to which reference is made in this chapter can be found in the Apocrypha or in *The Old Testament Pseudepigrapha*, edited by James H. Charlesworth, 2 vols. (Garden City, N.Y.: Doubleday; London: Darton, Longman & Todd, 1983-85).

Bauckham, Richard. "Early Jewish Visions of Hell." *Journal of Theological Studies* 41 (1990) 355-85.
————. "Resurrection as Giving Back the Dead: A Traditional Image of Resurrection in the Pseudepigrapha and the Apocalypse of John." In *The Pseudepigrapha and Early Biblical Interpretation*, edited by James H. Charlesworth and Craig A. Evans. Sheffield: JSOT Press, 1993, 269-91.
————. "Visiting the Places of the Dead in the Extra-Canonical Apocalypses." *Proceedings of the Irish Biblical Association* 18 (1995) 78-93.
————. *The Fate of the Dead: Studies on the Jewish and Christian Apocalypses.* Supplements to *Novum Testamentum.* Leiden: Brill, forthcoming.

Cavallin, H. C. C. *Life After Death: Paul's Argument for the Resurrection of the Dead in I Cor 15*. Part I: *An Enquiry into the Jewish Background*. Coniectanea biblica, New Testament 7/1. Lund: Gleerup, 1974.

Collins, John J. *Seers, Sibyls and Sages in Hellenistic-Roman Judaism*. Supplements to the *Journal for the Study of Judaism* 54. Leiden: Brill, 1997 (esp. chap. 5, "Apocalyptic Eschatology as the Transcendence of Death," and chap. 21, "The Root of Immortality: Death in the Context of Jewish Wisdom").

Himmelfarb, Martha. *Tours of Hell: An Apocalyptic Form in Jewish and Christian Literature*. Philadelphia: University of Pennsylvania Press, 1983.

——————. *Ascent to Heaven in Jewish and Christian Apocalypses*. New York/Oxford: Oxford University Press, 1993.

Martin-Achard, Robert. *From Death to Life: A Study of the Development of the Doctrine of the Resurrection in the Old Testament*. Translated by J. P. Smith. Edinburgh/London: Oliver & Boyd, 1960.

Nickelsburg, George W. E. *Resurrection, Immortality, and Eternal Life in Intertestamental Judaism*. Harvard Theological Studies 26. Cambridge, Mass.: Harvard University Press; London: Oxford University Press, 1972.

Puech, Émile. "Messianism, Resurrection, and Eschatology at Qumran and in the New Testament." In *The Community of the Renewed Covenant: The Notre Dame Symposium on the Dead Sea Scrolls,* edited by Eugene Ulrich and James VanderKam. Notre Dame, Ind.: University of Notre Dame Press, 1994, 235-56.

II. Portrayals of Jesus and His Teaching

CHAPTER 5

Gospel, Kingdom, and Resurrection in the Synoptic Gospels

DONALD A. HAGNER

IT IS surely one of the great surprises of the Synoptic Gospels that the death and resurrection of Jesus are only first explicitly announced in the second half of these documents. Yet it was the quite unexpected events of the death and resurrection of the Messiah — both of which could be seen as rude and unwelcome intrusions into the steady story-line of the setting up of God's kingdom on earth — that would become the cornerstone of the preaching of the church from the very beginning.

There was, of course, good reason for this focus in the early church's preaching. For the death and resurrection of Jesus are not mere interludes in the story of God's greater work, the establishment of his kingdom. Rather, they are themselves at the heart of God's saving work — being the basis, means, and demonstration of the restoration of God's rule. In particular, the resurrection of Jesus, which is an intrinsically eschatological event, is both the proper beginning of distinctly Christian eschatology and the foreshadowing of the coming resurrection of the dead.

The intention of this essay is to explore the theme of the resurrection in the Synoptic Gospels with the goals of (1) identifying its treatment in those Gospels, both as presented commonly by all three synoptic evangelists and as portrayed uniquely by each writer individually, and (2) coming to an understanding of the theological importance of the resurrection, both with respect to that of Jesus and that of believers in Jesus. We will, therefore, first treat the Synoptic Gospels together in discussing various aspects of the subject, then look at the individual resurrection narratives of the three evangelists, and, finally, attempt to put the resurrection message of these three Gospels into a larger biblical-theological perspective.

1. The Subject of Resurrection
Prior to the Resurrection Narratives

Resurrection Presupposes Death

It is one thing to speak of a future resurrection of the dead. It is another, however, to speak of the resurrection of the Messiah. As for the former, there was no agreement among the Jews. The Sadducees did not believe in a future resurrection. This is plain from explicit statements in all three Synoptic Gospels (cf. Mark 12:18; Matt 22:23; Luke 20:27). It is also clear from the violent dispute on the subject between the Pharisees and the Sadducees that was fomented by Paul, as recorded in Acts 23:6-10 (cf. also Acts 4:1-2), and from the writings of the Jewish historian Josephus (cf. *Jewish War* 2.164-65; *Antiquities of the Jews* 18.16-17). As for the latter, the resurrection of the Messiah, there could be no thought of such a resurrection on anyone's part since the idea of the death of the Messiah was in no one's mind (hence Peter's response in Mark 8:32 and Matt 16:22 to Jesus' statement about his impending death). After all, it was a commonplace among the Jews that the kingdom of the Messiah would have no end (cf. 1 Sam 7:13, 16; see also Luke 1:33).

There is in the early narratives of the Synoptic Gospels no hint — either in the portrayals of John the Baptist or of Jesus — that the announcement of the dawning of the kingdom of God would involve the death of the one who brings in that kingdom. There are, of course, a few anticipations of the death of Jesus prior to the first explicit announcement at Caesarea Philippi (which appears in Mark 8:31-32; Matt 16:21; Luke 9:22). Opposition to Jesus is indicated very early in Mark's narrative, where the scribes accuse Jesus of blasphemy (2:7). In Mark 3:6 the Pharisees and Herodians plot together to destroy him — though the parallel passages in the other Synoptic Gospels appear later in their respective narratives (cf. Matt 12:14; Luke 6:11). But the reference in Mark 2:20 to the bridegroom being "taken away" and the resultant fasting of Jesus' disciples (cf. Matt 9:15; Luke 5:35) could only have been enigmatic to those who first heard it.

If the disciples were not in a position to understand the death of the Messiah, they could hardly have made sense of statements about his resurrection. Only when the necessity of the death of the Messiah came to be realized (as will be spelled out below) would the idea of the resurrection of the Messiah make any sense. And only when it was understood that the Messiah's vocation included his death would there be any credence given to his resurrection from the dead.

Raisings from the Dead

In all three Synoptic Gospels Jesus is recorded as having raised the dead. All three include the story of the raising of the daughter of Jairus (Mark 5:41-42; Matt 9:25 [though Jairus is not named in Matthew]; Luke 8:54-55). Luke alone has the story of the raising of the widow's son at Nain (Luke 7:11-17). And in a Q passage, Matthew and Luke record the message of Jesus to the imprisoned John concerning his messianic ministry, including reference to the fact that "the dead are raised up" (Matt 11:4; Luke 7:22).

Matthew alone includes Jesus' instructions to the disciples to "raise the dead" (10:8) — with two dramatic instances of such raising given in Acts, where Peter raises Tabitha (9:36-42) and Paul raises Eutychus (20:7-12). Furthermore, common to all three Synoptic Gospels is the worry of Herod Antipas, when he heard about Jesus, that John the Baptist had been raised from the dead (Mark 6:14-16; Matt 14:1-2; Luke 9:7-9).

It is important to note that in all of these instances we have to do not with resurrections, but with resuscitations. That is, these people were raised to the old life, not to the life of the new eschatological order, and so they had to die again. There is no breaking in of the new age in these raisings from the dead. At the same time, however, in the radical movement from death to life, these events are in their own way signs and anticipations of the eschatological resurrection of the dead, for they display the authority of Jesus over death.

The story of the rising from the dead of the saints in Matt 27:51-53, which is highly problematic from a historical point of view, points theologically to the importance of the resurrection of Jesus for the resurrection of the dead. It is important because the death and resurrection of Jesus are presented as having inevitable consequences of an eschatological character and as pointing to an eventual resurrection of the dead.

The Sign of Jonah

Although the material about the sign of Jonah in Matt 12:38-42 and Luke 11:29-32 was apparently drawn by both Matthew and Luke from Q, only Matthew's redaction makes Jonah's circumstances into a sign having to do with the resurrection of Jesus. There is, of course, no actual reference to resurrection in Matthew's treatment. But it is implied in the parallel drawn by the evangelist between the three days and three nights spent by Jonah in the belly of the great fish and the statement that "so will the Son of Man be three days and three nights in the heart of the earth" (12:40; cf. 16:1-2 for a second Matthean reference to the sign of Jonah). Since, however, this passage in Matthew precedes by some four chapters the first passion prediction in 16:21 (cf. Mark 8:31-32; Luke 9:22), which incorporates the evangelist's first explicit reference to the death of Jesus, it must have been enigmatic to the disciples — perhaps even to the first readers of Matthew's Gospel.

Probably the original point of Q is captured by Luke, where the sign of Jonah is used (1) to parallel the preaching of Jonah and that of Jesus, and (2) to contrast the repentance of the people of Nineveh with the unbelief of the Jews (cf. Luke 11:30-32). Matthew appears to have adapted this saying, finding in its reference to three days and three nights an irresistible analogy to the time that the body of Jesus was in the tomb. In Matthew's redactional treatment, therefore, the sign of Jonah becomes the resurrection of Jesus. But even at this sign the Jews would not believe (cf. Matt 28:11-15; Luke 16:31).

It has often been pointed out that the parallels between Jonah and Jesus do not exactly fit at every point. Thus, for example, unlike Jesus, Jonah did not die. Moreover, the correspondence is not exact between "three days and three nights" with respect to Jonah and "after three days" (in Mark) or "on the third day" (in Matthew and Luke) with respect to Jesus (cf. also "after three days" in Matt 27:63 and "until the third day" in Matt 27:64). Matthew, however, was evidently not concerned with such matters. It was enough for him to ponder not only the correspondence between these two preachers and their respective audiences, but, more importantly, the divinely intended similarity of both Jonah and Jesus being returned to life after three days. For this evangelist, the sign of Jonah to unrepentant Jews is the resurrection of Jesus — a sign that they will come to know through the preaching of the early church.

The Three Passion Predictions

One of the most striking features of the synoptic narratives is that at a climactic point in the story there occurs the first explicit announcement of Jesus' imminent suffering, death, and resurrection — that is, immediately after the confession of Peter that Jesus is the Messiah. This initial announcement is then repeated two more times in parallel form in all three of the Gospels (cf. Bayer, *Jesus' Predictions*).

Matthew and Luke follow Mark in putting that initial announcement between Peter's confession and the transfiguration narrative (Mark 8:31; par. Matt 16:21; Luke 9:22). The sequence has a historical probability about it. For Jesus will not talk explicitly about his suffering and death until he elicits and affirms the confession that he is the Messiah. And then, once the necessity of his death has been made clear (note the Greek particle *dei*, "it is necessary," which appears in all three accounts), he reveals his glory to the disciples in the transfiguration — lest, evidently, the announcement of his death cancel out the disciples' conviction that he is, indeed, the Messiah.

What consumes the attention of the disciples in the first passion prediction of the Synoptic Gospels is, of course, Jesus' reference to his imminent suffering and death, not his statement about his resurrection. So mystified were they by the former that the latter hardly entered their minds. How could it be that the Messiah would suffer and die? The Messiah, in their view, was to conquer the enemies of Israel, overthrow the rule of the pagan Romans, and set up the everlasting throne of David. Surely the Messiah would go to Jerusalem for other purposes than to die!

The second passion prediction is essentially a repetition of the first, except for the replacement of the clause "suffer many things" with "delivered into the hands of men" (Mark 9:30-32; par. Matt 17:22-23; Luke 9:44, though in Luke the announcement consists only of the latter phrase). The third is the most elaborate of the three in its details concerning Jesus' death, for it includes references to the Gentiles and to mocking, spitting, and scourging (Mark 10:33-34; par. Matt 20:18-19, who alone uses the verb "to crucify"; Luke 18:31-33). It may well display some retrospective editing.

There are numerous other references and allusions to the death and resurrection of Jesus in the Synoptic Gospels outside of these three passion predictions, but they add little of significance for our purposes. More important are the allusions to the exaltation of Jesus (cf. Mark 12:10-11, par. Matt 21:42, Luke 20:17; also Mark 12:36, par. Matt 22:44, Luke 20:42-

43) and the parousia of Jesus (e.g., Mark 8:38, par. Matt 16:27, Luke 9:26; and Mark 13:26, par. Matt 24:30, Luke 21:27) — which, of course, presuppose the resurrection. Probably the easiest way to understand the difficult statement of Mark 14:62, "You will see the Son of Man sitting at the right hand of the Mighty One, and coming with the clouds of heaven" (par. Matt 26:64; Luke 22:69), is to take it as referring to the ascension of Jesus, but beginning with his resurrection.

The reference to the resurrection in the three synoptic passion predictions is formulaic. Mark is distinctive in that he uses the active verb *anistēmi,* "arise," and the phrase *meta treis hēmeras,* "after three days." Matthew, on the other hand, consistently uses the passive of the verb *egeirō,* "be raised," while Luke uses the passive of *egeirō* in the first prediction and *anistēmi* in the third (he does not refer to the resurrection in the second passion prediction). Both Matthew and Luke, against Mark, consistently use the phrase *tȩ tritȩ hēmerą,* "on the third day."

It would seem natural to conclude that the *egeirō* forms are divine passives, implying that God raised Jesus, and that the *anistēmi* forms refer to the power of Jesus himself to rise from the dead. Both ideas are clearly stated in the New Testament. Thus, it could be surmised, where God is the acting subject in raising Jesus both *egeirō* (e.g., Acts 3:15; Rom 10:9) and *anistēmi* (e.g., Acts 2:24; 13:34) are to be found, but where Jesus is the acting subject *egeirō* is used (e.g., John 2:19-20). Such a distinction between these verbs, however, cannot consistently be maintained, especially since the passive of *egeirō* can often have an intransitive sense, "he arose" (cf. Mark 14:28; 16:6; Matt 27:64; see N. Turner, *A Grammar of New Testament Greek* [Edinburgh: T. & T. Clark, 1963] 3:57). And that there is no consistent or essential difference between the two verbs can be further seen from Luke's ability to use them equivalently in his first and third passion predictions.

The preference of Matthew and Luke for *tȩ tritȩ hēmerą,* "on the third day," may be explained by the evangelists' tendency to reflect the more exact language used in the kerygma and liturgy of the early church (cf. 1 Cor 15:4, which also uses the passive of *egeirō;* see also Acts 10:40). Mark's *meta treis hēmeras,* "after three days," is essentially synonymous with "on the third day," because of the common manner of reckoning time inclusively (i.e., any part of three days may also be referred to as "after three days"). Thus no contradiction is involved in these different expressions.

A further explicit reference to the resurrection, the second in their respective narratives, occurs on the way down from the Mount of Transfiguration in Mark and Matthew. This time, however, it is the resurrection alone that is in view. The disciples are told not to speak about the transfiguration event "until the Son of Man is raised from the dead" (Mark 9:9; Matt 17:9). This command to silence is a part of what has been called the "Messianic Secret." Jesus can hardly allow the story about what had taken place to inflame popular Jewish expectations (cf. John 6:15), especially when his notion of the Messiah's vocation was quite the opposite of theirs.

Also to be noted here is the enigmatic statement of Jesus that is included in the report of Jesus' opponents in Mark 14:58 (par. Matt 26:61; cf. Mark 15:29; par. Matt 27:40): "I will destroy this temple [*naos*] that is made with hands, and in three days I will build another, not made with hands." As it appears in the Synoptic Gospels, this logion prompts the reader to think of two things: (1) Jesus' prophecy in the Olivet Discourse of the destruction of the temple (Mark 13:2; par. Matt 24:2; Luke 21:6), except for the fact that there Jesus did not say that *he* would destroy the temple, and (2) Jesus' resurrection sayings in the three synoptic passion predictions that refer to three days or the third day. It is the Fourth Gospel that solves the puzzle by explicitly applying this saying to Jesus' resurrection: "He was speaking of the temple [*naos*] of his body" (John 2:19-21) — though with the omission of the verb "I will" before "destroy." And John adds that "after he was raised from the dead, his disciples remembered that he had said this" (John 2:22). Thus John gives his readers the key to the right interpretation of this resurrection saying, which is expressed somewhat enigmatically in the Synoptic Gospels — where we may have a convergence of what seems to have been two originally independent sayings.

The incongruity of the death of the Messiah (note Peter's reaction in Mark and Matthew to such an announcement in the first passion prediction) appears to have virtually eclipsed all references to Jesus' resurrection. Even when resurrection is specifically in view, the evangelists note that the disciples did not know what to make of the idea. On being charged by Jesus "not to tell anyone about what they had seen, until after the Son of Man had risen from the dead," for example, Mark comments: "So they kept the matter to themselves, questioning what this rising from the dead could mean" (9:10). Likewise, after the mention of the resurrection in the second passion prediction, Mark records: "But they did not understand what he was saying and were afraid to ask him" (9:32). The Lukan parallel is even more suggestive: "But they did not understand this saying: its meaning was concealed from them, so that they could not perceive it. And they were afraid to ask him about this saying" (9:45). It was not, it seems, the concept of a future resurrection from the dead that was incomprehensible to them. Rather, it was the idea of the imminent resurrection of the one they had just confessed to be the Messiah, and whose glory they had seen on the Mount of Transfiguration.

Teaching the Sadducees

One of the very few passages in the New Testament that teach about the nature of resurrection life is found in the triple tradition of the Synoptic Gospels, in Mark 12:18-27; Matt 22:23-33; and Luke 20:27-40. The teaching here is prompted by a question of the Sadducees, who are identified as those who say that there is no resurrection. The question concerns a woman who had no children when her husband died. In keeping with the custom of levirate marriage (cf. Deut 25:5-6), because of her continued barrenness she successively married six of her original husband's brothers, as they died off one by one. The result was that she had had seven husbands. "Which of the seven," the Sadducees confidently asked, "would then be her husband in the resurrection?" — believing that in posing such a question they had shown how incredible the concept of a resurrection really was.

Mark, followed by Matthew (but not by Luke), records Jesus as accusing the Sadducees of being wrong in denying the resurrection because (1) they were ignorant of the Scriptures, and (2) they underestimated the power of God. With regard to the Scriptures, the passage ends with Jesus quoting from Exod 3:6: "I am the God of Abraham, and the God of Isaac, and the God of Jacob." The statement makes the point that long after their deaths God revealed himself to Moses as the God of the patriarchs. The implication that Jesus sees in the statement, however, is that the patriarchs were still alive, since God spoke of his relationship with them in the present tense ("I am") and would take no pleasure in being the God of the dead.

The patriarchs, therefore, are "alive in God" (cf. 4 Macc 7:19; 16:25; see also Luke 20:38b: "for all live to him"). And if they are alive, there can be no problem about their eventual resurrection. It is to this last point, the possibility of resurrection, that the remark about the Sadducees not knowing the power of God is directed. For God, who has the power initially to create, has also the power to give new, resurrection life (cf. 1 Cor 6:14).

The problem case posed by the Sadducees makes the wrong assumption that resurrection life will be exactly like human life as it is presently known. There will be, to be sure, continuity with this life. But also, as this passage shows, there will be features of discontinuity. Jesus reveals that in the coming resurrection life "they will neither marry nor be given in marriage." That is, in regard to marriage there will be discontinuity between this life and the life to come. The additional words, "but are like the angels in heaven," should not be taken as another discrete piece of information, but rather as stressing the point just made. For in resurrection life humans will resemble angels only in regard to no longer engaging in marriage, not necessarily in any other respect.

The Lukan redaction of Mark gives further information in setting out an apparent reason for there being no need for marriage in the coming resurrection: "Indeed, they cannot die anymore, because they are like angels [*isaggeloi*, literally: "equal to angels," which is unique to Luke] and are children of God, being children of the resurrection" (20:36). The age of the resurrection, in short, will involve a new order, an eschatological order, which corresponds to the hope of the prophets (cf. Isa 25:7; 26:19; see also Rev 21:4). Luke's version of Jesus' words also highlights a significant feature of that new eschatological order ("that age"): it will be inhabited by "those who are considered worthy of a place in that age" (20:35). The criterion whereby the worthiness of those inhabitants is established is not specified. What *is* clear, however, is that to be a "child of God" is to be, by definition, also a "child of the resurrection" (20:36).

2. The Resurrection Accounts

The major contribution of the Synoptic Gospels to the subject of the resurrection is, of course, to be found in the actual narratives of the resurrection of Jesus. Here we will look at certain significant themes that the three evangelists present in concert.

The Empty Tomb

Perhaps the single most important common element in the resurrection narratives of the Synoptic Gospels — apart, of course, from Jesus' resurrection appearances, which are found only in Matthew and Luke — is the empty tomb. The resurrection itself is neither witnessed nor described in any of the Gospels of the New Testament. (One can find a purely fictional description of the event in the *Gospel of Peter* 35-42, which indirectly demonstrates the historical sobriety of the canonical Gospels.) Rather, the resurrection narratives in the Synoptic Gospels and the Fourth Gospel begin with the empty tomb.

A great deal of debate has ensued regarding just how important the report of the empty tomb was among the early believers in Jesus, especially since it was not part of the kerygma of the early church and is referred to nowhere else in the New Testament outside of the Gospels. The silence of the remainder of the New Testament may well be due to the fact that the story rested on the testimony of women (cf. Osiek, "Women at the Tomb," 97-108). As Birger Gerhardsson notes, the testimony of women in that culture would have been "doubly incredible, doubly easy to ignore" ("Mark and the Female Witnesses," 225). Likewise, as has often been pointed out, the empty tomb is not used in the New Testament as a proof of Jesus' resurrection. And except for the Beloved Disciple in John 20:8, the empty tomb is not presented in our canonical Gospels — and particularly in the Synoptic Gospels — as the cause of faith in the resurrection of Jesus. All of this is quite true. At the same time, however, the empty tomb does have something important to say about the nature of the resurrection itself.

All three Synoptic Gospels (as well as John's Gospel) state that when the women came to the tomb they found the stone already rolled away and the tomb empty. It is always worth repeating the frequently made observation that the stone covering the opening to the tomb was not rolled away to allow Jesus to exit, but rather to reveal the empty tomb. Beyond the single main fact of the empty tomb with the stone rolled away, together with the important accompanying announcement "He is not here, but has risen!," the narratives differ considerably in their attendant details. Mark reports that at the tomb the women were met by "a young man . . . dressed in a white robe" (Mark 16:5). According to Matthew, they encountered "an angel of the Lord," who had "descended from heaven," whose appearance was "like lightning, and his raiment white as snow" (Matt 28:2f.); while in Luke's Gospel they encountered "two men . . . in dazzling apparel" (Luke 24:4; it is clear from 24:23 that angels are in view). It is not difficult to see how Matthew has simply made explicit that Mark's young man was an angel and that Luke has doubled the witness (something we might have expected Matthew to do, since he has been prone to such doubling elsewhere in his Gospel).

Matthew follows Mark fairly closely with regard to the angelic instructions to tell the disciples that they will see the risen Jesus in Galilee. Luke's messengers, however, mention Galilee only as the place where Jesus had foretold his death and resurrection. For in Luke, unlike Matthew and Mark (though the latter records no actual appearance), the appearance of the risen Jesus to the disciples occurs in Jerusalem rather than Galilee. Likewise, Matthew, again following Mark, notes the fear of the women (Matt 28:8), but adds to that their "great joy" — in contrast to Luke's omission of any reference to the reaction of the women.

The Women

That women were witnesses of the burial of Jesus and then also of the empty tomb in the Synoptic Gospels — and that, apart from the portrayal of Peter at the tomb in Luke 24:12 (cf. 24:34; John 20:3-7), they alone were witnesses of Jesus' empty tomb in these three accounts — is both (1) a testimony to the significance of women in the early Christian tradition, and (2) exceptionally strong evidence for the historicity of the empty tomb itself. The women were there for Jesus at his crucifixion, when most of his male disciples abandoned him. They came to the tomb where they had seen him buried not because they expected it to be empty, but because they were motivated by feelings of loyalty and reverence. And it is to these women that Jesus grants the first knowledge of the supremely important feature of the early Christian tradition, his resurrection, which would become the heart of the gospel.

Furthermore, the fact that it is women who are portrayed as the first witnesses of Jesus' resurrection underlines the historical truth of the story, for no one in that culture would have invented a story that gave such a key role to women. Even the disciples, at first, disregarded the report of the women, crediting it to be "an idle tale" not worthy of belief (Luke 24:11).

It has frequently been observed that there is no agreement among the Gospels concerning which or how many women came to the tomb — though all three of the Synoptic Gospels speak of the same women having witnessed the crucifixion at a distance. Mark has three women at the empty tomb, namely Mary Magdalene, Mary the mother of James (and Joses), and Salome (Mark 16:1; cf. 15:40). Matthew has only two: Mary Magdalene and "the other Mary" (Matt 28:1), who has been identified earlier as the mother of James and Joseph (Matt 27:56). Luke simply speaks of unspecified women "who had followed him from Galilee" (Luke 23:49, 55). And John has Mary Magdalene alone (John 20:1-2, 11-18).

Likewise, there are differences among the reactions of the women in the Synoptic Gospels. According to Mark, they were filled with "trembling and astonishment" and did not obey the command to tell the disciples, but "said nothing to anyone" (Mark 16:8). Matthew, on the other hand, records that they "ran to tell his disciples" (Matt 28:8), thereby making the women obedient to their commission. And in Luke, although there is no record of their reactions and no instruction given to tell the disciples, the women return to tell "the eleven" and "all the rest" (Luke 24:9).

The Appearances of the Risen Jesus

Matthew's Gospel records two appearances of the risen Jesus. The first is to the women, who worship him and are again told to tell "my brothers" that they will see him in Galilee (28:9-10). Then, climactically, Jesus appears to the eleven on a mountain in Galilee, where he gives them his famous commission to "make disciples of all nations" (28:16-20).

The first appearance of the risen Jesus in Luke's Gospel is to two disciples on the Emmaus road (24:13-35). The second is to a larger group of disciples at Jerusalem, which was made up of the eleven specially chosen by Jesus to accompany him during his ministry, the two from Emmaus, and probably others (24:36-49). In this episode we also find the Lukan form of Jesus' commission to his disciples (cf. vv. 47-49). These appearances in Luke 24 are then followed by a note at the beginning of Luke's second volume that tells the reader that Jesus "presented himself alive to them [i.e., his disciples] . . . appearing to them during forty days" before his ascension (Acts 1:3).

Both Matthew and Luke, in different ways, indicate the tangibility of the risen Jesus. Matthew, who alone has an appearance to the women, says that "they took hold of his feet and worshipped him" (28:9). In Luke's narrative, the disciples, who thought they were seeing a "ghost" (pneuma), are spoken to by Jesus in no uncertain terms. Pointing to his wounds he says: "Look at my hands and my feet; see that it is I myself. Touch me and see; for a ghost does not have flesh and bones as you see that I have" (24:39).

And then immediately after that he asks if they have any food, and he eats a piece of broiled fish — an episode undoubtedly staged to demonstrate the materiality of his body (cf. Talbert, "Place of the Resurrection").

The spiritual nature of Jesus' resurrection body, however, is also clear in the postresurrection accounts of the Synoptic Gospels. Luke, for example, records that Jesus "vanished from their sight" while eating with the two from Emmaus (24:31; cf. also the references to Jesus' ascension in Luke 24:51 and Acts 1:9). It is, in fact, clear from the synoptic narratives that the resurrection body of Jesus possesses a dual nature.

The shorter ending of Mark's Gospel, that is 16:1-8, which is attested by the best manuscripts, does not include a resurrection appearance of Jesus. The spurious longer ending that appears as 16:9-20 in many later manuscripts mentions three resurrection appearances: first to Mary Magdalene (vv. 9-11); then to "two of them as they were walking into the country" (vv. 12-13); and, finally, to the eleven "as they sat at table" (v. 14). There is nothing in these later accounts, however, to suggest that the body of Jesus was tangible. The unusual note in connection with the appearance to the two disciples that "he appeared in another form [*en hetera morphē*]" (v. 12) is probably only an allusion to the fact that in the Lukan story the Emmaus disciples were unable to recognize him (cf. Luke 24:16, 31), and nothing more.

The resurrection appearances of Jesus occur in the Synoptic Gospels to those who were expecting nothing — or, indeed, who were expecting only to see a dead Jesus. As George Ladd has appropriately put it: "Faith did not create the appearances; the appearances created faith" (*I Believe*, 39).

3. Distinctive Features of the Three Accounts

Before turning to a consideration of the theology of the resurrection in the Synoptic Gospels, it is necessary to focus on the distinctive features of each of the three evangelists in their respective resurrection narratives. Our concern here is not to attempt a harmonization of the well-known discrepancies between these accounts. Rather than weakening the case for the basic reliability of the resurrection portrayals, such discrepancies may be thought of as enhancing the credibility of the whole. Minute variations are to be expected in the reporting of any historical event by two or more witnesses.

And such diversities may be seen as pointing to a lack of collusion among the authors.

Mark's Narrative

The astonishing thing about Mark 16:1-8, which is accepted by most scholars as the original ending of Mark's Gospel, is the lack of an appearance of the risen Jesus. It may seem strange to us that the evangelist ended his Gospel with the words *ephobounto gar*, "for they were afraid" (v. 8) — unless, of course, the original ending was lost. Likewise, there can be no certainty as to why Mark wanted to end his narrative in such a fashion. Nonetheless, it has been shown that ancient writings could indeed end with the causal conjunction *gar* or "for," which in Greek cannot come first in a clause. And it has been well argued on the basis of narrative criticism that verses 7 and 8, when taken together and stressed equally, provide an appropriate closure to the Markan narrative and evoke a significant response on the part of its readers (cf. Lincoln, "The Promise and the Failure: Mark 16:7, 8").

Still, it remains somewhat strange that Mark has not recorded an actual appearance of the risen Jesus. Yet the announcement is clear both from 16:6, "He is risen, he is not here! " and 16:7, "He is going ahead of you to Galilee; there you will seem him, just as he told you." The rest is left to the mind of the reader (cf. Petersen, "When Is the End Not the End?"). And, after all, the claim of the early church that the earliest believers did see the risen Jesus was well known (cf. Best, *Mark* 73).

Some scholars are convinced that Mark would have had to refer to at least one resurrection appearance of Jesus. A few, therefore, have defended the "longer ending" of 16:9-20. But most of those who posit the need for a resurrection appearance in Mark have argued that this longer ending was composed as a replacement for an original, more extended ending, which evidently became lost. The oldest and best manuscripts, however, end at 16:8, and both Eusebius and Jerome regarded the verses that follow in the vast majority of later manuscripts as inauthentic. Francis Watson's conclusion is apropos: "The fragmentary nature of this particular narrative [i.e., 16:1-8] is therefore not an accident, but is integral to its meaning; it is an expression of the narrator's reticence in the face of the mystery of the divine action" (in Barton and Stanton, *Resurrection*, 101).

Accepting, then, the authenticity of the shorter ending, it needs to be noted that the emphasis at the end of Mark's Gospel is not on the disobedience of the women in saying nothing to no one. Rather, it is on their trembling, astonishment, and fear. And these emotions are regarded by the evangelist as being appropriate, and not at all blameworthy (cf. Smith, *Easter Gospels*).

Matthew's Narrative

The most distinctive feature in Matthew's account is the story about the posting of a guard at the tomb in 27:62-66. Before the resurrection narrative proper, Matthew relates that the chief priests and the Pharisees approached Pilate with their fears that the disciples of Jesus would steal his body and claim that he had risen from the dead. Their request was made on the day after the Day of Preparation, that is, on the Sabbath — hence their desire that the tomb be made secure "until the third day" *(heōs tēs tritēs hēmeras)*. Three days from the Sabbath would, evidently, provide some extra protection.

There is no little irony when later in the narrative, in 28:11-15, the chief priests and elders must invent the ludicrous story — which the Roman soldiers were supposed to have reported — that while they were sleeping the disciples had come during the night and stolen the body. The Jewish authorities and the Roman soldiers were confronted by an empty tomb. And dismissing the possibility of the resurrection of Jesus, they were forced to concoct a story to explain it.

Matthew notes that "this story is still told among the Jews to this day" (28:15). It is obvious that Matthew includes the story in order to provide an answer for his readers to the Jewish claim that Jesus' body had been stolen by his disciples. It is difficult to know, however, whether the evangelist created the story or not. It is, of course, only in Matthew's Gospel — and it fits well the needs of the Gospel's Jewish readership. Yet even events that occurred in history can also be used apologetically.

Unique and notable in Matthew's account of the empty tomb is his reference to an earthquake that rolled away the stone in front of the tomb (28:2). This reference to an earthquake, along with that of an earthquake at the crucifixion itself (27:51), lends an unmistakable apocalyptic character to the events narrated.

The final and climactic scene in Matthew's resurrection narrative is

Jesus' appearance to the eleven disciples on a mountain and his giving of the so-called Great Commission (28:16-20). Here for the second time in Matthew's Gospel we have the risen Jesus being worshipped — the first, of course, being that of the women in 27:9. This time, however, Matthew makes the interesting point that their worship was mixed with doubt (cf. v. 17). Two points in this verse should be noted. First, the definite article *hoi* in the Greek text is probably to be understood as "they" (i.e., "the disciples"), rather than "some" (for which Greek has a specific word). Second, what the verb *edistasan* ("they doubted") points to is not unbelief or uncertainty in what they saw, but rather their hesitation or indecision (which the word sometimes means in classical Greek). It is quite understandable that Jesus' disciples should be dumbfounded and unclear about what was to happen next. And, indeed, it is to their indecision and confusion that the immediately following words of the Great Commission are directed.

Jesus' commissioning of his disciples in 28:18-20, which are the last lines of Matthew's Gospel, explicitly opens up a mission to the Gentiles, thereby canceling the earlier restriction of the ministry of the disciples to the lost sheep of Israel (cf. 10:5-6). The commission itself is framed by a comforting statement and a promise. Jesus begins by informing the disciples: "All authority in heaven and on earth has been given to me" (28:18) — a statement reminiscent of an earlier statement: "All things have been committed to me by my Father" (11:27). Now, however, the glorious, risen Jesus embodies before them the reality of that authority. And after the commission itself to go, make disciples, baptize and teach (28:19-20a), he promises them: "Look, I am with you all the days until the consummation of the age" (28:20b; cf. 1:23).

The high Christology of the passage can hardly be missed — the possession of all authority, the commission itself, the call to baptize in the Trinitarian name, the call to teach what Jesus had taught them (cf. Smith, *Easter Gospels*), and the promise of his ongoing presence. All of this comes now from the risen, vindicated Jesus, who manifests his identity on the other side of death.

Luke's Narrative

Chapter 24 of Luke's Gospel is the most distinctive account among the three synoptic narratives of the resurrection and its aftermath. In the first pericope of 24:1-12, Luke includes the question posed by the two angelic figures: "Why do you look for the living among the dead?" (v. 5). The juxtaposition of the words "living" and "dead" points dramatically to the reality of the resurrection. Following this are again words unique to the Lukan account: "Remember how he told you, while he was still in Galilee, that the Son of Man must be handed over to sinners, and on the third day rise again" (vv. 6-7).

Only Luke records the response of the disciples to the report of the women about what they had seen: "But these words seemed to them an idle tale, and they did not believe them" (v. 11). Furthermore, Luke alone among the Synoptic Gospels (cf. John 20:3-7) refers to Peter running to the tomb, looking in, seeing the linen cloths, and returning home amazed (v. 12; cf. v. 34).

It is the story of the two disciples on the Emmaus road in 24:13-35, however, that is by far the most remarkable component of Luke's final chapter. (For a defense of the story's historicity, see Marshall, "Resurrection of Jesus in Luke.") Jesus meets them on the road, but incognito, because "their eyes were kept from recognizing him" (v. 16). This is reversed only toward the end of the story, when Jesus takes bread, blesses it, and gives it to them (*possibly* an allusion to the Eucharist) and "their eyes were opened, and they recognized him" (v. 31; cf. v. 35). With its wonderfully dramatic irony, the narrative provides the opportunity for a recapitulation of the entire gospel story. For when Jesus asks them what they were talking about, and when in obvious annoyance Cleopas replies, "Are you the only stranger in Jerusalem who does not know the things that have taken place in these days?" Jesus responds with the playful question: "What things?"

This is followed in 24:19b-24 by a brief summary of the events of Jesus' life and ministry as told by Luke in the preceding narrative. The summary ends with a very despairing assessment of the situation: "But we had hoped that he was the one to redeem Israel" (v. 21). Added to this is the report of the women, which was not believed by the two Emmaus travelers, that they had seen "a vision of angels who said that he was alive" (v. 23). Furthermore, as the two from Emmaus go on to report, some of their companions had gone to the tomb and found it empty (v. 24).

As the story progresses, Jesus chides these two disciples for being foolish and "slow of heart to believe all that the prophets have declared" (v. 25). In a rhetorical question he asks: "Was it not necessary that the Messiah should suffer these things and then enter into his glory?" (v. 26).

At this point Luke adds a narrative statement that serves to epitomize the heart of the Emmaus road episode: "Then beginning with Moses and all the prophets, he interpreted to them the things about himself in all the scriptures" (v. 27).

Here in 24:27, and again later in 24:45-47, Luke focuses on the death and resurrection of the Messiah as having taken place in fulfillment of the Scriptures. The evangelist wants to stress the fact that what had happened was neither accidental nor incidental. On the contrary, the strange events that had recently taken place were in accord with the will of God and in the fulfillment of what was promised to Israel in the Scriptures (cf. 18:31). So in narrating the event of his meeting with his disciples at Jerusalem in 24:36-49, Luke reports that Jesus "opened their minds to understand the scriptures" (v. 45). And then, again, the evangelist appends words of the risen Jesus regarding the necessity and importance of his own death and resurrection: "Thus it is written, that the Messiah is to suffer and to rise from the dead on the third day" (v. 46).

There has been a great deal of discussion regarding exactly which biblical passage or passages Luke — and the other evangelists — had in mind when he wrote of Jesus' death and resurrection being in fulfillment of the Scriptures. It may be impossible to say with certainty. But probably the suffering of Jesus was seen to have been prophesied in the servant song of Isa 52:13–53:12. The resurrection of Jesus may have been seen in Isa 53:10. More likely Hos 6:2, which says "on the third day he will raise us up," was used. Perhaps also the Psalm passages that are applied to the resurrection in the book of Acts were in mind — for example, Psalm 16, as used in Acts 2 and 13, and Psalm 2, as used in Acts 2. But whatever Scriptures were taken in support of the Messiah's resurrection, clearly a christocentric hermeneutic was in effect, whereby the Old Testament was understood through the lens of the risen Christ who is the goal of the whole of salvation history. The result is that the Scriptures were seen to have a *sensus plenior* or "fuller sense" wherein typological correspondences are viewed as not being coincidental but divinely intended, with the former understood as foreshadowing the latter. And Luke's approach in this matter is shared by the majority of New Testament writers.

In Luke 24:32 the Emmaus disciples remark poignantly on the effect of having heard Jesus interpret the Scriptures for them: "Were not our hearts burning within us while he was talking to us on the road, while he was opening the scriptures to us?" Perhaps they had not been among those who had heard Jesus earlier expound the Scriptures in reference to his destiny (cf., e.g., 18:31). What they came to realize through Jesus' interpretation, however, is that the strange events that had recently happened, and concerning which they had been wondering as they walked, were, in fact, the outworking of the great plan of God (cf. Talbert, "Place of the Resurrection"), and as such the fulfillment of what God had promised in the Scriptures.

Immediately, Luke reports in 24:33-34, the two Emmaus disciples returned to Jerusalem and found the eleven and their companions gathered together and talking about the resurrection, and especially about Jesus' appearance to Peter. Then in 24:36-49 the risen Jesus is portrayed as coming into that scene in a dramatic fashion. He proves to those gathered there that he is not an apparition, but a tangible reality, and again he states that what has happened is in fulfillment of the Scriptures. In the process, Luke states, "he opened their minds to understand the scriptures" (v. 45). Thus it is clearly the risen Christ who sets the church on its course of a christological interpretation of the Old Testament.

At this point in the narrative comes the Lukan version of Jesus' commissioning of his disciples. In Luke's Gospel a mission to the nations — that is, "that repentance and the forgiveness of sins is to be proclaimed in his name to all nations, beginning from Jerusalem" — is included in what was foretold in the Scriptures (cf. vv. 46-47). And Jesus climaxes his commission of his disciples with the words: "You are witnesses of these things. And see, I am sending upon you what my Father promised; so stay here in the city until you have been clothed with power from on high" (vv. 48-49).

Here in the final words of Luke's narrative — that is, in the commission of 24:47-49, the ascension narrative of 24:50-51, and the account of the disciples' return to Jerusalem in 24:52-53 — we have a collection of motifs that will emerge as key aspects of part two of Luke's story, namely the Acts of the Apostles. The opening chapters of Acts, which focus on the fulfillment of the promised coming of the Holy Spirit, provide a bridge between the Gospel of Luke and its aftermath. Indeed, throughout the narrative of Acts the important motifs of "witness" and "Holy Spirit" continue to be emphasized.

Not to be missed in these final words of Luke 24:47-53, of course, is the fact that it is the risen and ascended Jesus (v. 51) who will send the promised Spirit (v. 49). The risen, ascended Jesus will be the means of power in the proclamation of the forgiveness of sins, for it is with the death and resurrection of Jesus that such salvation becomes possible. Likewise not to be missed is the report that the disciples worshipped the risen Christ (v. 52a) and then returned to Jerusalem with great joy, being "continually in the temple blessing God" (vv. 52b-53). These are the motifs that Luke sets out at the end of his Gospel by way of introducing the accounts recorded in his Acts — motifs he evidently sees as characterizing the essential mission of the church.

4. Theological Retrospect

The Synoptic Gospels have as their common theme the establishment of the kingdom of God. The announcement of the coming of the kingdom means the new experience of God's rule or reign in the present age, in advance of its fullest coming at the end of the age. Everything in the Gospels — including the resurrection of Jesus — is to be related to that overarching theme. As Hans Bayer points out, "Jesus views his resurrection to immortality as a crucial event of foundational significance in the coming of the everlasting Kingdom of God" (*Jesus' Predictions*, 253).

This new realization and experience of God's sovereignty is eschatological in character. It involves the setting right of what went wrong in the Garden of Eden — indeed, an overturning of the effects of the Fall. Perhaps the most menacing of these effects is death itself. For just as the kingdom by definition promotes well-being and life, so the kingdom, or the rule of God, is the great enemy of death.

All the more surprising, then, is the necessity of the death of the Messiah. But the new reality of the kingdom, with its counteracting of the Fall and its effects, can only be established at the cost of the death of God's Son. The Messiah's death, in fact, is necessary as a sacrifice of atonement, "a ransom [*lytron*] for many" (Mark 10:45; par. Matt 20:28). His blood is "the blood of the new covenant, which is poured out for many for the forgiveness of sins" (Matt 26:28).

The Lukan version of the great commission specifically relates the death and resurrection of the Messiah to the early church's preaching of "repentance and forgiveness of sins . . . to all nations" (24:46-47). This conclusion, as Luke makes clear in 24:13-32 and 24:36-49, derives from a correct understanding of the Scriptures. For the death and resurrection of

118

Jesus are to be seen as the fulfillment of the Scriptures, and so reflect the accomplishment of the will of God and the achieving of the goal of salvation history. It is for this reason that the death and resurrection of Jesus constitute the heart of the kerygma. The gospel of the kingdom, in short, finds its basis in the death and resurrection of the Messiah.

The resuscitations of dead people that are recorded in the Gospels are a hint of the kingdom's victory over death, although they are only a foreshadowing and not a part of the new order. They are not the end of death. Rather, it is the resurrection of Jesus to a new order of life that is the irrefutable demonstration of the end of death. It is fundamentally a new eschatological reality that is signaled in Jesus' resurrection: that God, who created all that exists, will transform all that exists into a new creation where death will no longer be experienced. This new reality of the kingdom of God has already begun with the coming of Jesus and his resurrection from the dead. In the future, however, that new reality will produce children of God who are "children of the resurrection" and who "cannot die anymore" (Luke 20:36). The transformation of the old creation into a new creation will, therefore, involve the redemption of our corruptible bodies from their bondage to decay. And it is at this point that the tangibility of the body of Jesus, whose resurrection is prototypical, is important.

It is clear that the resurrection of Jesus is the high point in the Christology of the Synoptic Gospels. For it is the resurrection that vindicates all that Jesus said, believed, and did, and so is the definitive answer to the cross. It is obvious, as well, that the resurrection served as the impetus for the christological thinking of the early church (cf. Brian Hebblethwaite, "The Resurrection and the Incarnation," in Avis, *Resurrection of Jesus Christ*, 155-70).

Resurrection, ascension, and exaltation are sometimes difficult to distinguish. The Synoptic Gospels seem reluctant to call attention specifically to the glorious character of the resurrected Jesus. Nonetheless, Matthew's resurrection narrative refers to the women (28:6) and the disciples (28:17) as worshipping him. And Luke's accounts of Jesus' appearances to the Emmaus disciples (24:13-32) and then to a larger body of disciples at Jerusalem (24:36-49) call attention to the spectacular nature of what the disciples experienced. Even more significant are the commissioning scenes in both Matthew and Luke. Luke's version comes to its climax in the statement: "See, I am sending upon you what my Father promised; so stay here in the city until you have been clothed with power from on high" (Luke 24:49). Matthew's commissioning, however, is even more impressive, being framed, as we have seen, by the reference to the absolute authority of Jesus and his promise to be with the disciples unto the consummation of the age (Matt 28:18-20).

If the empty tomb does not have great apologetic significance, as we have noted above, the resurrection of Jesus certainly does. It is, in fact, the cornerstone of the gospel. And it is precisely for this reason the disciples are indispensable as "witnesses" (cf. Luke 24:48; Acts 1:8, 22; note also the importance of the verb "to see"). Yet it remains clear that not everyone will be persuaded, even by reliable witnesses and by what may be regarded as good and sufficient evidence. The Gospels themselves are not Pollyannaish on this point. In Luke's report of Jesus' parable about the rich man and Lazarus we find the words: "If they do not listen to Moses and the prophets, neither will they be convinced even if someone rises from the dead" (Luke 16:31). And in Matthew's redaction of the sign of Jonah, even resurrection will not convince "a wicked and adulterous generation" (Matt 12:39-42). Nor, in fact, does Jesus' resurrection itself compel faith, but rather it only serves to inspire the authorities to bribe the guards to spread a false story (Matt 28:11-15).

The disciples themselves experience considerable cognitive dissonance at the idea of the death and resurrection of Jesus (cf. Mark 9:10). After the first prediction, Peter reacts entirely inappropriately. After the second prediction, Mark records that "they did not understand what he was saying and were afraid to ask him" (Mark 9:32; par. Luke 9:45). At the same point Matthew notes "they were greatly distressed" (Matt 17:23). More surprising than this, however, is the fact that when the risen Jesus confronts them, they experience similar mixed reactions. Thus in all three synoptic resurrection narratives we find the mention of terror, amazement, and fear (Mark 16:8); great distress and doubt (Matt 17:23; 28:16); and fear and confusion (Luke 9:45; 18:34; 24:37). These we must regard as only natural human emotions experienced in the face of a totally new, glorious order that transcends what we otherwise know. Resuscitation, let alone resurrection, is not familiar territory.

The message of the resurrection of Jesus is that eschatological glory shall also be ours. The future belongs to us, death notwithstanding. The salvation that God has accomplished, the gospel of the kingdom, has been accomplished by the cross. Its full experience, however, is foreshadowed by the resurrection. For that reason the resurrection of Jesus produced in the disciples — as it should also produce in us — a distinct note of great joy (Matt 28:8; Luke 24:52).

Selected Bibliography

Avis, Paul, ed. *The Resurrection of Jesus Christ.* London: Darton, Longman & Todd, 1993.

Barton, Stephen C., and Graham N. Stanton. *Resurrection: Essays in Honour of Leslie Holden.* London: SPCK, 1994.

Bayer, Hans F. *Jesus' Predictions of Vindication and Resurrection.* Tübingen: Mohr-Siebeck, 1986.

Best, Ernest. *Mark: The Gospel as Story.* Edinburgh: T. & T. Clark, 1983.

Gerhardsson, Birger. "Mark and the Female Witnesses." In *DUMU-E2-DUB-BA-A: Studies in Honor of Åke Sjöberg,* edited by H. Behrens, D. Loding, and M. T. Roth. Philadelphia: Samuel Noah Kramer Fund, University Museum, 1989.

Heil, John P. *The Death and Resurrection of Jesus: A Narrative-Critical Reading of Matthew 26–28.* Minneapolis: Fortress, 1991.

Ladd, George E. *I Believe in the Resurrection of Jesus.* Grand Rapids: Eerdmans, 1975.

Lincoln, Andrew T. "The Promise and the Failure: Mark 16:7, 8." *Journal of Biblical Literature* 108 (1989) 283-300; reprinted in *The Interpretation of Mark,* edited by W. R. Telford. Edinburgh: T. & T. Clark, 1995, 229-51.

Marshall, I. Howard. "The Resurrection of Jesus in Luke." *Tyndale Bulletin* 24 (1973) 55-98.

O'Collins, Gerald. *Interpreting the Resurrection: Examining the Major Problems in the Stories of Jesus' Resurrection.* New York: Paulist, 1988.

Osiek, Carolyn. "The Women at the Tomb: What Are They Doing There?" *Ex Auditu* 9 (1993) 97-108.

Petersen, Norman R. "When Is the End Not the End? Reflections on the Ending of Mark's Narrative." *Interpretation* 34 (1980) 151-66.

Plevnik, Joseph. "The Eyewitnesses of the Risen Jesus in Luke 24." *Catholic Biblical Quarterly* 49 (1987) 90-103.

Smith, Robert H. *Easter Gospels: The Resurrection of Jesus according to the Four Evangelists.* Minneapolis: Augsburg, 1983.

Stuhlmacher, Peter. "The Resurrection of Jesus and the Resurrection of the Dead." *Ex Auditu* 9 (1993) 45-56.

Talbert, Charles H. "The Place of the Resurrection in the Theology of Luke." *Interpretation* 46 (1992) 19-30.

Wenham, David. "The Resurrection Narratives in Matthew's Gospel." *Tyndale Bulletin* 24 (1973) 21-54.

CHAPTER 6

"I Am the Resurrection and the Life": The Resurrection Message of the Fourth Gospel

ANDREW T. LINCOLN

THE DOMINANCE of the resurrection message in the Fourth Gospel is beyond dispute. While all the Gospel accounts are written from a post-resurrection perspective, the perspective in the Fourth Gospel is not only explicit in the narrator's asides (cf. 2:22; 7:39; 20:9) but also much more determinative for the shaping of the narrative than in the Synoptic Gospels. The preresurrection setting of Jesus and the postresurrection setting of the fourth evangelist and his readers have been telescoped together, so that much of the narrative is to be read on these two levels at the same time. Of the four Gospels, it is John's Gospel, in chapters 20 and 21, that allots the most space to the resurrection accounts and that provides the greatest number and variety of resurrection appearances.

Furthermore, the Fourth Gospel has eternal life — with its clear associations with resurrection — as a pervasive theme. The term "life" occurs thirty-six times in John's Gospel. On seventeen of those occasions it is accompanied by the adjective "eternal." And in a number of key sayings of Jesus, eternal life is linked explicitly to resurrection, with the most striking of these sayings being the "I am" formulation in 11:25: "I am the resurrection and the life."

1. Sharpening Our Focus:
The Role of the Resurrection in the Fourth Gospel

Despite the preponderance of resurrection material in the Fourth Gospel, the coherence of the resurrection message with other prominent features of the Gospel has frequently been a matter of dispute. This question arises principally because the structure of the plot in John's Gospel seems to find its resolution in Jesus' death on the cross. Likewise, the weight of the evangelist's theological point of view appears to fall on that death as being the moment of Jesus' glorification and exaltation. It is worth elaborating this matter briefly here so that the force of the question can be appreciated.

There are a number of ways in which Jesus' commission from God is formulated in the plot of John's Gospel — for example, to reveal God or make him known (cf. 1:18; 17:6, 26), to display God's glory (cf. 13:31, 32), to testify to the truth (cf. 18:37), and to give life (cf. 3:16; 10:10). In accomplishing his task, Jesus runs into opposition, primarily from "the Jews," who represent the unbelieving world. It is the dramatic irony of the narrative, however, that the opponents' counterplot to put Jesus to death only succeeds in bringing about the resolution of the story's main plot — which is the goal to which the narrative has been moving throughout the Fourth Gospel, as signaled by the evangelist's constant reference to Jesus' "hour" as being the decisive hour of glory (cf., e.g., 2:4; 7:6, 8; 12:23, 27; 13:1, 31, 32; 17:1). And in that resolution all opposition is overcome and Jesus' commission is completed.

It is, in fact, Jesus' cry from the cross — "It is finished!" (19:30) — that marks the actual resolution of the narrative plot of John's Gospel. Its force is that Jesus' mission is completed on the cross. Against all appearances, it is through Jesus' death that God is most fully known, that God's glory is supremely revealed, that the truth is most clearly testified to, and that life is abundantly given.

Add to such a scenario the facts (1) that the evangelist speaks of Jesus' death as a departure from the world to go to the Father, (2) that when he talks of the descent and ascent of the Son of Man he uses the double entendre of the Son of Man's being "lifted up" in both crucifixion and exaltation to indicate that that ascent is from the cross (cf. 3:14; 8:28; 12:32-34), and (3) that he describes Jesus as the resurrection and the life during his earthly mission, and it becomes clear why there is a puzzle about the role of the resurrection in the Fourth Gospel. What can the resurrection add that has not already been achieved in Jesus' mission, especially as that mission climaxes in his death?

We can allow Rudolf Bultmann to be the spokesperson for the perplexity felt by many scholars, when he says: "If Jesus' death on the cross is already his exaltation and glorification, *his resurrection* cannot be an event of special significance. No resurrection is needed to destroy the triumph which death might be supposed to have gained in the crucifixion. For the cross itself was already triumph over the world and its ruler" (*Theology of the New Testament,* vol. 2 [New York: Scribners, 1955] 56). Does the one who is the resurrection actually need to be raised? Are the resurrection accounts, strictly speaking, superfluous in the narrative of John's Gospel? Are they simply included, as many have argued, because of the pressure of the traditions that the evangelist inherited? Does the narrative of the Fourth Gospel deconstruct itself at the point of the resurrection? Such questions will help to sharpen our focus as we inquire about the role of the resurrection in John's Gospel.

2. Refining Our Method:
A Word about Narrative Criticism

In dealing with the resurrection message of the Fourth Gospel, one could start with inquiries about the history of the Johannine tradition, about the dependence or independence of John's Gospel vis-à-vis the Synoptic Gospels, about commonalities and differences between John's Gospel and the Synoptic Gospels, and about the theological reasons for such identifiable features. Source criticism, redaction criticism, and form criticism all have their place in Gospel study. Narrative criticism, however, has also become important for the study of the Gospels. And for our purposes, such an approach is probably more profitable.

Narrative criticism attempts to do justice to the shape of the canonical Gospels as narratives or stories. It focuses not so much on the real authors or readers as on what it calls the "implied authors" and "implied readers." These latter categories stand for the author and readers who are encoded in a particular text and whom we can reconstruct from the clues provided by the text itself. The implied author can sometimes take on a specific voice within the narrative, that of the narrator — the one who is actually relating the story. Narrative criticism also makes a distinction between "story" and "discourse." The story refers to the content of the narrative — its characters, settings, and events. The narrative discourse has to do with the way in which the implied author combines these elements into a particular plot, establishes the normative point of view necessary for a proper understanding of the plot, and attempts to guide and persuade the implied reader in the process of reading.

In what follows, therefore, we will pursue our inquiry along three main lines, concentrating on the narrative's "story" and "discourse" (i.e., how the story is told) in the conviction that it is through the narrative as we have it that the resurrection message of the Fourth Gospel is conveyed. We will ask in our first main section about the significance of the resurrection for the portrayal of Jesus himself ("Jesus and the Resurrection"). Then we will ask about the resurrection's significance for his followers, and, by extension, the narrative's implied readers ("Jesus' Followers and the Resurrection"). Finally, in our last main section we will highlight the episode of the raising of Lazarus, which brings together all of these issues and interests ("The Resurrection of Lazarus").

3. Jesus and the Resurrection

The Divine Life of the Logos

In treating the resurrection in its relation to Jesus, it is best, as with most matters in John's Gospel, to take our orientation from the prologue of 1:1-14, and not begin with the resurrection accounts themselves. For it is the prologue of the Fourth Gospel that gives its readers the vantage point from which to view all of the narrative that follows.

In the Gospel's prologue we are told not only that all things were created through the Logos (v. 3), but also that in the Logos was life (v. 4). As God's self-revelation, the Logos shares in the divine creative life. When the mission of the Logos is summarized in 1:10-13, it is depicted in terms of his coming into a world that has in some sense become separated from the divine life that created everything that exists, with the people of this world confirming that separation by rejecting the Logos. Yet at the same time the Logos is able to mediate life to those in the world who believe in him — that is, to put created life back into relationship with its source.

When the Logos enables humans to become children of God, this entails, the prologue stresses, something more than the ordinary process of human birth. Those who already possess created human life are to receive new life from the same origin as the Logos — that is, they are "born of God." How the life of the Logos is mediated to those who believe remains for the narrative to unfold. At this stage only one aspect of the process is emphasized: that "the Logos became flesh" (v. 14a). But this clause, though brief, is a huge interpretive clue. In fact, it is central to all that is portrayed in John's Gospel. For it serves to highlight the fact that there will be a new beginning of life among humans because the divine life of the Logos itself underwent something decisively new: it became identified with human bodily life in its temporality, weakness, and susceptibility to death. And concomitant with this central affirmation of the Fourth Gospel, two further questions arise: What will happen if the Logos returns to God? Will the Logos leave the flesh behind, or will he somehow retain this new identity as the incarnate Logos?

Jesus' Body as the New Temple

The reader of John's Gospel does not have to wait until the end of the narrative before these two further questions are answered. As early as the second major event of the narrative, the temple incident of 2:13-22, it is made clear that not only will the incarnate Logos die, but also that he will rise and that the bodily form of his resurrection will continue to be an essential feature of his identity. When asked for a sign to legitimize his action in the temple, Jesus says, "Destroy this temple, and in three days I will raise it up" (2:19). Over against the misunderstanding of "the Jews," who thought that Jesus was talking about the Jerusalem temple, the narrator makes sure that the reader has the insight that comes from a postresurrection perspective: "But he was speaking of the temple of his body. After he was raised from the dead, his disciples remembered that he had said this; and they believed the scripture and the word that Jesus had spoken" (vv. 21-22).

Although Jesus' death will be highlighted in the plot of John's Gospel, the reader is not allowed for one moment to divorce his death from his resurrection. The very first mention of Jesus' death, which appears here in the temple incident of 2:13-22, is accompanied by reference to his resurrection. And here the resurrection is formulated in terms of the Fourth Gospel's distinctive perspective. For the Logos, in whom is life, will be the agent of his own resurrection: "I will raise it up" (v. 19) — which suggests that not the

126

Jerusalem temple but now Jesus' crucified *and* raised body is to be the locus of God's presence and glory. So from as early as this point in the narrative, the reader expects to be given an account of this resurrection.

Given the emphasis in John's Gospel on the reliability of Jesus' word, it would be unthinkable for there not to be an account sometime later in the narrative of the fulfillment of the prediction of 2:19. Furthermore, it is now unthinkable that the future return and glorification of the Logos will mean the abandonment of his incarnate form, since the narrator has made it clear that the divine glory is inextricably linked to the body of Jesus in both its death and its resurrection. And, conversely, since the narrator has disclosed his point of view quite explicitly, what is also now unthinkable is that the story could be told in the way it is without the resurrection of Jesus being presupposed.

What is said in 2:21-22 to be a postresurrection insight into Jesus' crucified and raised body as being the temple in question is allowed to color the description of other aspects of the preresurrection mission of Jesus. In 4:21, for example, Jesus speaks to the Samaritan woman about a future time when she will worship the Father neither on Mt. Gerizim nor in Jerusalem; but then he follows this up with the assertion in 4:23 that "the hour is coming, *and is now here,* when the true worshipers will worship the Father in spirit and in truth." What is true of the crucified and raised body of Jesus, therefore, also holds for the period of his earthly mission — that is, that he is already the new locus for the worship of God. Similarly, believing that the divine glory is manifest in the temple of Jesus' risen body makes possible the attaching of that glory to the whole of Jesus' mission (cf. 1:14; 2:11), as well as, specifically, to his death as the supreme moment of glory rather than shame.

Thus from this early stage of the story, the reader is invited to see the resurrection not as being in competition with the death of Jesus for the spotlight, but as its necessary complement. Resurrection is both part and parcel of the mission of the incarnate Logos and the essential presupposition for the interpretation that his death receives in the narrative discourse of John's Gospel.

Jesus as Judge and Giver of Life

The perspective established by the conjunction of the prologue of 1:1-14 and the latter part of the temple incident in 2:19-22 is reinforced frequently in the ensuing narrative of the Fourth Gospel. We will here touch on just a few of these places, reserving the key Lazarus episode for discussion later.

In 5:19-29, in response to the charge that he was making himself equal to God, Jesus claims the two great divine prerogatives of judgment and raising the dead but also says that these prerogatives have been delegated to him by the Father. The reader is reminded of the earlier depiction of the Logos in 1:4, as the one in whom is life, when Jesus here declares: "For just as the Father has life in himself, so he has granted the Son also to have life in himself" (v. 26). As the living Logos/Son, Jesus has the power in both the present and the future to pronounce a positive verdict of life. Presently, it is his word that enables those who are spiritually dead to pass from death and experience eternal life through believing (vv. 24-25). What is more, at the end of history it will be his voice that inaugurates the physical resurrection of the dead for a judgment of either life or condemnation (vv. 28-29).

The great significance of these resurrection sayings in the Fourth Gospel needs to be underscored. For while resurrection and eternal life are correlated in the eschatological expectations of both Judaism and the Fourth Gospel, there is also an important difference to be noted between these two positions: in Judaism the resurrection precedes judgment with its verdict of either life or condemnation, whereas in the "realized eschatology" of John's Gospel not only is eschatological hope centered in Jesus but also divine judgment takes place ahead of time in his mission. Thus eternal life is presented in the Fourth Gospel as being able to be experienced in the present.

As is well known, eternal life in the Fourth Gospel signifies not simply duration. Rather, because it takes up the notion of the life of the age to come as having been inaugurated by Jesus' resurrection, it denotes the quality of life appropriate to that age. The present experience of eternal life is, therefore, an anticipation of — but not a substitute for — the physical resurrection. This means that eternal life for humans, while at present not simply the same as creaturely existence, cannot be viewed as divorced from physical life, and so existing on some totally separate "spiritual" level. The Logos mediates divine life to a world that, alienated from its Creator, is under the domination of death, both spiritually and physically (cf. vv. 21, 24, 25, 28). Therefore the experience of the renewal of life as a restored relationship to the Creator will also include the body in that relationship.

Jesus' Power to Lay Down and Take Up His Life

If eternal life involves resurrection for humanity — and the point is reinforced in the bread of life discourse in 6:25-59, where Jesus promises that those who come to him will have eternal life now and that he will raise them up at the last day (cf. vv. 39, 40, 44, 54) — then it would be exceedingly strange if, when its mediator died, he did not also experience resurrection. But, of course, it is also strange that the incarnate Logos, who is the source of eternal life, dies in the first place.

The narrative discourse about the good shepherd, particularly in 10:11-18, provides some illumination. Again, the death and resurrection of Jesus go hand in hand, with his resurrection seen as the necessary completion of his death (v. 18). But what is worthy of note here is that the life that Jesus as the good shepherd will, in sovereign power, lay down for the sheep — in order, then, to take it up again (vv. 11, 15, 17, 18) — is designated not as *zōē*, which is the term for eternal life, but as *psychē*, which is the term for human life that is temporal. *Psychē*, in fact, functions as an equivalent of *sarx* or "flesh," which is what the Logos in becoming truly human has taken on (1:14).

Thus in the portrayal of the Fourth Gospel, the Logos, in whom is "life" *(zōē)*, in taking on "flesh" *(sarx)* has taken on "temporal human life" *(psychē)*. He does not — indeed, could not — give up his divine life, which is imperishable. But he freely chooses to give up his human life in the flesh. Yet the point is that he lays down his human life only temporarily. He does not abandon it on the cross or in the tomb, but he takes it up. That is, he embraces it anew by his divine life in resurrection form.

The Whereabouts of Jesus' Body

In the farewell discourses of John 13:31–16:33, Jesus prepares his followers by talking not only about his departure but also about his return. One of the forms of that return will be as the risen one. In fact, the two sayings about seeing Jesus in "a little while" (cf. 14:18-19; 16:16-24) have the appearances of the risen Jesus as their primary referent. Furthermore, it will be on the basis of his resurrection life that the disciples will experience life — for, as Jesus said to them: "Because I live, you will live also" (14:19).

So it is that in "a little while" — that is, within three days (cf. 2:19) of the departure in glory of Jesus' death — Mary Magdalene finds the tomb empty on the first day of the week. Given what has already been said about Jesus' resurrection, the reader is not allowed to assume that the triumphant cry from the cross, "It is finished!" (19:30), and the glorification of Jesus' death are the whole story, nor that the ascent to the Father will simply entail the release of Jesus' soul from his body. Instead, the expectation has been raised that the incarnate form of the Logos will be involved. And so there remains the question of what has happened to Jesus' body.

At the level of the characters in the story, this is precisely the question of Mary Magdalene and the focus of the account in 20:1-18. Peter and the Beloved Disciple respond to Mary's anguished report that the body has been taken, and they head for the tomb. In line with his role as the ideal disciple, it is the Beloved Disciple who, on the basis of the linen wrappings from around the body being in one place and the cloth from around the head being rolled up in another, saw and believed (20:8).

Commentators have made heavy weather of what, in fact, the Beloved Disciple believed. Part of the difficulty in understanding what is meant by "he saw and believed" at the end of verse 8 lies in the relationship of this statement to the parenthetical comment of verse 9 that follows: "for as yet they did not understand the scripture, that he must rise from the dead." Nevertheless, because of his function as the perceptive witness, it is highly likely that the belief of the Beloved Disciple involved no less than what the reader is now expected to believe — and that verse 9 should be read as the narrator's comment on why, in contrast to the Beloved Disciple, the other disciples had not yet understood the necessity of the resurrection. So what the Beloved Disciple was the first to believe is that the position of the grave clothes meant not that others had taken Jesus' body away, but that he himself had demonstrated that death could not hold him by leaving death's symbols behind. And what the reader now knows is that this is the narrative demonstration of the earlier saying about Jesus' bodily life in 10:18: "I have power to lay it down and I have power to take it up."

Jesus' Resurrection as Ascension

In what follows in 20:11-18, as Jesus appears to her at the tomb, Mary Magdalene moves from not knowing where Jesus' body is to knowing the destination of his ascension. Essential to this transformation is the announcement she is given by Jesus in 20:17 to pass on to his followers. For after telling Mary not to hold on to him because he was not yet ascended, Jesus says: "I am ascending to my Father and your Father, to my God and your God" (v. 17). Significantly, the message Mary is to pass on is not that Jesus is risen, but that he is ascending. This puts the resurrection account squarely within the framework of the earlier narrative discourse about Jesus' ascent (cf. 3:13; 6:62) and his return to the Father who sent him (cf. 7:33; 13:1, 3; 14:28; 16:17, 28; 17:11, 13).

The climax of John's story about Jesus is neither his death itself nor his resurrection itself. Rather, the climax of the story focuses on the return of the crucified Jesus in a resurrected body to the Father. For the implied author, Jesus' death, his resurrection, and his ascension are all stages in the one event of glorification and together constitute the one hour of glory. Jesus' appearance at the empty tomb is depicted as only a temporary stop *en route* to the Father. It is only one movement of ascent from the cross that returns the Logos, who was with God, back to this same God in transformed incarnate form.

The later resurrection appearances in John's Gospel are, therefore, appearances of the already ascended Jesus. In the two Jerusalem appearances of 20:19-23 and 20:26-29 the risen and ascended Jesus shows his hands and side (cf. 19:34). This demonstrates that, whatever were the new properties of the resurrection that allowed Jesus to appear in a room with locked doors, there was (and is) a continuity between the earthly Jesus and the risen Lord. Just as back in 2:19-22 it was made clear to the reader that the Gospel's message about Jesus entailed both the death and resurrection of his body, so now in the resurrection appearances that inextricable link is reinforced. For the transformed body of the risen Jesus is also the body of the crucified one.

The glory to be seen in Jesus' death does not obviate the need for his resurrection. But neither does the resurrection triumphalistically supersede his death. The new life that Jesus achieves bears the marks of the pain and woundedness that he experienced.

4. Jesus' Followers and the Resurrection

The Fourth Gospel is primarily a story about Jesus. It is also, however, a story about his immediate followers, for whom the resurrection message was clearly essential. Interpreting the resurrection message of John's Gospel in terms of Jesus' followers also sheds light on the relevance of this message for the Gospel's implied readers, since their situation of needing to make an appropriate response to Jesus' self-revelation is similar to that of Jesus' immediate followers.

The Disciples' Struggle for Adequate Faith and Understanding

In the narrative of the Fourth Gospel, it soon becomes clear that those who were Jesus' immediate followers by no means understood the implications of either their striking confessions in chapter 1 (cf. esp. vv. 15, 29, 34, 35, 41, 45, and 49) or their early belief after Jesus' first sign at Cana of Galilee (cf. 2:11). Yet the loyalty and faith of the core group of disciples is highlighted later in the narrative. For when others defect because they are offended at Jesus' words, Peter, representing the Twelve, confesses that Jesus is the Holy One of God and that his words are the words of eternal life (6:68-69). Nevertheless, these immediate followers continue to be characterized by their frequent misunderstandings of Jesus. As late as the farewell discourses — which were meant to prepare them not only for Jesus' departure but also for their own future lives of discipleship and mission, as well as for the coming of the Paraclete — their imperfect faith and lack of insight are woefully apparent. And although at the end of Jesus' instruction they acknowledge that Jesus knows all things and has come from God (16:29-30), they, at the same time, indicate that they really have no clue about his going to God the Father.

The reader's doubts about the disciples' lack of preparedness are reinforced by Jesus' prediction that they will be scattered and leave him alone (16:32). This is followed by Peter's three denials (18:15-18, 25-27), which occur despite his earlier protestation about laying down his life for Jesus (cf. 13:37), and by the absence from the crucifixion of all but the Beloved Disciple and the three women. Adequate belief and understanding on the part of the disciples await the resurrection. But this is, of course, what the reader has already been told in the two asides of the narrator that bracket the public ministry of Jesus in 2:22 and 12:16 — the first stressing the disciples' postresurrection faith; the second, their postresurrection understanding.

The implied readers of John's Gospel have the advantage of knowing the prologue. Nonetheless, following out in the narrative the disciples' struggle to come to full belief, as well as recognizing some of the disciples' shortcomings also in themselves, have the effect of reinforcing the initial perspective on Jesus that they were invited by the prologue to share. And implied readers are not disappointed in their expectation that the resurrection accounts will (1) resolve the issues of discipleship that arose for Jesus' first followers, and (2) illumine what it means to continue to follow Jesus.

The Resurrection and Faith

The resurrection of Jesus completes the faith of Jesus' followers. It is at the empty tomb, as we noted earlier, that the Beloved Disciple comes to the belief that qualifies him to be the ideal witness regarding the significance of the events of the narrative and that narrative's ideal author (20:8-9; cf. 21:24).

But if the Beloved Disciple has primacy with respect to a faith connected with the empty tomb, Mary Magdalene has primacy with respect to a faith connected with a resurrection appearance. Her recognition of Jesus comes through his utterance of her name (20:16). Like the good shepherd of chapter 10, Jesus calls his own sheep by name (v. 3); and Mary, turning to face him directly, because she now knows his voice (v. 4), answers, "Rabbouni!" And when Mary takes the message with which she is entrusted to the disciples, she also announces to them, "I have seen the Lord" (20:18). These two designations, "Rabbouni" and "Lord," reflect Jesus' earlier statement to his disciples in 13:13: "You call me Teacher and Lord — and you are right, for that is what I am."

The need and grounds for faith are to the fore in the account of Jesus' appearance to Thomas in 20:24-31. In his first appearance to the disciples (20:19-23), there had been no explicit confessional response. Afterwards, however, the disciples take up Mary's words to them in their testimony to Thomas: "We have seen the Lord" (v. 25). When after eight days Jesus appears again, and this time Thomas is present, Jesus says to him: "Do not be unbelieving but believing" (v. 27c). Why does Thomas need this exhortation? After all, by asking to see Jesus' hands and side, he was requesting no more than what was given to the other disciples (cf. 20:20). His statement, "Unless I see the mark of the nails in his hands, and put my finger in the mark of the nails and my hand in his side, I will not believe" (20:25), may be understood as simply making his desire more graphic.

There is, however, a real problem evident in Thomas' desire to see and touch Jesus. For his statement incorporates an adamant disbelief of the other disciples' testimony and a setting out of his own conditions for accepting testimony. The force of Jesus' final words to Thomas in 20:29 concerns the acceptance or rejection of the disciples' testimony: "Have you believed [their testimony] because you have seen me? Blessed are those who have not seen and yet have come to believe [their testimony]." The narrator then drives home the significance of this saying in his conclusion of 20:30-31, which highlights (1) that faith in the risen Lord is not limited to Jesus' immediate followers, and (2) that the narrative itself — with its recounting of Jesus' signs, including these resurrection episodes — has been written as the testimony through which "you," the readers, may come to appropriate belief in Jesus, and thereby enjoy the life made available through his death and resurrection (20:30-31).

What that appropriate belief entails is set out in terms of believing in Jesus as the sort of Messiah who is "Son of God." And what that confession means in its full Johannine sense has just been spelled out in the account of Jesus' appearance to Thomas. For despite his strange missing out on the commissioning and the reception of the Spirit, and despite his initial unbelief, Thomas is not only granted faith but also given the privilege of making the climactic christological confession: "my Lord and my God" (20:28).

This is the first time in the narrative of John's Gospel that a character calls Jesus "God." For the Gospel's readers, of course, this unique status of Jesus has been made clear from the beginning. The prologue had already stated that the Logos was God (1:1) and that it is the "only God" who has made the Father known (1:18). But the readers have then had to wait to see whether any of the characters of the story are able to come to a full recognition of Jesus' identity.

The earlier confessions that Jesus is "Son of God" and "Lord" amount to much the same thing because of the connotation of these titles in the narrative discourse. Nonetheless, it remains striking that it takes the resurrection of Jesus before a character in the narrative makes fully explicit the Son's unique relationship with the Father that is depicted by the implied author in the prologue.

The Resurrection and Mission

His own mission having been vindicated, the risen Jesus, in the commissioning words of 20:21 ("As the Father has sent me, so I send you"; cf. 17:18), tells his followers that the story is by no means over. They are to carry on where he has left off. They are to continue his mission.

As to just *how* his followers are to carry on where he left off, the reader needs to recall how the narrative of the Fourth Gospel has portrayed the mission of Jesus himself. There are a variety of ways in which that mission is depicted, but the dominant framework of the narrative of John's Gospel, and its most pervasive motif, is that of a lawsuit or trial on a cosmic scale (cf. my "Trials, Plots and the Narrative of the Fourth Gospel"; see also Trites, *New Testament Concept of Witness*, 78-124). In that lawsuit or trial, God initiates a process of judgment that is meant to have a positive outcome. As always, however, two sorts of judgment are possible: (1) a positive verdict of life, or (2) a negative verdict of condemnation, which comes on those who condemn themselves by refusing to acknowledge the truth about God and the world as it is now revealed in Jesus. The main witness in this trial is Jesus himself. Thus the most striking and emphatic description of Jesus' mission in the whole narrative of John's Gospel is expressed as follows: "For this I was born, and for this I came into the world, to testify to the truth" (18:37).

So for Jesus to send his disciples as the Father has sent him means that they, too, are sent to be witnesses in the trial of truth. Do we simply have to infer this? No, it has been made explicit in the farewell discourses of chapters 13-16 that look out beyond Jesus' departure to the future of his followers. The double witness that was always necessary under Jewish law is now to be carried out both by the Spirit, who acts also as the Advocate, and by Jesus' followers. This was Jesus' promise in 15:26-27: "When the Advocate comes, whom I will send to you from the Father, the Spirit of truth who comes from the Father, he will testify on my behalf. You also are to testify because you have been with me from the beginning." The cosmic trial is, in fact, to go on beyond Jesus' death. And the risen Jesus commissions his followers to be witnesses in it, just as he has been.

While Jesus, like God in the Jewish Scriptures, is both witness and judge in that cosmic trial, his followers' role is primarily that of being a witness — though there is also, of course, a secondary feature of judgment attached to the message to which they are to bear witness. This is indicated by Jesus' words in 20:23: "If you forgive the sins of any, they are forgiven them; if you retain the sins of any, they are retained." In this narrative's discourse, sin is primarily failing to acknowledge the revelation of God in Jesus. So as the disciples in their witness announce God's verdict in Jesus, they will be pronouncing forgiveness for those who receive their witness, but they will also be retaining the sins of those who reject their witness.

Jesus' followers, then, are to press home the implications of the verdict that the Judge has already given in the death and resurrection of Jesus. The passive forms of the verbs *apheōntai* (literally, "they have been forgiven") and *kekratēntai* (literally, "they have been retained") in the two main clauses in 20:23 are clearly to be taken as divine passives. God stands behind the disciples' witness, so that their forgiveness or retention of sins reflects God's forgiveness or retention. And just as Jesus' mission constituted a realized judgment of either salvation or condemnation, so the disciples' witness to that mission will entail a realized judgment of either the forgiveness or the retention of sins. The disciples do not forsake the witness stand for the judgment seat. But by pointing to the Lamb of God who takes away the sin of the world, the disciples also point to the One into whose hands judgment has been given — and thereby they play their part in the ongoing process of the trial.

In chapter 21, which in many ways forms an epilogue for the Fourth Gospel, the disciples — who had been sent on a mission — are now found fishing back in Galilee. At his first sign in Cana of Galilee, the reader was told that Jesus had manifested his glory (2:11). That this fishing episode is to be considered a final sign in the narrative is indicated by the fact that the evangelist states twice, in the form of an *inclusio* in verses 1 and 14, that Jesus manifested himself to his disciples. The activity of fishing is now treated as a sign of the task for which the disciples have been commissioned.

To appreciate fully the symbolism inherent in 21:1-14, the implied reader needs to be familiar with Jesus' words in the Synoptic Gospels about making the disciples those who will fish for people (cf. Mark 1:17; Matt 4:19; Luke 5:10). Likewise, it needs to be recognized that behind those words lie the traditions from the Jewish Scriptures that picture God's eschatological judgment in terms of fishing or catching people in nets (cf. Jer 16:16; Ezek 29:4-5; Amos 4:2; Hab 1:14-17). A saving as well as a judging function, however, now attaches to God's eschatological mission, of which Jesus and the disciples are agents.

At this symbolic level of the narrative, the fact that the disciples catch nothing during the night suggests the failures and frustrations of their mission. The reader is reminded of Jesus' words in the farewell discourse of John's Gospel regarding fruitfulness: "Apart from me you can do nothing" (15:5). The sovereignty and supernatural knowledge frequently seen in the earlier narrative of the Gospel now reappear in the command of the risen Jesus to cast the net on the right side of the boat. And the compliance of the disciples with Jesus' command results in the miracle of a great haul of fish.

According to Ezek 47:10 (LXX), one of the consequences of the life-giving waters that will flow from the eschatological temple in Jerusalem is that the fish of those waters will be like the fish of the great sea — that is, there will be an exceedingly great number. Thus as the disciples obey the word of the risen Jesus, who is the new temple from which life-giving waters flow, they are unable to haul in the net because of the great number of fish (21:6). And when Peter responds to Jesus' request to "bring some of the fish that you have just caught" (21:10), he hauls from the boat one hundred and fifty-three fish in a net that remains untorn (21:11). The stress on the number of fish and the condition of the net not only attests to the magnitude of the miracle. It also, at the level of the symbolism of the sign, suggests the completeness and unity of those drawn in by the disciples' mission.

The rest of the narrative involving the risen Jesus in 21:15-25 both completes the story-line about Peter and the Beloved Disciple and indicates their future roles in the continuing witness of the church. In the passion narrative, Peter had been singled out for his three denials of Jesus. Now in the resurrection narrative, however, he is singled out for rehabilitation in a conversation that draws out from him a threefold affirmation of his love for Jesus (vv. 15-17). And the presence of a charcoal fire as the backdrop on both occasions (cf. 18:18; 21:9) underscores the parallel.

Peter is to demonstrate the genuineness of his love by being an undershepherd to God's people — protecting, nourishing, and tending the flock of the good shepherd himself. Not only so, but Jesus predicts that Peter will also later follow in the footsteps of the good shepherd by laying down his life (vv. 18-19a). His rehabilitation is rounded off by Jesus' command: "Follow me" (v. 19b). This picks up on Peter's earlier question and claim in 13:37, "Lord, why can I not follow you now? I will lay down my life for you." The resurrection has produced a changed situation. Jesus now deems Peter ready to be the sort of follower who is able to go all the way and to lay down his life for him.

But dying a martyr's death is not the only significant form of witness. The narrator corrects the rumor about the Beloved Disciple remaining until the coming of Jesus and confirms the truth of that disciple's written witness in the form of this Gospel's narrative itself (vv. 20-25). Despite his death, the Beloved Disciple's witness, as contained in the Fourth Gospel, will have a continuing role in the further playing out of the cosmic trial within history.

The Resurrection and the Spirit

The presence of the risen Jesus is vital for the launching and directing of the church's mission of witness. But equally vital is the presence of the Spirit in that witness. For it is through the Spirit that the presence and power of the risen Jesus remain with those who are Jesus' followers.

After his words of commissioning at his first postresurrection appearance to the disciples (20:21), the narrator reports that Jesus "breathed on them and said to them, 'Receive the Holy Spirit'" (20:22). In this way the resurrection brings about the fulfillment of the predictions about Jesus and the Spirit from earlier in the narrative of John's Gospel. For John the Baptist had been told that "he on whom you see the Spirit descend and remain is the one who baptizes with the Holy Spirit" (1:33). Now in the narrative of 20:22 Jesus confirms the Baptist's identification by baptizing his disciples with the Spirit.

Furthermore, in connection with Jesus' citation of Scripture in 7:38 — "Out of his belly shall flow rivers of living water" — the narrator had observed: "Now he said this about the Spirit, which believers in him were to receive; for as yet there was no Spirit, because Jesus was not yet glorified" (7:39). Now in 20:22 the disciples' reception of the Spirit indicates that Jesus has indeed been glorified. At his death, of course, water flowed from his side (19:34), showing the Spirit had become available. But it is only after his resurrection that Jesus specifically confers this Spirit on his disciples.

In the farewell discourses, four passages had promised the presence of the Paraclete: 14:16-17; 14:26; 15:26; and 16:7-15. The Paraclete was depicted as the Spirit of truth who would abide with and be in the disciples. He would teach them and remind them of what Jesus had said, guiding them into all truth. He would testify on behalf of Jesus and glorify Jesus. He would convict the world of sin, righteousness, and judgment. Now in 20:22, with Jesus' bestowal of the Spirit on the disciples, the work of this Advocate who will take Jesus' place can begin. Thus the resurrection message of John is clearly a message about the Spirit. Indeed, in this narrative Easter and Pentecost come together.

The manner in which Jesus is said to have conferred the Spirit — that is, by breathing on the disciples — recalls the creation narrative of Gen 2:7, where God breathed into the man and he became a living being (cf. also Wis 15:11). Ezekiel's vision of Israel's end-time renewal also involved a resurrection in which new life was to be breathed into dry bones (Ezek 37:5; see also vv. 9-10). The bestowal of the Spirit by the risen Jesus here in 20:22, therefore, signals the eschatological new creation. The God who endowed humanity with life is now through Christ's gift to the disciples endowing humanity with new life.

Such an endowment of new life takes the reader back to the prologue's statement that in the Logos was life (1:4). The incarnate Logos has shown through the resurrection that the divine life in him overcomes death, and he gives this life through his Spirit to the disciples. Their reception of the Spirit, therefore, is also their birth from above, or their birth by the Spirit (cf. 3:3-8), through which they participate in the eternal life that the Logos has with God. "Because I live, you also will live," Jesus had said in 14:19. And now his followers know what it is to experience this connection through Jesus' breath of life.

5. The Resurrection of Lazarus

Central in the narrative of the Fourth Gospel, and pivotal for its plot, is the Lazarus episode, which extends from 11:1 to 12:11. Whereas in the Synoptic Gospels it is the temple incident that provokes Jesus' arrest and condemnation, in John's Gospel it is the raising of Lazarus that is the catalyst for the decision of the Sanhedrin to put Jesus to death. This seventh and climactic sign of Jesus' public ministry is recounted creatively and dramatically by overlaying it with the theme of Jesus' own destiny and with the concerns of later followers about the death of believers.

The Raising of Lazarus and the Death of Jesus

The raising of Lazarus is linked to Jesus' death. This is evident most clearly from the divided reactions depicted in 11:45-57. For whereas, on the one hand, it is said that many Jews believed in him (v. 45), on the other hand, a report given by others to certain Pharisees — and through them to "the chief priests and Pharisees" — leads to the decision of the Sanhedrin to kill Jesus (vv. 46-53, 57). But the linking of these two events is also evident from the very start of the narrative.

Lazarus is introduced in 11:2 as the brother of the Mary who anointed Jesus, with that anointing then being made part of the whole episode in 12:1-8 and explained as an anointing for Jesus' burial. Furthermore, in 11:4 the first words of Jesus on hearing of Lazarus' illness are: "This illness does not lead to death; rather it is for God's glory, so that the Son of God may be glorified through it." The implied reader knows that the hour of glory for both God and the Son of God is Jesus' death (cf. esp. 12:23, 28; 13:31-32). And so the reader sees a connection between the coming sign and Jesus' mission — a connection that is highly ironic, for Lazarus' illness will not end with his death, but, rather, will lead to Jesus' death.

Then in the ensuing dialogue between Jesus and the disciples in 11:7-16, the expectation that in going to Judea Jesus is going to his death is underlined by the comment of Thomas, "Let us also go, that we may die with him" (v. 16). Since it is Lazarus' death that has just been mentioned, Thomas' words may well refer to dying with Lazarus. But even if that be so, they still receive their force from the view that to go to Lazarus is to go to death, because it is to go back to the region where Jesus will inevitably again face death. So from the beginning of the episode, all the indications are in place that life for Lazarus will mean death for Jesus.

The Raising of Lazarus and the Resurrection of Jesus

If the links with Jesus' death are crucial for an understanding of the Lazarus episode, the links with Jesus' resurrection are just as vital. The raising of Lazarus is a sign, a symbolic action. The extraordinary last part of the episode in 12:9-11 makes this emphatically clear by raising the possibility that the one who has just been raised will be killed shortly thereafter! This serves as a sharp reminder that Lazarus' resurrection is only temporary. In fact, at the end of the story he returns to the situation he occupied at the beginning — that is, he is again under the threat of death. So Lazarus' resurrection is only a sign. His temporary restoration to normal human life points beyond itself to the full resurrection and eschatological life that Jesus provides.

Yet the sign also indicates that human bodily life is significant, because it points to the belief that eternal life will not finally involve an escape from the body but will entail physical resurrection. When Jesus, "with a loud voice," cries out: "Lazarus, come out!" (v. 43), this is a narrative embodiment of his words in 5:28-29: "For the hour is coming when all who are in their tombs will hear his voice and will come out."

This sign anticipates the final resurrection. In so doing, however, it also anticipates the anticipation of that resurrection in Jesus' resurrection. In both cases there is a tomb and a stone has to be removed. In both cases the grief and faith of women disciples are to the fore. And in both accounts the grave clothes — particularly the head cloth — are singled out for mention (cf. 11:44; 20:7). But here the difference is telling: Lazarus exits from the tomb still bound in these wrappings, whereas in Jesus' resurrection they are left behind and rolled up, indicating Jesus' own sovereignty over death.

The Raising of Lazarus and the Death of Believers

So the raising of Lazarus is integrally related to both the death and the resurrection of Jesus. But it also has to do with the death of Jesus' followers. For the implied readers of John's Gospel also face the possibility of martyrdom, like Peter (16:2-3; cf. 21:18-19), and they have to deal with questions regarding the death of believers before the Parousia, such as those raised about the Beloved Disciple (cf. 21:22-23).

Mary and Martha can be seen as representative figures who share the concerns of Jesus' later followers about his delay in coming and his absence, and about what these factors mean for the death of those they love (cf. 11:21-22, 32). Mary's weeping reflects the continuing painful reality of the loss of a loved one through physical death. Weeping is totally appropriate, as is demonstrated by Jesus' own inner anger and anguish in response to death and the pain it causes — emotions that turn into his own tears (11:33-35, 38).

It is in the earlier dialogue with Martha that the theological issues inherent in the Lazarus episode are confronted. When Jesus assures Martha that her brother will rise again, she takes Jesus' words to be a reference to Lazarus' participation in the end-time resurrection (11:24). Her misunderstanding serves as the introduction to the key self-identification of Jesus in the "I am" saying of 11:25: "I am the resurrection and the life." For in so claiming, Jesus declares himself to be the fulfillment of traditional Jewish eschatological expectations, the one who embodies the power to raise from the dead, and the one who is the source of the positive verdict of eternal life. No longer are these eschatological features solely reserved for the last day; they are now presently available in and through Jesus.

The significance of this saying is elaborated in the parallel clauses of 11:25b and 26a: "Those who believe in me, even though they die, will live; and everyone who lives and believes in me will never die." The final question of 11:26b, "Do you believe this?," underscores that Jesus' words in verses 25-26 unlock a true understanding of the episode. For this reason, the question can be seen as addressing not only Martha but also the reader.

Martha answers with a praiseworthy christological confession that reflects what the reader is meant to believe about Jesus (cf. 20:31). Yet her answer makes no explicit mention of what Jesus has said about resurrection and life. And her later reaction to Jesus' command that the stone be removed from the tomb, as well as Jesus' response (cf. 11:39-40), suggests that she still has not seen the significance of her own confession for the raising of her brother.

The force of the words that Martha is meant to believe turns on the different meanings of "to live" and "to die" in 11:25b-26a. Believers in Jesus may undergo physical death, but that cannot affect the eschatological life they already have in him. They will continue to live beyond death. In fact, as the second clause in verse 26a almost tautologically asserts, to have such life through believing in Jesus means that believers will never experience spiritual death, because the quality of life they enjoy is eternal. Death does not entail an absence from Jesus' presence until the Parousia. Neither does it mean that Jesus has lost his hold on a person until the last day. Nor does it disrupt the experience of eternal life with God until the final resurrection.

What is missing in Martha's response to Lazarus' death is a true grasp of the believer's connection with Jesus. That connection changes everything, because faith links Jesus' followers to the one who *is* the resurrection and the life. Death has lost its sting, because it is swallowed up in the life that God has already made available through Jesus. By means of such life, believers who die continue to live and at the last day that life will take on a new bodily form. Both outcomes are made possible — and Jesus' claim to be the resurrection and the life is substantiated — by the event of which Lazarus' raising is a sign: the decisive defeat of death in Jesus' own resurrection.

6. Conclusion: The Resurrection Message of the Fourth Gospel

If it can be said that the Fourth Gospel is the "Gospel of Life," then the Lazarus episode constitutes this Gospel's message in miniature. The return of Lazarus to human mortal life is a sign of the giving of eternal life and of the death and resurrection of Jesus through which such life is made available. The interweaving of these themes in an episode so central to the narrative's structure amply demonstrates that there is no basic incoherence between this Gospel's highlighting of the death of Jesus in its plot and the place that it gives to the resurrection accounts. Indeed, were it not for the account of his resurrection, Jesus' claim in this episode to be the resurrection and the life would ring rather hollow.

"I am the resurrection and the life" sums up the christological focus of the resurrection message of the Fourth Gospel. But because that message is christological, it also has both Trinitarian dimensions and consequences for humanity. Resurrection life has its source in the Logos, who is one with the Creator God; it is manifested in the body of Jesus, the incarnate Logos; and it is mediated through the risen Jesus' bestowal of the Spirit. Faith in Jesus as the Christ, who has this unique relationship to God, makes life now available to believers. And just as for the incarnate Logos divine life overcame death in a bodily resurrection, so for believers, too, eternal life will triumph over physical death through resurrection.

The focus of this chapter has been on the narrative of the Fourth Gospel — that is, on its structure and flow, its storylines about Jesus and the disciples. But such an analysis would be deficient if it left the impression that the Gospel's resurrection message could simply be distilled from the narrative by summarizing its theological points. Rather, the resurrection message is to be encountered through the narrative itself. The narrative form of the Fourth Gospel invites readers into its story and challenges them to believe. When Jesus says, "I am the resurrection and the life" — and when the whole narrative witnesses to this claim — we, along with Martha, are being asked: "Do you believe this?" (11:26; cf. 20:31). To believe is to find our own story in this Gospel's story of Jesus. And to find our story in the story of the crucified Jesus, who is the resurrection and the life, is to be linked to the life of the triune God, to be empowered for mission and witness, and to be given profound assurance in the face of the present painful reality of death.

ANDREW T. LINCOLN

Selected Bibliography

Ashton, John. *Understanding the Fourth Gospel.* Oxford: Clarendon, 1991, esp. 214-20, 501-14.

Beasley-Murray, George R. *John.* Waco: Word, 1987.

Brown, Raymond E. *The Gospel According to John.* 2 vols. New York: Doubleday, 1966-70.

Culpepper, R. Alan. *Anatomy of the Fourth Gospel.* Philadelphia: Fortress, 1983.

Evans, C. F. *Resurrection and the New Testament.* London: SCM, 1970, esp. 116-28.

Heil, John P. *Blood and Water: The Death and Resurrection of Jesus in John 18–21.* Washington: Catholic Biblical Association, 1995.

Lee, Dorothy A. *The Symbolic Narratives of the Fourth Gospel.* Sheffield: JSOT Press, 1994, esp. 188-226.

Lincoln, Andrew T. "Trials, Plots and the Narrative of the Fourth Gospel." *Journal for the Study of the New Testament* 56 (1994) 3-30.

MacDonald, J. I. H. *The Resurrection: Narrative and Belief.* London: SPCK, 1989, esp. 117-35.

Morris, Leon. *Jesus Is the Christ.* Grand Rapids: Eerdmans, 1989, esp. 190-209.

Perkins, Pheme. *Resurrection: New Testament Witness and Contemporary Reflection.* New York: Doubleday, 1984, esp. 169-86, 205-6, 311-15.

Schnackenburg, Rudolf. *The Gospel According to St. John.* 3 vols. New York: Seabury, 1980; New York: Crossroads, 1982.

Schneiders, Sandra M. "Death in the Community of Eternal Life." *Interpretation* 41 (1987) 44-56.

Stibbe, Mark W. G. "A Tomb with a View: John 11.1-44 in Narrative-Critical Perspective." *New Testament Studies* 40 (1994) 38-54.

Thompson, Marianne Meye. "Eternal Life in the Gospel of John." *Ex Auditu* 5 (1989) 35-55.

Trites, Allison A. *The New Testament Concept of Witness.* New York: Cambridge University Press, 1977.

III. The Message of Paul

CHAPTER 7

Resurrection and Immortality
in the Pauline Corpus

MURRAY J. HARRIS

"RESURRECTION" AND "immortality" in the Pauline corpus find their focus in the risen Christ. For Paul the resurrection of Jesus Christ is absolutely foundational for the proclamation of the Christian gospel and for living the Christian life. Christ's resurrection is the basis for the hope of Christian believers in their own forthcoming resurrection and future immortality.

The aim of this essay is (1) to show that in Paul's teaching about the destiny of believers both resurrection and immortality have an honored place, (2) to point out that these two concepts must be understood as being inseparable and complementary features in Paul's eschatological message, and (3) to explicate Paul's thought regarding the resurrection and immortality of believers, dealing with these matters first separately and then in concert. In so doing, we will range widely throughout the traditional Pauline collection of thirteen letters, though our focus will be on the undisputed letters of the apostle.

1. Resurrection

Terminology

Our English term "resurrection" translates the Greek word *anastasis* (1 Cor 15:42), where the prefix *ana*, which may mean "up" or "again," signifies either a rising *up* (i.e., standing erect) of someone who has been in a reclining position or a coming to life *again* of someone who has died. In its basic sense, "resurrection" denotes a person's restoration to life after an interval spent in the realm of the dead. Paul's favorite verb to denote resurrection is *egeirō* ("rouse," "rise up"), which he uses to refer to either the resurrection of Christ or the resurrection of believers — with the verb being applied to both in 2 Cor 4:14 (see further Harris, *Raised Immortal*, 269-71).

Three Types and Levels of Resurrection

Three types of resurrection can be distinguished in Paul's usage. First, there is the past bodily resurrection of Christ *from* the grave *to* immortality: "We know that because Christ was raised from the dead *(egertheis ek nekrōn)*, he will never die again" (Rom 6:9). Second, there is the past spiritual resurrection of believers with Christ, which was *from* slavery to sin *to* newness of life: "In baptism you were raised with him *(synēgerthēte)*" (Col 2:12; cf. Rom 6:4, 6, 13, 17). Third, there is the future bodily resurrection of believers *from* the dead *to* immortality: "The dead will be raised immortal *(egerthēsontai aphthartoi)*" (1 Cor 15:52). In each of these cases, it needs to be noted, resurrection involves both a "from" and a "to."

Resurrection, however, should not be regarded as both an event and a process, for the present tense of the verbs that denote the act of raising or rising is never found in the New Testament. Rather, resurrection is an event that leads to a state. The perfect passive verb *egēgertai* (which stems from *egeirō*) appears seven times in 1 Corinthians 15 and can literally be translated "he has been raised." It signals the past event of Christ's resurrection and so is to be equated with *ēgerthē* or *anestē*, "he arose." But *egēgertai* also, as a perfect passive, highlights the present consequences of that event and so can be translated "he is risen" (cf. also 2 Tim 2:8, where the perfect passive participial phrase *egēgermenon ek nekrōn*, "risen from the dead," is used of Jesus Christ). We may, therefore, legitimately paraphrase 1 Cor 15:52 this way: "The dead will experience a resurrection (i.e., an event), and so they will become permanently immortal (i.e., live in a state of "risen-ness").

This leads us to suggest that in Paul, as in other New Testament writers, there are three levels of meaning in the concept of resurrection:

1. In its most elementary sense, resurrection denotes *resuscitation* — the regaining of a physical life that has been forfeited through death (cf., e.g., Mark 5:41-42; John 5:28-29; Heb 11:35; Rev 20:5). When Paul speaks of bodily resurrection, such a resuscitation or reanimation is certainly implied.
2. Resurrection involves *transformation,* since "flesh and blood cannot inherit the kingdom of God" (1 Cor 15:50). Accordingly, Paul indicates that believers will be "raised immortal" (1 Cor 15:52), which suggests that the transformation or change that results in immortality is coincident with resurrection — and, in fact, is part of the resurrection event itself.
3. A third level of meaning, that of *exaltation,* is also involved. The raising up of believers is from the dead (resuscitation) in newness of life (transformation) into the presence of Christ (exaltation).

This three-stage process also applies to believers' present spiritual resurrection, as well as to their future bodily resurrection. For from spiritual death the Christian is raised up (Eph 2:1, 6) to new life (Rom 6:4) in the heavenly realm (Eph 2:6).

So it is that, for Paul, resurrection implies not only restoration to life but also transformation and exaltation. In its full theological import, resurrection signifies the raising of persons from the dead to a new and permanent life in the presence of God. Such a definition applies first of all to the resurrection of Christ, but it also applies to both the present spiritual resurrection and the future bodily resurrection of believers.

The Subjects of Resurrection

Paul never explicitly says that "bodies" will be raised. When he qualifies the noun "resurrection," it is once with the phrase "from [i.e., out from among] the dead" (*ek nekrōn,* Phil 3:11) and several times with the phrase "of the dead" (*tōn nekrōn;* e.g., 1 Cor 15:42). In both of these usages, the expression "the dead" refers not to impersonal corpses but to dead persons. So when Paul speaks of "the resurrection of the dead," he is not envisaging the mere revitalization of corpses. Rather, he has in mind the emergence of deceased persons from the realm of the dead in a transformed bodily state.

The nearest Paul comes to speaking of "the resurrection of the body"

— which is a formulation that was introduced into the Apostles' Creed in 1552 — is when the verb "raise" is associated with the term "body" in 1 Cor 15:44, where he writes *egeiretai sōma pneumatikon*. This phrase has been translated either "it [i.e., the body that is sown] is raised a spiritual body" (so NASB, NIV, NAB[2]) or "a spiritual body is raised up" (so C. K. Barrett, *The First Epistle to the Corinthians* [New York: Harper, 1968] 369, 372). But however we translate these words of 1 Cor 15:44, it seems that Paul would more readily speak of "the resurrection of the spiritual body" than "the resurrection of the physical body" or "the resurrection of the flesh."

We should, therefore, distinguish between that with which the resurrection begins and that with which it ends. For "the resurrection of the body" can refer to the physical body (i.e., the *terminus a quo* of the resurrection) or to the spiritual body (i.e., the *terminus ad quem* of the resurrection). In traditional usage, "the resurrection of the body" has referred primarily to the earthly body. 1 Cor 15:44, however, shows how appropriately it can be applied to the heavenly body.

But if the term "resurrection" is to be qualified at all, Paul prefers to qualify it by the phrase "of the dead" *(tōn nekrōn)*. This qualification has the effect of juxtaposing two virtual opposites — namely, "raising to life" and "the dead." Thus it draws attention to God's magnificent victory over death by means of resurrection. More than that, however, the phrase "of the dead" is personal in reference and plural in form (unlike the formulas "of the body" or "of the flesh"), and so it aptly highlights the communal and interpersonal nature of the resurrection state.

Throughout Paul's letters, those who are raised from the dead in an immortal, spiritual body are invariably believers. Even in the celebrated resurrection chapter of 1 Corinthians 15, only believers are in view — only "those who belong to Christ" *(hoi tou Christou)*, as in verse 23. It might seem that verse 22 contradicts this: "As in Adam all die, so in Christ shall all be brought to life" *(zōopoiēthēsontai)*. On a first reading, it might be possible to interpret this statement as referring to a resurrection of all human beings prior to judgment. But given Paul's belief that on the day of judgment there will be a permanent separation between those who have done good and those who have done evil (Rom 2:5-10), the statement cannot be understood as speaking of a universal resurrection that leads to eternal life for all. Rather, the crucial words "all shall be brought to life" in verse 22 must be taken as being parallel to "the resurrection of the dead" in verse 21 — a phrase which in 1 Cor 15:12-13 and 42-44 refers solely to believers. Moreover, the "all" of the statement in verse 22 is defined in verse 23 as "those who belong to Christ." Thus the sense of the statement in verse 22 seems to be: "Just as it is *in Adam* that all who die now die *(apothnē-skousin)*, so also it is *in Christ* that all who are to be brought to eternal life will be made alive."

The situation is complicated, of course, by a passage in Luke's summary of Paul's defense before Felix in Acts 24. For in replying to the accusation of the Jewish lawyer Tertullus that he was "a ringleader of the Nazarene sect" (v. 5), Paul is portrayed as having insisted that he had not deviated from the faith of his fathers as set out in the Scriptures and that he shared with the Pharisaic elders in the retinue of Ananias a hope in God "that there will certainly be a resurrection including *both* the righteous *and* the unrighteous" (v. 15, italics mine, in order to highlight the passage's *te kai* construction). In defense of this statement as an accurate summary of Paul's words, we may observe, first, that Luke's knowledge of Paul was sufficiently personal and prolonged to prevent his attributing to Paul a sentiment out of keeping with the apostle's own theology. Furthermore, a partial explanation as to why this one unambiguous testimony to Paul's belief in a resurrection of the unjust appears outside of the Pauline letters themselves is that here Paul is addressing a Roman procurator who could not have been expected to know the basic doctrines of Judaism, much less the teachings of those who were followers of "the Way, which they call a sect" (v. 14).

Thus Paul, like John (John 5:29; Rev 20:4-6), believed in two resurrections — the one issuing in eternal life (Rom 2:7; Tit 1:2; 3:7); the other resulting in condemnation (Rom 2:8; 2 Thess 1:8-9). The "resurrection" of those who are to be raised and subsequently condemned will involve their appearance before God to receive their rightful judgment, presumably in some (undisclosed) bodily form that permits a continuity of personal identity. The silence of Paul and the other New Testament writers about the nature of that embodiment of the wicked for judgment is in keeping with their concentration on the facts of humanity's universal accountability to God and the final state of the righteous, as well as their total silence on matters of physiology. Furthermore, if Paul does not regularly speak of a "resurrection of judgment," that is because "resurrection" for him was not a purely neutral term signifying mere reanimation — merely "coming to life again" after death — but a positive concept denoting the receipt of a permanent spiritual body like Christ's, with the concomitant enjoyment of eternal life.

151

The Resurrection Body

The classic passage dealing with the resurrection body is 1 Corinthians 15. Although we have already discussed certain verses in this chapter, it will now be appropriate to give an overview of Paul's argument with regard to its structure, background, focus, and teaching.

The chapter falls into two clear parts: verses 1-34 treat the fact or *that*-ness of the resurrection of believers (*hoti*, "that," vv. 4, 12), and verses 35-58 the *how* of that resurrection (*pōs*, "how," v. 35). In the first part, Paul enunciates the premise that he shares with his opponents: their foundational conviction regarding the fact of Christ's resurrection (vv. 1-11); then he draws a major conclusion from that premise: the dead in Christ will, like Christ, also be raised (vv. 12-32). In this latter section he argues that a denial of this conclusion leads inevitably to a denial of the basic premise that is accepted by all Christians regarding the resurrection of Christ (vv. 12-19). Furthermore, he goes on in this latter section to specify what an acceptance of this conclusion means for an understanding of the fullness of Christ's work, particularly as Christ "the Son" brings to culmination the divine program of redemption in the Last Days (vv. 20-28). And he concludes the first part of 1 Corinthians 15 with two *ad hominem* arguments that are set out in support of this conclusion — the first having to do with certain Christians being "baptized for the dead" (v. 29); the second, regarding his own apostolic labors and the perils involved (vv. 30-32) — and then with a warning to avoid bad company and conduct (vv. 33-34).

Part two of the chapter (vv. 35-58) spells out two difficulties that were evidently being raised by certain believers at Corinth regarding this conclusion. The first, it seems, had to do with the nature of the resurrection body (vv. 35-50). The question posed in verse 35a, "How are the dead raised?," is answered in verses 36-41 with a discussion of the conceivability of the resurrection — particularly, with the possibility of a resurrection body. This leads to Paul's reply to the question of verse 35b, "With what kind of body [*poiǭ sōmati*] do they come?," in which he expounds the manner of the future resurrection of believers and the properties of their resurrection bodies (vv. 42-50). The second difficulty posed had to do, evidently, with the destiny of Christian believers who would still be alive at the time of the Second Advent (vv. 51-57). For having asserted quite categorically that "what you sow is brought to life only if it dies" (v. 36),

Paul needed further to explain how those who will be alive at the time of Christ's return will be prepared to enter the kingdom. His answer to that latter question is that the transformation of believers who are alive at Christ's coming will be analogous to the resurrection-transformation that will be experienced by those believers who have died. The chapter then ends with a call to unflagging and enthusiastic devotion to the Lord's work (v. 58).

The precise nature of the denial of the resurrection at Corinth continues to be a matter of scholarly debate. Nonetheless, it is clear that Paul, in addressing the problems posed, lays stress on two central matters with regard to the resurrection of Christian believers: (1) that it lies in the future, and (2) that it involves a body. But what does Paul tell us about this body of the resurrection? Four emphases can be identified.

In the first place, it is a body *provided by God* (v. 38). The phrase "God gives it a body" applies primarily to the "bare kernel" that is sown in the ground (v. 37). But given the wider context of the whole chapter, it must also be applicable to human beings whose life and death are comparable to sowing. The diverse types of "bodies" in the universe (vv. 39-41) illustrate God's ability and willingness to provide human beings with a bodily organism that is different from their earthly bodies and suitable for their residence in heaven.

Secondly, it is a *sōma pneumatikon* or "spiritual body" (vv. 44, 46). Both of the terms in the expression need careful definition. For Paul, the noun *sōma* ("body") normally refers to the human person viewed as a whole, though with special emphasis on the corporeal and outward aspects of existence. The adjective *pneumatikon* ("spiritual") does not mean "composed of spirit," as though "spirit" were some ethereal, heavenly substance. Rather, it signifies "animated and guided by the spirit," with *pneuma* ("spirit") denoting either the Spirit of God or the human spirit as revitalized by the divine Spirit. The spiritual body, then, is the organ of the resurrected person's communication with the heavenly world. It is a form of embodiment that is fully responsive to the Christian's perfected spirit and perfectly adapted to its heavenly environment.

A third element in Paul's description of the resurrection body in 1 Corinthians 15 is found in the threefold antithesis of verses 42b-43. In those three antitheses the "sowing" of our life on earth, which terminates in death and burial — or, in other words, "the physical" or "natural body" — is characterized, on the one hand, by perishability, dishonor, and weakness. But the reaping of the harvest through the resurrection — or, in other words, "the spiritual body" — is characterized, on the other, by imperishability, glory, and power.

Because it is constantly renewed by the Spirit, the spiritual body will be, first of all, *imperishable* (vv. 42, 50, 52-54). We will no longer be characterized by physical decay (*phthora*, "perishability"). And because it will be completely suffused with the Spirit (cf. 1 Pet 4:14), the spiritual body will be *glorious* (v. 43a; cf. Phil 3:21). No more will existence be marked by physical indignity (*atimia*, "dishonor"), or what Paul elsewhere calls the condition of "lowliness" (*tapeinōsis*, Phil 3:21). The animal aspects of human life and the indignities associated with our physical constitution will, in fact, never again be present. Furthermore, because it is permanently energized by the Spirit, the spiritual body will be *powerful* (v. 43b). Believers will be forever delivered from physical weakness (*astheneia*, "weakness"). Gone for ever will be the dependence of childhood, the distressing infirmity associated with illness and old age, and the frustration of physical limitations felt by even the healthy.

Paul is saying in these three antitheses, then, that in place of an earthly body that has been always characterized by physical decay, indignity, and weakness, the resurrected believer will have a heavenly body that is incapable of deterioration, beautiful in form and appearance, and with limitless energy and perfect health. Once believers who have died experience a resurrection from the dead and a transformation by God's Spirit — or, if they are alive at Christ's coming, a transformation analogous to that of other believers, even though they are still alive physically — they will know perennial rejuvenation. At their resurrection they will be given a body that will be a perfect vehicle for God's deathless Spirit and invariably responsive to their transformed personality.

But the apostle's threefold description of our earthly, physical life in verses 42b-43 should not be understood simply in physical terms. For life on earth is also marked by moral corruptibility (*phthora*; cf. Rom 8:21), spiritual wretchedness (*atimia*; cf. Rom 7:34; Phil 3:21), and spiritual disability (*astheneia*; cf. Rom 7:14-23). Correspondingly, life in heaven in the resurrection body provided by God will be free from the taint of sin and from the frustrations of spiritual powerlessness.

A fourth emphasis of Paul in describing the future resurrection body of believers is that it will be a *heavenly* body (vv. 40, 47-49). As he develops his contrast between the first man, Adam, and the second Man, Christ, Paul emphasizes that these two archetypal representatives share the characteristics of their places of origin. Formed from the dust of the ground, Adam and his physical descendants are earthlings, liable to sin, decay, and death. Being from heaven, however, the risen Christ bears a heavenly image that is sinless, incorruptible, and immortal — an image to be shared by his spiritual descendants. Heaven is, therefore, the natural habitat of the resurrection body, its normal sphere of operation. And this "heaven" is not simply a condition, but also, although secondarily, a place. As Paul Badham rightly insists, the concept of a resurrected body and the concept of a non-spatial heaven are incompatible. The real options are a resurrected body in a place or an immortal soul existing without location, for "a body is spatial and a soul is non-spatial" (*Christian Beliefs about Life after Death* [London: Macmillan, 1976] 91; see his full discussion on pages 90-94).

What is the relation between the physical body and the spiritual body? The seed analogy Paul uses in 1 Cor 15:36-38 suggests that there is *some* relation between these successive forms of Christian embodiment. Outwardly, of course, the full-grown plant may appear unconnected with the seed buried in the ground. Inwardly, however, the plant is continuous with the seed. And while the seed analogy may highlight not so much the factor of identity as that of difference, it nevertheless suggests both continuity (v. 36) and discontinuity (vv. 37-38) between what is sown and what is raised — or, perhaps more aptly stated, it suggests *identity with a difference.*

If, then, complete material continuity cannot be claimed between the present physical bodies of believers and their future spiritual bodies, what is the extent of that continuity? On this question there has never been unanimity in the church. Some affirm that everything necessary for the integrity of human nature will be retained, including physical organs and senses (e.g., Thomas Aquinas, *Summa Theologica,* Supplement, Q. 80. 5). Others hold that the substratum of the resurrection body will be formed by some of the decomposed matter of the earthly body (e.g., Hermann Bavinck, *Gereformeerde Dogmatiek* [Kampen: Kok, 1918] 4:776, as cited by Schep, *Resurrection Body,* 195). Others are convinced that Paul taught an "essential continuity and identity," although the "how" remains God's secret (e.g., J. A. Schep, *Resurrection Body,* 195-96). And not a few assert that there will be a personal, but not a material, continuity between these two forms of embodiment (e.g., George Ladd, *I Believe in the Resurrection of Jesus* [Grand Rapids: Eerdmans, 1975] 129).

The Resurrection of Believers and Christ's Resurrection

The intimate connection between the past resurrection of Christ and the present *spiritual* resurrection of believers is evident from the fact that believers are said to have been raised "with Christ" (Col 3:1) or "with him" (Eph 2:6; Col 2:12). This prepositional phrase indicates not only an identification or solidarity in destiny between Christ and his own, but also a grounding of the resurrection of Christians to new life in Christ's resurrection. Without a risen Christ who rose supreme over "all rule and authority and power and dominion" (Eph 1:20-21), believers could never in their present earthly lives, before their deaths, experience a resurrection life of victory over all the powers of evil (Eph 2:1-6; Col 3:1, 5-8).

Having experienced such a resurrection event, believers now live their lives in a resurrection state. For after noting that God "made us alive together with" Christ (with the aorist verb *synezōopoiēsen* signaling a past event), Eph 2:5 adds: "by grace you are now in a state of salvation" (with the perfect participial phrase *este sesōsmenoi* indicating a present resurrection state). In this state, too, there is an integral association with Christ. For it is "in Christ Jesus" — that is, in union with the risen Jesus — that Christians are presently alive to God (Rom 6:11). The present life of believers, therefore, is based on the risen life of Christ (Rom 5:10). So then, just as the event of a spiritual resurrection in the experience of believers is founded exclusively on the resurrection of Christ, so also the ensuing state of a spiritual resurrection in their lives is totally dependent on Christ's vibrant new life.

But what about the future *bodily* resurrection of believers and Christ's resurrection? In Paul's teaching, the resurrection of believers will be both like and unlike Christ's. The most important similarity is that they both have a single cause — the creative power of God. It is the God whom Paul characterizes as the one who "gives life to the dead" (Rom 4:17) or "raises the dead" (2 Cor 1:9) who will display his life-giving power and his concern for the body in raising dead believers, just as he raised the Lord Jesus (1 Cor 6:14; 2 Cor 4:14).

What is more, some of the aspects or results of resurrection will be the same for Christian believers as they were in the case of Christ. The most significant analogies between Christ's resurrection and the resurrection of believers — beyond the obvious fact of reanimation — are those of transformation (cf. Luke 24:31 and Acts 1:3, of Christ; 1 Cor 15:42-43, 51-54, of believers), ascension to heaven (cf. Acts 1:9-11, of Christ; 1 Thess 4:17, of believers), and exaltation (cf. Acts 2:32-33, of Christ; 2 Tim 2:12, of believers). Then the renewed life gained by resurrection will never be terminated by death (cf. Rom 6:9, of Christ; 1 Cor 15:42, 52-54, of believers). It will be expressed through a spiritual or glorified body (1 Cor 15:48-49; Phil 3:20-21), and its natural habitat is heaven (Eph 1:20-21, of Christ; 2 Cor 5:1, of believers).

There are, however, certain differences between Christ's resurrection and the future resurrection of believers. Most obvious, of course, is that in Christ's case his body remained relatively intact, whereas the bodies of the great majority of believers who have died will have decomposed and their atoms or material particles dispersed. More theologically relevant is the fact that Christ was raised "on the third day" (1 Cor 15:4), whereas his people will experience resurrection on the Last Day. Furthermore, only of Christ can it be said that he was constituted a "life-giving spirit" (1 Cor 15:45) through his resurrection, or that resurrection marked his conquest over death (Rom 6:9). And only of Christ is it true that his resurrection was the occasion of his public installation as Son of God (Rom 1:4), as universal Lord (Rom 14:9; Eph 1:20-21; Phil 2:9-11), and as judge of the living and the dead (Acts 17:31).

These twin ideas of similarity and difference are implied in the metaphor of "firstfruits" *(aparchē)*, by which Paul in 1 Cor 15:20 picturesquely sums up the relationship between the resurrection of Christ and the resurrection of Christians: "Christ has been raised from the dead, the firstfruits of those who have fallen asleep" (cf. v. 23). In the Old Testament, the firstfruits were the initial portions of the produce of the field and flock, which were offered to God in acknowledgment of his ownership of all and in thanksgiving for his generous provision (cf. Exod 23:16, 19; Lev 23:10; Num 18:8, 12; Neh 10:37). As used by Paul, the metaphor of firstfruits establishes two basic points: (1) that the resurrection of Christ and the resurrection of his people are essentially one, and yet (2) that these two resurrections are distinguishable with regard to time.

This essential unity between the firstfruits and the harvest is central to the whole argument of 1 Corinthians 15. To affirm Christ's resurrection is to affirm that of his people (vv. 12, 20, 23). To deny their resurrection is to deny his (vv. 13, 15-16). Each implies and is involved in the other. Paul, of course, cannot contemplate the full harvest without the firstfruits. But neither can he envisage the firstfruits without the full harvest.

Nonetheless, the resurrection of Christ and the resurrection of believers remain distinguishable. The term *"firstfruits"* itself implies a priority in time. Firstfruits were gathered before the remainder of the harvest was ripe. Jesus' resurrection inaugurated "the last days" (Acts 2:16-17, 32-33), which will be terminated by the resurrection of the righteous (1 Cor 15:23-24). So Paul specifies two "ranks" or "orders" *(tagmata)* that are to be understood as being related by succession: "Each in his own rank: Christ the firstfruits, then *(epeita,* or, "next in sequential order"), at his coming, those who belong to Christ" (1 Cor 15:23). This priority of Christ in a resurrection to deathlessness is an important Pauline theme. For as "the first to rise from the dead" (Acts 26:23; cf. Rom 6:9), Jesus inaugurated the new creation (2 Cor 5:17; cf. John 20:22).

One important question remains to be asked: "If the resurrection of Christ and the resurrection of believers are intimately connected, can Christ's resurrection be termed the *cause* of the resurrection of believers?" There are three personal causes of the resurrection, and thus the transformation, of the righteous mentioned by Paul: God (1 Cor 6:14), Christ (Phil 3:20-21; perhaps also 1 Cor 15:45 and 1 Thess 4:14), and the Spirit (Rom 8:11; perhaps also 2 Cor 3:18; Gal 6:8). The ostensibly impersonal causes include the power of God (1 Cor 6:14; Eph 1:19-20; cf. 2 Cor 13:4) and the glory of the Father (Rom 6:4). Probably the most satisfactory way to accommodate all these data is to distinguish between God the Father, acting powerfully, as the ultimate cause of resurrection, and Christ and the Spirit as proximate causes.

If, then, the category of cause-effect is not fully relevant to the relation between Christ's resurrection and that of believers, what is their precise interrelationship? Nowhere does Paul use the word "pledge" *(arrabōn)* of the resurrected Christ (as he does of the Spirit indwelling the believer in 2 Cor 1:22; 5:5). Nonetheless, this expression aptly characterizes the relation in question. For the risen Lord — or his rising from the dead — is in Paul's thought the guarantee of the bodily resurrection of all Christ's followers.

One expression that seems to capture much of this idea is found in the prepositional phrase "with Jesus" *(syn Iēsou),* which appears in two Pauline passages. In 2 Cor 4:14 Paul claims that he declared "the good news" with confidence because he knew that the God who raised the Lord Jesus would raise him as well "with Jesus" (2 Cor 4:14). Then in 1 Thess 4:14 he asserts that through the power of Jesus *(dia tou Iēsou)* God would bring (i.e., raise) "with him" those who had fallen asleep. Obviously, "with him" in these passages cannot mean that Jesus will undergo a second resurrection. Probably we should paraphrase it: "as pledged by the resurrection of Jesus," or "by virtue of association with the risen Jesus." In addition, the very notion of firstfruits hints at a divine pledge that as Christ rose, so too will his people rise. As surely as the harvest follows the firstfruits, the resurrection of the members of the Body will follow the resurrection of the Head. At least, this is how the fifth-century Antiochian commentator Theodoret understood 1 Cor 15:20: "In the resurrection of our Savior we have a guarantee *(echegguon)* of our resurrection" (*Commentary,* ad loc.).

Another term that would have suitably expressed the relation of Christ to his people is "archetype," "prototype," or "pattern" *(typos)*, though it is not used in the New Testament of the relation of Christ's resurrection to that of believers. At times, however, the destiny of Christians is defined by Paul as being in conformity to the "image" *(eikōn)* of the glorified Christ, as in Rom 8:29; 2 Cor 3:18; and Col 3:10, or as bearing "the image of the man from heaven," as in 1 Cor 15:49. In such passages, Christ's resurrection and resurrected state are clearly adduced as exemplars of the Christian's resurrection and immortality. For as Paul says in 1 Cor 15:48b: "Corresponding to the man from heaven are those who belong to heaven." Thus, to paraphrase the message of 1 Cor 15:48: Just as those who have Adam as their head share his nature and likeness, so those who acknowledge Christ as their head will share his nature and likeness.

2. Immortality

Terminology

There are two nouns in the New Testament that may be rendered "immortality," and all ten occurrences of these nouns are within the Pauline corpus. *Athanasia,* "deathlessness" (three uses), denotes the immunity from death enjoyed by God (1 Tim 6:16) and by resurrected believers (1 Cor 15:53-54). *Aphtharsia,* "incorruptibility" or "imperishability" (seven uses), signifies the immunity from decay that characterizes the divine state (Eph 6:24) and the resurrection state (1 Cor 15:42, 50, 53-54). In addition, the adjective *aphthartos,* "imperishable" (four Pauline uses), describes the quality of the divine nature (Rom 1:23; 1 Tim 1:17), the Christian's reward (1 Cor 9:25), and the future state of resurrected believers (1 Cor 15:52).

Although all of these terms are formed with a negative prefix — the Greek letter *a-* (the so-called "alpha-privative"), which functions like *in-* or *un-* before an English word — each takes on positive overtones relating to "eternal life." For just as God is "never-dying" because he is "ever-living," so believers are destined to become free from decay and death because they will participate fully in the eternal divine life. Immortality, therefore, implies the presence of life as well as the absence of death. This correlation of "immortality" and "life" can be seen particularly in the significant juxtaposition of these two concepts in two Pauline passages: in Rom 2:7, "To those who by persistence in doing good seek for glory and honor and immortality, he [God] will give eternal life"; and in 2 Tim 1:10, "Christ Jesus, who abolished death and brought life and immortality to light through the gospel."

It may come as a surprise to some to learn that the terms for immortality — whether as nouns translated "deathlessness," "incorruptibility," or "imperishability," or as an adjective translated "imperishable" — are never used in connection with the word "soul" *(psychē)*, but are associated only with the resurrected spiritual body (eight times, all in 1 Corinthians 15). And never do we find Paul or any other New Testament writer using the verb *athanatizō*, "I make immortal" or "I immortalize," or, in the passive voice, "I am or become immortal" — even though in such passages as Rom 8:11 and (especially) 2 Cor 5:4 the verb would have proved suitable. Perhaps the New Testament writers avoided this verb because it could have so easily been misunderstood as implying that immortality, as a natural property of the soul, was procurable apart from resurrection.

Immortality, therefore, may be defined as the immunity from decay and death that results from having (in the case of God) or sharing (in the case of human beings) eternal divine life.

The Immortality of God

In 1 Tim 6:16 there is a clear assertion of the uniqueness of God's immortality. He is "the blessed and only Sovereign . . . who alone has immortality" *(athanasia)*. What constitutes God's immortality?

Behind each negative definition of God's character lies some implicit positive truth. For instance, when we say that God is invisible, we are not merely saying that he cannot be perceived by human gaze or human inquiry, but also implying that he is perceivable and knowable through his self-revelation. Likewise, when we say that God is immaterial, we are not merely saying that he is not composed of matter, but also implying that he has a spiritual existence. What, then, is Paul affirming when he denies God's propensity to decay and death? We propose that he is implying two things: (1) his incessant life and action, and (2) his inviolable holiness of character.

Immortality in God is not an inherent protection from death, nor simply the guarantee that traces of mortality will never appear in his character or conduct. Rather, in the first place, it is the assurance that God's incessant activity will never end. He perpetually "gives life to all things" (1 Tim 6:13) — a statement that occurs, significantly, in the same Greek sentence as "who alone has immortality." Furthermore, he has in himself a constant supply of creative energy that will never be depleted, far less exhausted. "He is the living God and the everlasting King" (Jer 10:10); he is the "living God" who acts in both the physical realm (Acts 14:15-17) and the spiritual realm (1 Tim 4:10). The notion of immortality, in fact, is inextricably tied to the ideas of life and eternality. For immortality implies that life and activity are constantly present, as well as that inactivity and death are permanently absent.

The second positive truth implied by the Pauline affirmation of God's "nonmortality" is his holiness. One of the principal ways that the Greeks distinguished between human beings and the gods was by reference to death. People are mortal *(hoi thanatoi)*, whereas the gods are immortal (*hoi athanatoi;* see, e.g., Plutarch, *Moralia* 960B). At the root of all other differences between humans and the gods in Greek thought was this essential difference of subjection to or immunity from death.

In a Christian context, of course, the distinction between human beings and God remains (cf., e.g., Rom 1:23). But there is an important difference. For humans are mortal *as sinners* (Rom 5:12), whereas God is immortal *as the Holy One.* It is both that God "alone has immortality" and that he "dwells in unapproachable light" (1 Tim 6:16). It is because of sin, rather than simply because of mortality, that "flesh and blood" cannot inherit the kingdom of God (cf. 1 Cor 15:50). Death is inexorably linked with sin, so where there is sin there is death. The complementary truth, however, is that where there is no sin, there is no death. Immortality, therefore, is a corollary of holiness.

161

The Immortality of Humans

If, then, only God is inherently immortal, it follows that any immortality that may be ascribed to humans is gained as a gracious gift of the divine will (cf. Rom 2:7; 6:23). That is, the corollary of the fact that only God is essentially immortal is the truth that humans can be only derivatively immortal. Their immortality is not essential or intrinsic, but derived or extrinsic.

But were human beings created immortal? In few places is it more important to have precise definitions of terms than in discussing this question. For if "immortal" is defined as being "with a soul that persists after bodily dissolution" or "without the seeds of decay and death," many would be willing to answer with an unequivocal "Yes!" But if "immortal" is defined as "immune from decay and death as a result of sharing the divine life," fewer would be content with an unqualified answer.

Three views of the immortality of humans have been argued:

1. Some hold that human beings were created "immortal" but forfeited that immortality through disobedience to God. But there seems to be a logical difficulty in the idea of losing immortality. However defined, immortality implies the permanence and irreversibility of the immortal state. It is hardly satisfactory to affirm that if Adam had proved obedient in his probation he would have gained "permanent immortality," as J. Barton Payne proposed (*The Theology of the Older Testament* [Grand Rapids: Zondervan, 1962] 216). It is very difficult, in fact, to conceive of degrees of immortality, nor can it be a momentary or temporary state.

2. Others allege that human beings were created mortal, yet were "immortable" — able not to die in that they had the possibility of gaining immortality through obedience to God (cf. F. S. M. Bennet, *The Resurrection of the Dead* [London: Chapman and Hall, 1929] 1-53).

3. Still others affirm that human beings were created neither immortal (see Gen 3:22-24) nor mortal (see Gen 2:17), but with the possibility of becoming either, depending on their obedience or disobedience to God. They were created *for* immortality rather than *with* immortality. Being potentially immortal by nature, humans actually become immortal through grace. To use the classical distinctions, humans were not created unable to die *(non posse mori)* but able not to die *(posse*

non mori), although after the Fall they were unable not to die *(non posse non mori).* Of the views cited above, the third seems to fit best Paul's insistence on the futurity of immortality.

A second issue, however, arises when one talks about the futurity of human immortality and receiving immortality only through God's grace. The question is this: Who will be the recipients of this immortality? Is it the prerogative of all humanity, or is it a privilege reserved only for the righteous?

Romans 2:7-8 delineates two categories of persons who will appear before God on the day of judgment: "To those who seek for glory, honor, and immortality by perseverance in doing good, he will give eternal life; but for self-seeking people who resist the truth and yield to wickedness, there will be wrath and fury." The implication of this distinction is clear. For just as those who pursue immortality will not experience wrath, so those who fail to obey the truth will be denied eternal life — which here includes immortality, as the parallelism shows.

In 1 Corinthians 15, as well, the dead who are raised are described as "those who have fallen asleep in Christ" (v. 18), "we who are in Christ" (v. 19), "those who belong to Christ" (v. 23), and "those who are of heaven" (v. 48). In each case, the stress is on relationship to "the man from heaven." Even those who find some reference to a general resurrection in this chapter agree that verses 51-54 must refer only to those in Christ, for the transformation alluded to in verses 51-52 denotes a conformity to the image of Christ, which is a destiny that is reserved for those on whom God has fixed his affectionate regard (Rom 8:29). Investiture with imperishability and immortality (vv. 53-54), therefore, is denied to those who are "separated from Christ" (Eph 2:12).

Immortality includes sharing the life of God. It is inconceivable that any who are doomed to suffer the punishment of eternal exclusion from the presence of the Lord (cf. 2 Thess 1:9) should simultaneously enjoy the blessings of his immediate presence and life. Thus we must conclude that the focus of Paul's teaching with respect to human immortality is on those who "belong to Christ" or are "in Christ," and so those "of heaven," as being the recipients of God's gift of immortality, and so sharing in the life of God.

Finally we may ask: When is this gift of immortality received by the righteous? 2 Timothy 1:10 indicates that life and immortality were "brought to light" by Christ Jesus "through the good news" of his death and resurrection. It is not that Easter brought universal immortality. But it did inaugurate an era marked by the promise of eternal life and immortality. Only with the appearing of Christ did the idea of immortality emerge from Old Testament shadows into the full light of New Testament day. Nonetheless, the fact of the availability of immortality is not the same as its possession.

Many scholars have interpreted 2 Cor 4:7–5:10 and Phil 1:19-26 to be primarily concerned with the state of Christians between death and the Parousia (e.g., L. Cerfaux, *The Christian in the Theology of St. Paul* [London: Chapman, 1967] 191-212, 223). Under the stimulation of his contact with Greek thought, Paul is seen in these passages to be developing a view of the intermediate state in which the personal Christian "self" acquires immortality at death and — deprived of embodiment but in conscious fellowship with Christ — awaits the resurrection of the body at the Parousia. This "self" that becomes immortal at death is described by these scholars by such epithets as the "inward man," the "self" independent of the body, the intellectual soul as a subsisting subject, and the "ego" in relationship with Christ.

But 1 Corinthians 15 clearly places the receipt of immortality at the resurrection, for it juxtaposes resurrection and immortality in the phrases "what is raised is immortal" of verse 42 and "the dead will be raised immortal" of verse 52. This latter verse does not mean that "the dead will be raised and thus will be seen to be already immortal" but, rather, that "the dead will be raised and thus become immortal." It is possible, of course, to argue that Paul linked immortality with regeneration, thereby affirming that the seed of immortality is implanted by regeneration with the full flower appearing only after resurrection — or that the immortality gained potentially at the moment a person comes to be in Christ (cf. 1 Cor 15:22; 2 Cor 5:17) becomes an actual possession in the resurrection of the dead. But on the evidence of 1 Corinthians 15, it seems more probable that Paul simply portrays immortality as a divine gift that is gained through bodily resurrection. That is, immortality is a gift reserved for the afterlife. Far from already possessing immortality or deserving it, Christians are described as those who "seek" it (Rom 2:7).

Two important consequences follow from viewing immortality as a divine gift that is gained only through bodily resurrection and therefore reserved for the afterlife. The first is that the concept of "a natural immortality of the soul" does not accord with the tenor of Paul's teaching. Often it is claimed, "By immortality of the soul is meant the infinitely prolonged existence of that center of awareness to which the term 'I' refers" (W. L. Reese, *Dictionary of Philosophy and Religion. Eastern and Western Thought* [New Jersey: Humanities, 1980] 247). But in the New Testament generally and Paul's teaching in particular:

1. Only God inherently possesses immortality (1 Tim 6:15-16).
2. Immortality is never predicated of the "soul"; "this mortal body" is destined to "put on" immortality (1 Cor 15:53-54). It is not by birth, but by grace and through resurrection that immortality is gained.
3. Immortality is a future gift (1 Cor 15:53-54).
4. The highest good *(summum bonum)* is not equated with freedom from embodiment but with the receipt of a spiritual body as a perfect instrument for the knowledge, worship, and service of God (Rom 8:23; 1 Cor 15:43-54; Phil 3:20-21). What Christians eagerly await is their "heavenly dwelling" (*to oikētērion hēmōn to ex ouranou*, 2 Cor 5:2), not incorporeal bliss (2 Cor 5:2-4).

When a naturally immortal soul — viewed as having an independent existence either before or after death, or both — is posited, several serious implications usually result. Most serious are that any lively sense of the soul's dependence on God is eclipsed and that the need for a relationship to Christ is removed. But also of great significance — particularly for the issues being dealt with here — are the implications that (1) death comes to be regarded as either illusory or beneficial; (2) corporeality is likely to be seen as an impediment; (3) the afterlife tends to become the prolongation of the present life, and so only a perpetuation of the status quo; and (4) divine judgment is rendered inconsequential.

Under Plato's influence, the Christian church has often affirmed the "immortality of the soul" in the sense that the soul of every person, by divine fiat, will survive death and exist forever. For example, the Westminster Confession (XXXII.1) speaks of the souls of persons as having "an immortal subsistence." Although the concept behind these phrases is biblical, that is, that individual human beings do not cease to exist, either at or after death, there is no biblical precedent for attaching the terms "immortal" or "immortality" to the word "soul." According to Paul and the New Testament, what is immortal when one uses that term with regard to humanity is the resurrected believer.

A second consequence of viewing immortality as a divine gift gained only through bodily resurrection, and so reserved for the afterlife, is that immortality is conditional — only "those who belong to Christ" are destined to share God's immortality. "Conditional immortality" of this variety, of course, is quite different from the traditional or popular meaning of that expression. For, as commonly understood, "conditional immortality" is the view that only the righteous will live forever, the unrighteous being consigned to annihilation — either at death or after suffering divine punishment for a period. Paul, however, teaches that immortality is conditional, but *only* in the sense that there is no eternal life apart from Christ. This does *not* imply that existence beyond death is conditional or that unbelievers will be annihilated.

In Paul's usage, immortality has a positive content, being more than mere survival beyond death. Its opposite, however, is not nonexistence, but exclusion from God's presence (2 Thess 1:9). Forfeiture of immortality means the deprivation of eternal blessedness, not the destruction of personal existence. All human beings survive beyond death, but not all will become immortal in the Pauline sense.

3. The Relation of Resurrection and Immortality

Paul does not present resurrection and immortality either as opposites or as synonyms. They may be distinguished, yet they are closely related. At this point we should note again, in the light of our earlier discussion of the resurrection of the unjust and the relation between the resurrection of the dead and the transformation of the living, that it is necessary for the sake of precision to speak not simply of "resurrection" but of "resurrection-transformation." This is a category that embraces only Christians — not just Christians who will experience death before resurrection, but also, by analogy, those who will be transformed without dying.

Resurrection and Immortality as Inseparable

Several important features regarding the relations of resurrection and immortality in Paul's thought need to be noted. First, since the resurrection-transformation of believers is the only means of gaining immortality, there can be no immortality without a prior resurrection-transformation (Rom 6:9; 1 Cor 15:42, 52-54). Second, since immortality is the inevitable result of the resurrection-transformation of believers, there can be no resurrection-transformation without a subsequent immortality (Rom 6:9; 1 Cor 15:53-54). We have also seen that although *conceptually* resurrection and immortality may be related by succession (as implied in the preceding use of the words "means" and "result"), in *reality* the moment of final transformation is also the moment when immortality is attained. This is because the resurrection-transformation event itself involves the state of having put on the garment of immortality (1 Cor 15:53-54), the swallowing up of mortality by eternal life (2 Cor 5:4).

From a Christian perspective, then, the two doctrines stand or fall together. It is a case of resurrection to immortality and immortality through resurrection. To deny resurrection is to deny immortality, since the embodiment involved in the event of resurrection-transformation is, from a Christian outlook, necessary for the enjoyment of the meaningful existence implied by immortality. On the other hand, to deny immortality is to deny resurrection, since the permanent supply of the divine life pledged by immortality is necessary to sustain the resurrection life of transformed persons.

It is, therefore, illegitimate to choose between resurrection and immortality, as if they were separable alternatives. Each involves the other, so that choosing between them is not only unnecessary but also impossible.

Resurrection and Immortality as Complementary

In Paul's thinking resurrection and immortality are distinct yet inseparable ideas. Each of these doctrines prevents some misunderstanding of the other. Each protects the other. But what is the precise nature of their relation? Three matters need to be highlighted.

In the first place, Paul's doctrine of resurrection prevents an impersonal interpretation of immortality, as has been argued by most of the major competing views. Some people hold to an immortality of influence, wherein the abstract ideas for which they stood live on after their deaths. Others hope for a simple generational immortality, wherein a person lives on in his or her posterity. Still others look for a pantheistic immortality in which the individual is reabsorbed into some sort of universal divine life. But belief in

God's power to restore dead persons to life and to impress on them the image of "the man from heaven" (1 Cor 15:48) — without compromising their individuality — leaves no room for a less than personal immortality.

Second, Paul's view of resurrection forestalls an individualistic understanding of immortality. Paul knows nothing of a neo-Platonic immortality of "the alone with the Alone." Resurrection in a Christian sense does not mark the receipt of a beatific vision in which individual believers dwell in fellowship with Christ but are in isolation from fellow worshippers. Rather, it is a corporate experience of "those who belong to Christ" (1 Cor 15:23), leading to their corporate dwelling with the Lord (1 Thess 4:17).

Third, resurrection as described by Paul excludes the view that immortality may be seen as a disembodied or purely spiritual existence. The Christian's desire and destiny is not for release from embodiment, but for the redemption of the body through resurrection (Rom 8:23) — not for the divestiture of the physical body but for investiture with the spiritual body (2 Cor 5:2-4).

Conversely, however, Paul's doctrine of immortality protects against certain inadequate or aberrant views of resurrection. First, it prevents resurrection from being regarded simply as a single, isolated event. For directly resulting from the event of resurrection is the state of immortality, which, in Paul's teaching, is the immediate and permanent participation of the believer in the eternal divine life that leads to incorruptibility and deathlessness. By passing through the door of resurrection-transformation, the believer has entered the realm of immortality. There is no other means of entry into that realm. No one can pass through that door without also entering this new realm. Immortality, therefore, *is* the resurrection state.

Second, belief in the Christian view of immortality precludes any equation of resurrection with the mere restoration of the dead to transient physical life. Immortality guarantees the permanence of the resurrection state. Jesus is not only "the resurrection" but also "the life." Just as the divine life is unending, so those who share that life also share its "unendingness" — and so will enjoy the benefits of resurrection for ever. Once resurrected, Christians will permanently bear the image of God's Son (Rom 8:29; 1 Cor 15:49).

Third, to understand immortality as Paul does forestalls the idea that resurrection life may languish from lack of sustenance. The concept of immortality enshrines the truth that the divine power displayed in the initial act of raising the dead (1 Cor 6:14; Phil 3:21) will continue to support the new life of those raised (1 Cor 15:43). It will be as true of the resurrected believer as it is true already of the risen Christ: "he lives by the power of God" (2 Cor 13:4). God does not impart the heavenly body only to allow it to falter for want of constant invigoration. It is a spiritual body precisely because it is fully dependent on God who is Spirit and because it is completely energized and controlled by the Spirit. God sustains what he gives as surely as he completes what he begins.

4. Conclusion

There are, then, at least three ways in which Paul's doctrine of resurrection informs the idea of immortality. It ensures that immortality is seen (1) as personal, not impersonal; (2) as corporate, not individualistic; and (3) as involving a body and not merely a soul. Similarly, the view of immortality found in Paul informs the doctrine of resurrection in at least three ways. It guarantees that resurrection is seen (1) as a state rather than simply an event; (2) as a permanent condition rather than a temporary state; and (3) as a state sustained by the life and power of God.

With such a hope and confidence, the exhortation of Paul at the end of his famous death-resurrection-immortality chapter takes on a new significance: "So then, my dear brothers and sisters, stand firm. Let nothing move you. Always devote yourselves completely to the Lord's work, since you know that your toil in the Lord is certainly not in vain" (1 Cor 15:58).

Selected Bibliography

Benoit, Pierre, and Roland E. Murphy, eds. *Immortality and Resurrection.* New York: Herder, 1970.

Charles, R. H. *Eschatology: The Doctrine of a Future Life in Israel, Judaism, and Christianity — A Critical History.* 1913. Reprint, New York: Schocken, 1963.

Cooper, John W. *Body, Soul, and Life Everlasting: Biblical Anthropology and the Monism-Dualism Debate.* Grand Rapids: Eerdmans, 1989.

Cullmann, Oscar. *Immortality of the Soul or Resurrection of the Dead?* New York: Macmillan; London: Epworth, 1958.

Darragh, J. T. *The Resurrection of the Flesh.* New York: Macmillan; London: SPCK, 1921.

Duthie, C. S., ed. *Resurrection and Immortality*. London: Bagster, 1979.

Gaffin, Richard B., Jr. *The Centrality of the Resurrection: A Study in Paul's Soteriology*. Grand Rapids: Baker, 1978.

Guntermann, F. *Die Eschatologie des Hl. Paulus*. Münster: Aschendorff, 1932.

Harris, Murray J. *Raised Immortal: Resurrection and Immortality in the New Testament*. London: Marshall, Morgan & Scott, 1983; Grand Rapids: Eerdmans, 1985.

Kennedy, H. A. A. *St. Paul's Conceptions of the Last Things*. 2d ed. London: Hodder & Stoughton, 1904.

Lewis, H. D. *The Self and Immortality*. London: Macmillan, 1973.

Lincoln, Andrew T. *Paradise Now and Not Yet: Studies in the Role of the Heavenly Dimension in Paul's Thought, with Special Reference to His Eschatology*. Cambridge: Cambridge University Press, 1981. Reprint, Grand Rapids: Baker, 1991.

Schep, J. A. *The Nature of the Resurrection Body*. Grand Rapids: Eerdmans, 1964.

Stanley, David M. *Christ's Resurrection in Pauline Soteriology*. Rome: Pontifical Biblical Institute, 1961.

Stendahl, Krister, ed. *Immortality and Resurrection*. New York: Macmillan, 1965.

Vos, Geerhardus. *The Pauline Eschatology*. Princeton: Princeton University Press, 1930. Reprint, Grand Rapids: Eerdmans, 1953.

CHAPTER 8

Is There Development in Paul's Resurrection Thought?

RICHARD N. LONGENECKER

WHEN DEALING with the resurrection of believers in Paul's letters, the question inevitably arises: "Is there development in Paul's thought?" The question has been asked for over a century and a quarter, and it continues to be asked today.

The question is not, "Did Paul view the Christian life in terms of growth and development?" That seems to be answerable in the affirmative by appeal to such features as his illustration of the course of salvation history in Gal 4:1-3, the imagery he uses to describe believers at Corinth in 1 Corinthians 3, and the prayers he prays for his converts in Phil 1:9-11, Col 1:9-14, Philm 6, and Eph 1:15-23. Nor is it, "Did Paul grow and mature in his own Christian experience?" Again, that seems answerable in the affirmative by appeal to such passages as 1 Cor 13:9-12 and Phil 3:12-16.

Likewise, our question is not: "Is there evidence of development in Paul's letters with regard to a number of other crucial matters at the core of his thought — such as about Jesus Christ, the Gentile mission, the nature of God's salvation, God's covenant with his people, the Mosaic law, the Holy Spirit, women in God's redemptive program, Christian ethics and lifestyle, or even about eschatology generally?" Each of these matters requires careful explication (cf. *The Road from Damascus: The Impact of Paul's Conversion on His Life, Thought, and Ministry,* ed. R. N. Longenecker [Grand Rapids: Eerdmans, 1997]). And what can be said about Paul's development of thought in any of these areas cannot be claimed to apply directly to the question at hand, but only, at best, by way of analogy.

171

Rather, our question concerns quite specifically Paul's resurrection message. It seeks to determine the parameters of that message and to what extent his thought about the resurrection of believers may have changed during the period represented by his extant letters. Our investigation must necessarily ask regarding (1) *the circumstances* that gave rise to writing about the resurrection in his letters, (2) *the basis for his thought* about the resurrection as expressed in those letters, (3) *central features* of his various resurrection statements, and (4) *discernible shifts of focus, emphasis, or expectation* in his resurrection message. (For pedagogical reasons, in fact, our discussion of the relevant passages in Paul's letters will be largely organized in terms of these four issues.) And if in our investigation certain changes or developments can be identified, we must then ask: "Of what nature are they?" and "How does one account for them?"

Development in Paul has often been identified in terms of shifts in his statements: (1) from a Jewish anthropology and cosmology in his earlier letters to a Hellenistic anthropology in his later letters; (2) from Jewish apocalyptic imagery in his earlier letters to more Hellenized expressions in his later letters; (3) from an apocalyptic, world-renouncing mind-set to a world-affirming mind-set; (4) from a collective eschatology to a personal, individual eschatology; (5) from focusing on Christ's coming (the Parousia) to focusing on his own death; (6) from anticipating fulfillment "with Christ" in the future to experiencing fulfillment "with Christ" and "in Christ" here-and-now; and (7) from expecting that he himself would be alive at the time of the Parousia, and so be personally involved in the resurrection without dying, to a consciousness that he would probably die before Christ's coming, and so be among those raised from the dead at the final resurrection. The data claimed in support of each of these proposals need to be carefully evaluated as we proceed. Furthermore, our question requires us to ask: "What exactly do we mean by 'development' in Paul — that is, whether dichotomous or discontinuous changes of opinion, or, in some manner, changes that occurred within a continuum of thought?"; and, "How are matters of 'continuity' and 'development' to be related when dealing with Paul's resurrection statements in his various letters?"

1. A Brief History of Pauline Developmental Theories

The history of Pauline developmental theories can be set out in terms of two phases. The first occurred during the latter part of the nineteenth century and the first part of the twentieth — that is, from 1870 to about 1932. The second has been taking place during the latter two-thirds of the twentieth century, from 1932 to the present.

Phase One: 1870-1932

The second half of the 1800s was a time when ideas of development and progress were "in the air." People were conscious of achievements in science, technology, exploration, trade, and the arts, and so began to view all human endeavor in terms of progress, both quantitatively and qualitatively. More important for our purposes, a number of works were written during this time by eminent theologians representing all shades of the theological spectrum that advocated a developmental understanding of the course of Christian doctrine — usually focusing on developments after the New Testament period, though often, as well, arguing for developments throughout the Scriptures. John Henry Newman's *An Essay on the Development of Christian Doctrine* (1845) was, of course, seminal. But just as important were Robert Rainy's *The Delivery and Development of Christian Doctrine* (1874), Adolf Harnack's *History of Dogma* (1886; English translation, 1905), and James Orr's *The Progress of Dogma* (1901).

It was Auguste Sabatier who first proposed a developmental hypothesis for the understanding of Paul and attempted to trace out what he called the "progressive character of Paulinism" (*The Apostle Paul: A Sketch of the Development of His Doctrine* [French original, 1870; English translation, 1896]). In opposition to "the orthodoxy of the past" and "the rationalistic criticism of the Tübingen School" — both of which, he asserted, denied "the existence of progress and development in Paul's doctrine," and so turned the figure of the apostle into something resembling the frigid, stone statuary of Europe's cathedrals — Sabatier took as his purpose "to write not a general biography of Paul, but a biography of his mind, and the history of his thought" (ibid., v-xiv, 1-2).

A number of German scholars followed Sabatier's lead and attempted to work out a developmental understanding of Paul's thought generally. Among them were Hermann Karl Lüdemann (*Die Anthropologie des Apostels Paulus und ihre Stellung innerhalb seiner Heilslehre: Nach den vier Hauptbriefen*, 1872), Otto Pfleiderer (*Der Paulinismus: Ein Beitrag zur Geschichte der urchristlichen Theologie*, 1873), and Bernhard Weiss (*Lehr-*

buch der Biblischen Theologie des Neuen Testaments, first published in 1868, but revised extensively through 1893). More particularly, Ernst G. G. Teichmann (*Die paulinischen Vorstellungen von Auferstehung und Gericht,* 1896) and Heinrich Julius Holtzmann (*Lehrbuch der neutestamentliche Theologie,* 1897) focused on the development of Paul's eschatological thought.

Likewise, a number of British scholars at the end of the nineteenth century added their voices in support of a developmental approach to Paul. Among them were J. B. Lightfoot (see particularly his "The Chronology of St. Paul's Life and Epistles," which was taken from his lecture notes and published posthumously in *Biblical Essays,* 1893, 213-33) and George Matheson (*The Spiritual Development of St. Paul,* 1897). Special attention was given to Paul's eschatological development by Henry St. John Thackeray (*The Relation of St. Paul to Contemporary Jewish Thought,* 1900) and R. H. Charles (*A Critical History of the Doctrine of a Future Life in Israel, in Judaism, and in Christianity,* 2d rev. ed., 1913).

Not everyone, however, understood Paul in such a fashion. On the Continent, for example, Albert Schweitzer, surveying scholarship "From Baur to Holtzmann," expressed the following opinion:

> There is in works of this period much assertion and little proof regarding the development within Paulinism. One almost gets the impression that the assumption of different stages of thought was chiefly useful as a way of escaping the difficulty about the inner unity of the system (*Paul and His Interpreters: A Critical History,* trans. W. Montgomery [1912] 32).

Likewise, Johannes Weiss, pointing out the need to recognize distinctions between the early Paul (about whom we know little) and the later Paul (about whom through his letters we know a lot), argued:

> It cannot be too much insisted upon that the real development of Paul both as a Christian and as a theologian was completed in this [early] period which is so obscure to us, and that in the letters we have to do with the fully matured man. . . . We cannot watch Paul's growth during these [early] years. By contrast, the 'development' which some think they can discern in the period of the letters — ten years, at the most — is not worth considering at all (*The History of Primitive Christianity,* 2 vols., trans. and ed. F. C. Grant et al. [1936] 1:206).

In the early twentieth century, English speaking developmental approaches to Paul were also receiving a bad press. In Britain, for example, James Moffatt pointed out that "the extant letters of the apostle fall . . . in the late afternoon of his career" (*An Introduction to the Literature of the New Testament,* 3rd rev. ed. [1918] 62); and he went on to insist: "To arrange the [Pauline] epistles in the order and for the reasons suggested, e.g., by Lightfoot, is to confuse the parade-ground with the battlefield" (ibid., 170). Similarly in North America, as witness Ernest Findlay Scott's statement on the matter:

> Attempts have often been made to trace out a development of Paul's thought, as reflected in the Epistles, but this, on the face of it, is a somewhat futile task. When he wrote the earliest of these letters, Paul was a mature man, perhaps approaching fifty. He had been thinking out his message for twenty years, and had arrived at strong convictions which he was not likely now to change (*The Literature of the New Testament* [1932] 112).

Likewise, Geerhardus Vos, in an article entitled "Alleged Development in Paul's Teaching on the Resurrection" (*Princeton Theological Review* 27 [1929] 193-226) — in which he characterized developmental views of Paul as "consisting in the elimination of error, each successive stage of belief contradicting the preceding stage, and in turn being superseded by the following one" (ibid., 193) — argued that for contextual reasons Paul did not say everything that could be said in each of his resurrection texts, but that it can be assumed that his views, though somewhat different in the various texts, were not contradictory.

Phase Two: 1932 to the Present

A second phase of developmental approaches to Paul began with C. H. Dodd's John Rylands lectures on "The Mind of St. Paul: A Psychological Approach" in 1932 and "The Mind of St. Paul: Change and Development" in 1933 (*Bulletin of the John Rylands Library* 17 [1933] 3-17 and 18 [1934] 3-44). At the beginning of his second lecture, Dodd acknowledged that (1) developmental theorists of a previous generation perhaps "over-pressed the evidence in the interests of a neat scheme of development," and (2) "the

modern tendency is to deny that the thought of Paul underwent any substantial development during the period covered by the extant epistles, and
to explain the acknowledged differences as due merely to differences of aim,
or to the different circumstances in which the epistles were written"
("Change and Development," 3). Nevertheless, Dodd went on to argue for
"real development" in Paul's thought during his mature years, with that
development being "not merely the result of the circumstances or the
particular aim of the several epistles," but to have resulted, in the main,
from "a significant spiritual experience which left its mark" about the time
of his writing 2 Corinthians (ibid., 4). And he identified that experience as
being not just the stinging rebuke he experienced at Corinth, as reflected
in 2 Corinthians 10–13, but principally a grave illness that left him almost
dead at Troas, as referred to in 2 Cor 1:8-10 and alluded to elsewhere
throughout the first seven chapters of 2 Corinthians (esp. 1:3-7 and 4:7-12)
— with these two factors combining to constitute in his life a "spiritual
crisis" that resulted in "a sort of second conversion," which effected a
"change of temper" in his personality and ministry ("Psychological Approach," 14-17; "Change and Development," 4, passim).

In Dodd's understanding, Paul's "spiritual crisis" caused him to re-
evaluate his outlook as a Christian missionary and to move from a world-
renouncing attitude, with personal fulfillment of being united "with Christ"
reserved for the future, to a world-affirming attitude, with salvific fulfillment understood in terms of the here-and-now (or, "Realized Eschatology"). Many other implications, as Dodd saw it, were also involved in
this "second conversion." For example, (1) temperamentally, Paul moved
from lingering feelings of resentment, frustration, self-vindication, pride,
and seeking to excel (cf., e.g., 1 Thess 2:18; 1 Cor 4:21; 7:8-9; 2 Cor 12:7)
to a final abandonment of any claim to achievement, success, or satisfaction
in his own life, in full surrender to God in Christ (as in Philippians);
(2) politically, he moved from a view that believers ought not to have
recourse to pagan courts (1 Cor 6:1-11) to a view that human governments
exist by God's ordinance (Rom 13:1-10); (3) sociologically, he moved from
advocating a strict separation of believers from unbelievers (1 Cor 5:9;
perhaps also 2 Cor 6:14–7:1) to arguing that unbelievers can do some good
before God because of divine law having been written on their hearts (Rom
2:14-15) and that Christians ought to have a generous attitude toward
"whatever is true, whatever is noble, whatever is right, whatever is pure,
whatever is lovely, whatever is admirable" (Phil 4:8-9); and (4) with regard

to marriage, from a depreciation of the value of marriage (1 Cor 7:1-9), with those who had wives being exhorted to live as though they were unmarried (1 Cor 7:29), to actually using marriage as an illustration of divine love and exhorting husbands to "love your wives, just as Christ loved the church and gave himself up for her" (Eph 5:25-33). More particularly with regard to eschatology, Dodd argued that before his near fatal sickness at Troas Paul had a Parousia fixation and expected he would personally experience resurrection without dying, but that after his traumatic illness his focus was on death, on gaining immortality at death (rather than at the Parousia through resurrection), and on being now "in Christ."

While not espousing all that he proposed, a number of scholars have generally followed Dodd in tracing out developments in Paul's thought during the period of his mature Christian ministry — particularly in positing some sort of shift between 1 Corinthians 15 and 2 Corinthians 5, but also in identifying developments in his views of Christ, the Gentile mission, the nature of God's salvation, and the church. Many of these are British scholars who have been influenced, either directly or indirectly, by Dodd — such as W. L. Knox, H. E. W. Turner, T. W. Manson, A. M. Hunter, George B. Caird, W. D. Davies, R. F. Hettlinger, J. A. T. Robinson, and F. F. Bruce. Others are Germans, who were rooted in the developmental approach of a previous generation and found in Dodd a catalyst to their thinking — such as Hans Windisch, Hans-Joachim Schoeps, Adolf Schlatter, Joachim Jeremias, and Oscar Cullmann. Still others are North Americans who have attempted to wed Dodd's developmental approach to John Knox's "Three Jerusalem Visit" chronology, and so to argue for an earlier (though more compressed) period for Paul's western mission (in the early 40s) when the apostle's thought was presumably less mature and therefore still being formed — such as Charles H. Buck, Greer Taylor, H. L. Ramsey, Frederic R. Crownfield, M. Jack Suggs, and John C. Hurd.

But though there have been many advocates of a developmental understanding of Paul during the last two-thirds of the twentieth century, there have also been many who have opposed such an approach. John Loewe's "An Examination of Attempts to Detect Developments in St. Paul's Theology" (*Journal of Theological Studies* 42 [1941] 129-42), which was written in direct opposition to C. H. Dodd and W. L. Knox, is a classic example. For though Loewe acknowledged that Paul certainly developed in his mental history, he insisted that those developments took place before the apostle's mature thought as expressed in his letters. And though he recognized shifts in what Paul presents in his letters — which could even be called inconsistencies — Loewe argued that those seeming inconsistencies should be viewed as due to (1) changes in the apostle's mood when writing, (2) differing circumstances of those addressed, (3) tensions between Jewish and Christian elements of faith, and/or (4) the paradoxical character of the gospel message itself.

Somewhat more idiosyncratically, C. L. Mearns has argued that Paul's earliest eschatology — that is, what he believed and taught prior to the writing of any of his extant letters — was that all of the expected eschatological events had already taken place in the experience of Jesus (or, what has been called "Realized Eschatology"), and that it was only as Paul encountered the problem of believers dying at Thessalonica that he revised his stance to speak of events yet future ("Early Eschatological Development in Paul: The Evidence of I and II Thessalonians," *New Testament Studies* 27 [1981] 137-57). Mearns rightly latches on to certain realized features in 1 and 2 Thessalonians, which appear even amidst Paul's futuristic teachings, crediting those realized features to the apostle's earliest convictions. The fatal flaws with his argument, however, have to do with (1) ascribing to Paul the belief that Jesus' resurrection was his Parousia, and (2) assuming that Paul (and other earlier Christians) never really thought about the death of believers until confronted by the concerns of those at Thessalonica — both of which seem highly unlikely.

2. Problems in Tracing Out Development in Paul

Part of the difficulty today in even raising questions about development in Paul is that contemporary New Testament scholarship is almost exclusively concerned with the task of identifying the circumstances of each of the churches to which the apostle wrote — the particular church's interests, problems, needs, misunderstandings, failures, and triumphs. These are matters that are highly relevant and important. But consideration also needs to be given to Paul's own situation and thought at the time when he wrote each letter — his interests, problems, needs, hopes, fears, and maturing experience as Christ's ambassador. For the special circumstances of the various churches and the differing situations of Paul when writing those churches can never be divorced from one another in our interpretation of what is written. Furthermore, part of the difficulty in dealing with development in Paul resides in the fact that many New Testament scholars have become wary of a synthetic, holistic, or so-called "Biblical Theology" treatment of the apostle, preferring, rather, to treat in a more modest fashion only aspects of his thought. This saves them, of course, from dangers of an overly systematized portrayal and unfounded speculation. But it also forces them to remain somewhat agnostic regarding the overall course of Paul's thought.

Nonetheless, even when one attempts to take into consideration not only (1) the circumstances of the churches addressed, but also (2) the situation and mental temper of the apostle himself in writing each of his letters and (3) the contours of the overall course of his thought, there still remain significant problems in trying to trace out developmental features in Paul's thought. Chief among these are the following:

1. That all of Paul's extant letters, however identified and whenever dated, fall within a relatively brief period of his later adult life (roughly speaking, somewhere between eight to fifteen years) when he was extensively engaged in ministry and when his thought might reasonably be supposed to have reached maturity;

2. That the extent of the Pauline corpus is debated, with seven letters commonly accepted but the Pastoral Epistles usually set aside and 2 Thessalonians, Colossians, and Ephesians often questioned;

3. That a relative chronology between the letters — in certain cases, also within the letters (e.g., 2 Corinthians; perhaps also Philippians; less likely 1 and 2 Thessalonians) — is a frequent matter of dispute;

4. That the pastoral and polemical nature of much of what Paul writes in his letters requires interpreters to treat his statements more circumstantially than systematically, both as regards their subject matter and as regards their manner of argumentation;

5. That an argument from silence, which has been used frequently in support of various developmental theories, is notoriously insecure; and,

6. That the paradoxical nature of Christian truth makes it exceedingly difficult to classify Paul's thought, either as a whole or in part, according to any schema of successive stages of development.

Probability debates as to whether Paul's thought on any particular subject could or could not have developed during a relatively brief period of time in his later adult life as Christ's ambassador are interesting, but not highly productive. Numerous analogies can be provided in support of either stance, and deductive reasoning does not take us very far. It is the data from his letters themselves that must be appealed to, keeping in mind the caveats listed above. And while the data on many other significant Pauline themes (e.g., Christ, the Gentile mission, soteriology, God's covenant, the Mosaic law, the Holy Spirit, women, ethics, ecclesiology, and even eschatology generally) may be spread over a more expansive body of Pauline writings (whether ten or thirteen canonical letters), the question of development when held to the apostle's resurrection thought is essentially confined to passages within those letters that are commonly accepted: 1 Thess 4:13-18, 1 Cor 15:12-58, 2 Cor 4:14–5:10, Rom 8:19-25; 13:11-12, and Phil 1:21-26; 3:10-11, 20-21; 4:5 (in some such order). So it is to those passages that we must now turn.

3. 1 Thessalonians 4:13-18

In 1 Thessalonians we have the earliest explicit statements about the resurrection of believers in Paul's letters, and so it is to that letter that we must turn first. John Hurd's attempt to show that the "Previous Letter" to Corinth, referred to in 1 Cor 5:9, contained the same type of teaching "concerning bodily resurrection" as 1 Thess 4:13-18 is interesting, informative, and suggestive (*Origin of I Corinthians,* 50-53, 213-40; esp. 229-33). But it remains unproved. Likewise, a "South Galatian" view of the provenance of Galatians, which would allow for Galatians to be seen as the earliest extant letter of Paul, need not be invoked here. For even if Galatians is earlier than 1 Thessalonians, as I believe (cf. my *Galatians* [Dallas: Word, 1990] lxi-lxxxviii), its few allusions to eschatology (e.g., Gal 5:5, 21; 6:8) cannot be taken as a basis for Paul's words about the resurrection in 1 Thessalonians or as detailing in any adequate fashion the nature of his early eschatological thought. At best, Galatians is only supplementary to 1 Thessalonians in matters of eschatology generally and not directly relevant when evaluating Paul's resurrection message in particular.

The Circumstances Behind Paul's Statements

It is frequently taken for granted that futuristic eschatology is the dominant theme of 1 Thessalonians and that Paul's main purpose in writing the letter was to teach and reinforce apocalyptic doctrines about the future. Such an understanding can be buttressed by appeal to 2 Thess 2:1-12 (whether written before or after 1 Thessalonians), for apocalyptic imagery is even more to the fore in that passage, and Paul explicitly says that this type of teaching was part of his evangelistic preaching, even to Gentiles (cf. 2:5: "Don't you remember that when I was with you I used to tell you these things?"). But though Parousia references rest easily on his lips when praising and praying for his converts in 1 Thessalonians (cf. 2:19; 3:13; 5:23), an analysis of the letter indicates that eschatology was not Paul's main concern in writing that letter. Or, as A. L. Moore aptly observes, futuristic eschatology "is not the high peak" of the letter (*Parousia in the New Testament*, 108) — though, of course, "it is not, however, unimportant" (ibid.).

What was of major concern to Paul when writing 1 Thessalonians was what he speaks about in chapters 2 and 3 — that is, a defense of his own and his companions' conduct while at Thessalonica, against certain charges made against them, and a message of encouragement to his converts who were facing some type of persecution. His discussions of ethics in 4:1-12 and eschatology in 4:13–5:11 seem almost tacked on as afterthoughts (cf. the colloquial expression *loipon oun*, "finally then," of 4:1, which appears to signal a transition from the main concerns of the letter to an additional topic or topics), being appended to express further concerns for believers at Thessalonica (see further my "Paul's Early Eschatology").

Having founded the church at Thessalonica about A.D. 49 on his second missionary journey, Paul was forced by Jewish opposition to leave the city after only a brief residence there — perhaps staying only three weeks, though possibly up to three months (cf. Acts 17:1-15). The church seems to have developed quickly and in a gratifying manner (1 Thess 1:3-4; 2:13), and Paul characterizes the Christians there as examples for other believers throughout the provinces of Macedonia and Achaia (1 Thess 1:7-8). But rumors discrediting him and his companions and some type of persecution against believers in the city seem to have arisen. Furthermore, the deaths of some of these new believers — whether because of persecution or natural causes — raised the question: Is there a resurrection hope for believers who die before Christ's Parousia?

So a few months after leaving them, Paul writes back to his Thessalonian converts, probably in the spring of A.D. 50 from Corinth, instructing them about his own and his companions' motivations and how they should live amidst rising persecution (1 Thess 2:1–3:13, with a formal

181

closing at 3:11-13). Then, as something of an addendum, he goes on to speak about two or three other matters that he knows were of concern to them — and which, of course, were also of concern to him: (1) their life-style in a pagan city (1 Thess 4:1-12); (2) the situation of believers who die before Christ's coming, and so might (presumably) miss out on the resurrection (1 Thess 4:13-18); and (3) the nearness of the Parousia and a believer's proper response (1 Thess 5:1-11, with this latter topic perhaps only to be seen as a continuation of the topic in 4:13-18).

The Basis for Paul's Statements

Paul's argument for the inclusion of the believing dead in the final resurrection builds on two premises. The first is what appears to be an early church confession, "Jesus died and rose again," as included in 4:14. The verb *anistēmi*, "rise again," suggests something other than Paul's own formulation, for elsewhere in his letters he usually uses *egeirō*, "rise" (about forty times, and normally in the passive), when speaking about Christ's resurrection and the resurrection of believers. Likewise, his use of the singular name "Jesus," which is common in the confessional portions elsewhere in the New Testament, supports such a view, for usually Paul speaks of "Jesus Christ," "Christ Jesus," or simply "Christ." Only rarely does he use "Jesus" alone — as in Rom 8:11, 2 Cor 4:14, and 1 Thess 1:10, passages that may also reflect portions of early confessional material, and in the latter part of our verse here (v. 14b), whose phraseology is conditioned by the confessional language of the first part of the verse (v. 14a). Furthermore, the *hoti* that introduces the statement "Jesus died and rose again" seems to be a *hoti recitativum*, which would indicate that Paul is here quoting an early Christian confessional portion.

The second premise on which Paul's argument is based is a "word of the Lord," which seems to be set out in 4:15-17. Exactly what is meant by *en logō kyriou*, "by the word of the Lord," and how this teaching came to Paul have been hotly debated. The possibilities are usually narrowed down to three: (1) that this "word" was a revelatory teaching from the exalted Jesus; (2) that it was a teaching of the historical Jesus that was not incorporated into the four canonical Gospels — that is, a so-called "agraphon" (literally, an "unwritten" word); or, (3) that it was a deduction drawn by Paul himself from teachings that were later recorded in the canonical

Gospels? With Joachim Jeremias (cf. his *Unbekannte Jesusworte* [1948, 1951; English translation, *Unknown Sayings of Jesus,* 1957; idem, "Isolated Sayings of the Lord," in *New Testament Apocrypha,* 2 vols., ed. W. Schneemelcher, trans. R. McL. Wilson [London: Lutterworth, 1963] 1:85-90), I believe this "word" to be an "agraphon."

But however we spell out the specifics of the case, it is likely that in 4:13-18 when Paul speaks about the believing dead and their relation to the final resurrection, he does so on the basis of an early Christian confession (4:14) and Jesus' own word (4:15-17). From the first he argues that since it is true that "Jesus died and rose again," the corollary follows: "God will bring with Jesus [who himself died and rose again] those who sleep in him" (v. 14). Highlighting the teaching of Jesus — though, evidently, substituting "we" for "those" and "they" in the words quoted — his points are that at the Parousia (1) living believers will have no advantage over deceased believers, but rather (2) "the dead in Christ will rise first," and (3) both living and dead believers will be joined to meet the Lord and will then be with him forever (vv. 15-16).

Central Features of Paul's Statements

The content of 1 Thess 4:13-18 is pastoral, with a stress on encouraging Christians who are grieving (cf. 4:18; 5:11). Central features of the passage are (1) its focus on Christ's coming, (2) its direct association of the resurrection of believers with Christ's Parousia, (3) its depiction of believers being "with the Lord" as a future reality, and (4) its hint that Paul's own personal expectation was that he himself would be alive at the time of the Parousia and so experience at that time the resurrection without dying — as witness the twice repeated words "we who are alive and remain" (4:15, 17).

Furthermore, the imagery of 1 Thess 4:13-18 is highly apocalyptic: "the Lord will come down from heaven" (cf. Mic 1:3), "with the voice of the archangel" (cf. *4 Ezra* 4:36), "with the trumpet call of God" (cf. *4 Ezra* 6:23), "we will be caught up in clouds" (cf. *2 Enoch* 3:1), "to meet the Lord in the air . . . [and to] be with the Lord forever" (cf. *1 Enoch* 62, esp. vv. 13-16). Adding the imagery of 2 Thess 2:1-12 to this list, the apocalyptic nature of Paul's Thessalonian statements is heightened: "the coming of our Lord Jesus Christ," "our being gathered to him," "the day of the Lord," "the apostasy," "the man of lawlessness," "that which restrains," and "the one who restrains."

All of this, of course, is expressly futuristic in orientation — as is also Paul's reference to his earlier preaching at Thessalonica in 2 Thess 2:5. But the presence of such futuristic features should not be taken to mean that the apostle only thought in a futuristic fashion when discussing eschatology with his Thessalonian converts. As Ernest Best points out, Paul's eschatology in 1 Thessalonians also evidences a number of realized motifs — as, for example, (1) calling believers "children of the light and children of the day" in 5:5, thereby signifying that they have a new existence; (2) associating closely the indicative and the imperative of the gospel throughout 5:1-12; and (3) highlighting the close relationship of believers to Christ, as in 4:14 and 5:10 — items that Best calls "the basic structural patterns" of Paul's thought (*A Commentary on the First and Second Epistles to the Thessalonians* [London: Black, 1972] 12-14, 222). And when we add the two sets of exhortations that immediately follow the eschatological portions of 1 Thess 5:1-11 and 2 Thess 2:1-12 — that is, the exhortations of 1 Thess 5:12-22 and 2 Thess 2:13-15 — it becomes even more evident just how engrained these "basic structural patterns" were in Paul's thinking.

Discernible Shifts in Paul's Statements

In what follows, our question will be: "Are there discernible shifts in Paul's resurrection thought from what appears in his Thessalonian correspondence?" 1 Thess 4:13-18, together with the cognate materials of 1 Thess 5:1-11 and 2 Thess 2:1-12, therefore, function as the base for our investigation of development in Paul's letters. So confining ourselves only to the Thessalonian letters, it is impossible to speak of shifts in 1 Thess 4:13-18, for that is the passage from which we are working.

Yet when one considers the question of development in Paul more broadly, it needs always to be noted that the most significant shift in the apostle's thought with respect to the resurrection occurred prior to the writing of any of his extant letters, and that this occurred in connection with his conversion to Christ. For while the concept of a bodily resurrection was a rising feature within the Judaism of Paul's day, no Jew would have spoken of belief in the resurrection as being based on the fact that "Jesus died and rose again" (4:14). Nor would any Jew have repeated a "word of the Lord" that referred to the future Parousia of Christ, that identified the godly dead as "the dead in Christ," or that spoke of believers being "caught up . . . to meet the Lord in the air" and being "with the Lord forever" (as in 4:15-17). Indeed, some fifteen to seventeen years before he wrote 1 Thess 4:13-18, Paul experienced as a result of his conversion to Christ a shift in his thinking about the resurrection of the righteous that went far beyond any shift of thought that might be found in his later, extant letters.

4. 1 Corinthians 15:12-58

In 1 Cor 15:12-58 Paul deals with a matter that was very much on his mind and that he believed was needful for Christians at Corinth: a proper understanding of the resurrection of believers. It may be that the topic was raised by the Corinthian believers themselves in their letter to Paul and that we should understand his statements in 1 Corinthians 15 as being in response to their agenda, and so in line with his other responses in 1 Corinthians 7–14. More likely, however, this matter regarding the resurrection of believers is to be understood as reflecting Paul's own agenda — though, of course, he thought it to be a topic of great importance for his converts as well.

The Circumstances Behind Paul's Statements

The church at Corinth, like that at Thessalonica, was founded by Paul on his second missionary journey (cf. Acts 18:1-18a). Unlike his stay at Thessalonica, however, his evangelistic ministry at Corinth lasted "for some time" (Acts 18:18a), probably during A.D. 50-51. Later, during his third missionary journey, Paul wrote to his Corinthian converts the letter we know as 1 Corinthians, writing it toward the close of his ministry at Ephesus (cf. 16:5-9), probably in A.D. 56 or 57.

We know from 1 Cor 5:9 that Paul had written the Corinthian church an earlier letter (the so-called "Previous Letter"), whose content can only be surmised (perhaps it is partly contained in 2 Cor 6:14–7:1). That Paul wrote any other letters to his converts at Corinth before writing 1 Corinthians may seem plausible, but it is impossible to tell. We do, however, have 1 Corinthians, and its unity seems assured and its content known.

185

1 Corinthians is largely dominated in its order and form by the polemics of the situation — that is, by Paul's need to respond to reports received from members of the household of Chloe about divisions in the church (1:10–4:21), to rumors that were widely circulating about certain evils in the church (5:1–6:20), and to specific questions asked him by the Corinthian believers themselves in their letter (7:1–14:40). In 15:12-58, however, it seems that Paul speaks to an issue that went beyond what he was specifically told or asked about, but a matter that he knew was an issue among the believers at Corinth — a matter that he probably knew about from being with them earlier: that of the resurrection of believers.

Evidently some Christians at Corinth were claiming that a future, personal, corporeal resurrection of believers in Jesus was (1) *irrelevant*, since the eschatological hope of the gospel was already fulfilled in a believer's present, spiritual experience; (2) *impossible*, since the corporeal body in Greek religious thought was excluded from divine redemption — perhaps, also, in reaction to crude Jewish ideas about resurrection as being simply revivification, reanimation, or resuscitation; and (3) even *unnecessary*, since believers were thought to possess already an immortal soul, which, now being redeemed by Christ, made any further action by God superfluous. Such a scenario seems evident from a "mirror reading" of Paul's statements in the passage. For in 1 Cor 15:12-58 the apostle sets out (1) the *fact* of a Christian's future, personal, corporeal resurrection in vv. 12-34 (as signaled by the use of *hoti*, "that," which appears twice in v. 12), (2) the *manner* of a Christian's resurrection in vv. 35-49 (as signaled by the use of *pōs*, "how," which appears in v. 35), and (3) the *necessity* for a Christian's resurrection in vv. 50-58 (as signaled by the use of *dei*, "necessary," which appears in v. 53).

The Basis for Paul's Statements

Paul's resurrection statements in 1 Cor 15:12-58 are undoubtedly rooted in a number of factors, both Jewish and Christian. Evident in the substructure of the passage are (1) a Jewish anthropology, which laid stress on the essential wholeness of a person — with both "body" and "soul," the "material" as well as the "immaterial," being required for true personhood, and (2) a rising Jewish understanding of a future resurrection for the righteous, which was developing in the period of Second Temple Judaism. This rising

Jewish understanding of resurrection appears to have often taken the form of the revivification, reanimation, or resuscitation of a deceased person (cf., e.g., 2 Macc 7:9-23; *2 Baruch* 50:1-2; *Sibylline Oracles* 4.179-91) — though, at times, it was expressed in terms of immortality (cf. *Jubilees* 26:30-31; *Wisdom of Solomon* 2:1–3:9) and even reincarnation (cf. Josephus, *Jewish War* 2.163; *Antiquities of the Jews* 18.14). Also evident in the passage, however, is a Christian reinterpretation of that Jewish heritage, which saw the resurrection of Jesus as the true validation of hope for a bodily resurrection and focused on Jesus as the agent of that resurrection.

Yet what needs to be noted beyond such a general background is the fact that in 15:12-58 Paul bases all of his arguments on an early Christian confessional portion that he incorporates in 15:3b-5:

> That Christ died for our sins according to the Scriptures;
> that he was buried;
> that he was raised on the third day according to the Scriptures; and,
> that he appeared to Peter and then to the Twelve.

In particular, Paul focuses on the statement "he was raised" (v. 4; cf. also v. 12) and uses it as the immediate basis for his own statements — highlighting in the process both the fact and the prototypical nature of Christ's resurrection. Thus in verses 12-34 he asserts the reality of a future and personal resurrection of believers (i.e., because Christ was raised from the dead and is the "firstfruits" of the righteous, believers in Christ will also be resurrected). Then in verses 35-49 he argues by analogy for the bodily nature of their resurrection (i.e., because Christ was transformed in his resurrection, believers will also be transformed to "bear the likeness of the man from heaven"). And then in verses 50-58, by derived implication, he presents the necessity for the resurrection of believers if they are ever to be clothed with immortality (i.e., because it was necessary for Christ to be raised, it is also necessary for believers to experience resurrection in order to gain immortality).

Central Features of Paul's Statements

A number of features of importance in Paul's argument of 1 Cor 15:12-44 can be paralleled, to one extent or another, by statements found in some of the apocalyptic writings of Second Temple Judaism and the later rabbinic materials of the Talmud. Certainly the fact of a bodily resurrection of the righteous — at times, as well, of the unrighteous — was a growing doctrine within the Judaism of Paul's day. Likewise, the insistence that it is God who is both the Creator and the Re-Creator of the righteous was a common tenet of Judaism. And probably the seed analogy of verses 35-44a was, as W. D. Davies has argued, "a rabbinic commonplace" (*Paul and Rabbinic Judaism: Some Rabbinic Elements in Pauline Theology* [4th ed.; Philadelphia: Fortress, 1980] 305).

In the talmudic tractate *b. Sanhedrin* 90b, for example, Queen Cleopatra is claimed to have asked Rabbi Meir whether the dead rise naked or clothed, and R. Meir is credited with replying:

> Thou mayest deduce by an *a fortiori* argument [the answer] from a grain of wheat: for if a grain of wheat, which is buried naked, shooteth forth in many robes, how much more so the righteous, who are buried in their raiment [i.e., their bodies]?"

Likewise, Rabbi Eliezer in *Pirqe de Rabbi Eliezer* 33.245 is represented as using the same seed analogy with the same logic to argue that the dead do not rise naked:

> All the dead will arise at the resurrection of the dead, dressed in their shrouds. Know thou that this is the case. Come and see from [the analogy of] the one who plants [seed] in the earth. He plants naked [seeds] and they arise covered with many coverings; and the people who descend into the earth dressed [with their bodies], will they not rise up dressed [with their new bodies]?

What distinguishes Paul from his Jewish compatriots on the resurrection of the dead, however, comes to the fore in verses 45-57 and has to do with two matters. The first concerns the centrality of Christ in Paul's thought, with that centrality being evident in his contrast between the First Adam and the Second Adam (vv. 45-49), his allusions to Christ's Parousia (v. 52), and his references to the victory that God has effected and will yet effect "through our Lord Jesus Christ" (vv. 54-57). Thus, while his Jewish compatriots spoke of God as the agent and the End as the time of the resurrection of the dead, Paul — without denying either God or the End as being important — focused on Christ and his Parousia when talking about the resurrection of believers.

But joined with an emphasis on the centrality of Christ is a further matter of great importance for Paul, which also may be claimed to have gone beyond what many of his Jewish compatriots were explicitly teaching and what Christians generally of his day were explicitly stating: that resurrection has to do with the transformation of a person's whole being, and is not to be thought of as merely the revivification, reanimation, or resuscitation of one's former self. It is at this point in his presentation, it should be noted, that Paul speaks of relating to his readers a "mystery" — that is, of explicating, as verses 51-52 have it, an enigma in Christian thinking about how the resurrection of believers should be understood:

> Listen, I tell you a mystery *(mystērion):* We shall not all sleep, but we shall all be transformed *(allagēsometha)* — in a flash, in the twinkling of an eye, at the last trumpet. For the trumpet will sound, the dead will be raised imperishable, and we shall be transformed *(allagēsometha).*

In biblical parlance, "mystery" *(mystērion)* does not mean a "secret" that can only be disclosed to the initiated, as in Greek thought. Rather, it signifies something "enigmatic" that was earlier only partially understood, but now has been clarified by God through a further revelation, as in Jewish thought (cf. R. E. Brown, *The Semitic Background of the Term "Mystery" in the New Testament* [Philadelphia: Fortress, 1968]). And Paul's twice repeated statement "we shall [all] be transformed" serves to highlight the importance of this feature in the explication of that "mystery."

While many of his Jewish compatriots spoke of the resurrection of the dead in terms of revivification, so that the righteous might live their lives on a reconstituted earth and be able to recognize one another — with some also suggesting that some type of transformation would take place at some later time, so that the righteous might then be able to live their lives in a reconstituted heaven (cf. *1 Enoch* 90:28-42; *2 Baruch* 51:1-16) — Paul speaks of the resurrection in terms of the transformation of all believers at the time of Christ's Parousia. Evidently he saw in Christ's resurrection the eschatological revelation that clarifies a former enigma, which had always been associated with the subject of resurrection. And so he conceives of the believer's resurrection as being patterned after Christ's transformation when he was raised from the dead — for, as he says in verse 49, "just as we have borne the likeness of the earthly man [the First Adam], so we shall bear the likeness of the man from heaven [the Second Adam]."

Discernible Shifts in Paul's Statements

Writing six or seven years after having written 1 Thess 4:13-18, Paul says much in 1 Cor 15:12-58 that corresponds to what he said earlier to his Thessalonian converts. His purpose in writing each of these passages, of course, differed — consoling grieving Christians in 1 Thess 4:13-18, correcting confused Christians in 1 Cor 15:12-58. But Paul's Jewish heritage (i.e., God as Creator and Re-Creator; the fact of a future resurrection of the dead; human personality as inseparably connected with both body and soul; and the use of the seed analogy to illustrate the resurrection reality) and a common Christian reinterpretation of that heritage (i.e., Christ as validating the hope of the resurrection and the One who will bring about the resurrection at his Parousia) are evident in both passages. Likewise, in both passages Jewish apocalyptic imagery abounds — as, for example, in 1 Corinthians 15: Christ is the "firstfruits" of the dead (vv. 20, 23); death is "the last enemy" (v. 26); Adam is the historical, natural, earthly "first man" (vv. 45-49); and the resurrection takes place "in a flash, in the twinkling of an eye, at the last trumpet" (v. 52).

Where Paul differs in 1 Corinthians 15 from what he wrote in 1 Thessalonians 4, and so where a discernible shift seems to have taken place in his resurrection thought, is to be found at verse 51 — at that very place where he himself says he is explicating an enigma or "mystery": that resurrection has to do with transformation, not merely with the revivification, reanimation, or resuscitation of a dead corpse. As Joachim Jeremias concluded in comparing Paul's statement in 15:51 with what he wrote in 1 Thess 4:13-18 and what appears in the Jewish apocalyptic writings:

> In I Thess. iv nothing is said about the change. As a matter of fact, the change at the parousia is not met within the Jewish apocalyptic literature. There, the conception is — as may be seen for example from the Syriac Apoc. of Baruch xlix–li — that the dead are raised in their earthly state. Literally, Syr. Bar. 1, 2 says "nothing being changed in their appearance." This is, as Syriac Baruch continues, to secure their identity (1.3f.). Only after the judgment the righteous are changed.

190

This, then, seems to be the mystery, the new revelation: the change of the living and the dead that takes place immediately at the parousia ("'Flesh and Blood Cannot Inherit the Kingdom of God' (I Cor. XV.50)," *New Testament Studies* 2 [1956] 159).

Paul does not speculate in 1 Corinthians 15 as to the anatomical or physiological makeup of transformed believers at the time of their future resurrection. Such details, as Murray Harris points out, "were of no more consequence to Paul and the early Christians than was the geography of heaven" (*Raised Immortal,* 124). Rather, what Paul highlights in this chapter is not only that believers will be resurrected at the Parousia, but also that the resurrection of believers will be patterned after Christ's resurrection — with the paradigm of Christ's resurrection being seen as having to do principally with transformation.

It is, in fact, on this point of resurrection as transformation that 1 Cor 15:12-58 evidences a development of thought over that expressed in 1 Thess 4:13-18. And it is with respect to this teaching on transformation that one can speak of a discernible shift in Paul's statements here. Probably, it may be speculated, Paul's thought matured in the six or seven years between the writing of 1 Thessalonians and 1 Corinthians to the point where he focused not only on Christ's resurrection as the basis for the actuality of a future resurrection of believers, on Christ's Parousia as the time of that resurrection, and on Christ as the agent of resurrection (cf. 1 Thess 4:14-17), but also came to see Christ's resurrection as revealing the paradigm or pattern for what the believer's resurrection will be like.

5. 2 Corinthians 4:14–5:10

2 Corinthians is a difficult writing to analyze, chiefly because of uncertainties regarding its compositional character. For while there is no external attestation in support of any partition theory, there are a number of internal features that have suggested to many that the work should be seen as composed of various Pauline letters (or, portions of letters), which have been brought together to form our present canonical letter. These internal matters have to do with (1) the sudden changes of tone, topic, and rhetorical styles in the writing, most obviously between chapters 1–7 (or, 1–9) and 10–13, (2) the seemingly disparate character of some portions of the

191

writing, chiefly that of 6:14–7:1, (3) the separate treatments of Titus and the brothers in chapter 8 and the collection in chapter 9, and (4) certain references to events in Paul's life and allusions to relations with his Corinthian converts that seem to suggest various times for the writing of what we have as 2 Corinthians — principally (1) his statement of 13:1, "This is the third time I am coming to you"; (2) his reference in 2:1-4 to having written the Corinthians a letter "out of great distress and anguish of heart and with many tears," after having had a "painful visit" with them; and (3) certain allusions throughout the writing to the varying reactions of his converts at Corinth to his person and ministry that seem to suggest various incidents or differing circumstances in their relations with one another.

There have been a number of scholars who have argued forcefully for the unity of 2 Corinthians, usually positing some type of "compositional hiatus" between chapters 1–7 (or, 1–9) and 10–13. The major problem with such a view has always been: Why, then, did Paul retain the conciliatory section that speaks of his joy over his Corinthian converts' repentance (chaps. 1–7) in a letter that concludes in such a severe, harsh, and sarcastic manner (chaps. 10–13)? Most scholars today, therefore, have invoked some type of "partition theory" and postulated some such order of letters as the following: (1) a "Previous Letter," which is referred to in 1 Cor 5:9 (being now either "lost" or represented to some extent by 2 Cor 6:14–7:1); (2) our present 1 Corinthians (a unified letter); (3) an "Intermediate Letter," which is possibly referred to in 2 Cor 2:3-4; (4) a "Severe Letter," which now appears as 2 Corinthians 10-13; and (5) a "Conciliatory Letter," which now appears as 2 Corinthians 1–7 and was written about A.D. 57-58 — with, perhaps, chapters 8 and 9 appended to that final letter.

We need not here get bogged down in the current critical debates regarding the composition of 2 Corinthians. The integrity of what is written — that is, that Paul is the author of all that we have in 2 Corinthians — is not in question. It is primarily only the historical order of the "Conciliatory Letter" (chapters 1–7) and the "Severe Letter" (chapters 10–13) that is of any importance for a discussion of development in Paul. And even that is not of overwhelming significance for dealing with Paul's resurrection thought, since most of the explicit data on the topic in 2 Corinthians is contained within chapters 1–7.

The Circumstances Behind Paul's Statements

However we relate the various portions of 2 Corinthians to one another, it seems obvious that Paul's relations with his Corinthian converts were often strained. Even if chapters 10–13, with their clear indications of a breakdown in relations, are ignored, there still runs throughout chapters 1–7 a refrain of difficulty and distrust between Paul and his converts — as, for example, in his reference to a former "painful visit" (2:1), his statements about the distress caused by that visit (2:2-4), his allusions to grief caused by someone in some particular situation at Corinth (2:5-11), and the various hints throughout these chapters that he was aware of a growing unhappiness among his converts regarding his ministry (e.g., 3:1-3).

Of more importance for an understanding of the circumstances behind Paul's resurrection statements in 2 Corinthians, however, is the traumatic situation that he speaks about as having taken place "in the province of Asia" — at some time when he was away from Corinth and probably shortly before writing what he wrote in (at least) chapters 1–7. He refers in 1:8-11 to that situation as a time when he was "under great pressure, far beyond our ability to endure, so that we despaired even of life" — when, in fact, he "felt the sentence of death" and experienced "deadly peril." And he continues to allude to that situation elsewhere in chapters 1–7, principally in 1:3-7 and 4:7-12.

The Basis for Paul's Statements

The basis for Paul's resurrection statements in 2 Cor 4:14–5:10 must, first of all, be judged to be his Jewish heritage as reinterpreted by his basic Christian convictions, with that background evidently being common to all early Jewish believers in Christ. Such a commonality of background is evident in 4:14-18, where he says, "The one who raised the Lord Jesus from the dead will also raise us with Jesus and present us with you in his presence" (v. 14) — which seems to echo early Christian confessional material. Likewise, it is evident when he exhorts believers to allow "thanksgiving to overflow to the glory of God" (v. 15), not to "lose heart" (vv. 16-17), but to fix their eyes "not on what is seen, but on what is unseen" (v. 18).

More particularly, however, Paul's statements in 4:14–5:10 need to be seen as motivated by certain difficulties he encountered with believers at

Corinth and by a traumatic personal experience he had "in the province of Asia" sometime shortly before writing, which he refers to directly in 1:8-11. Evidently that latter experience was a situation unlike anything he had experienced before, for his reaction of distress and despair (cf. 1:6-11) seems quite different from how he responded to the litany of sufferings he sets out in 11:23-27 — imprisonments, floggings, beatings, stripes, stonings, shipwrecks, perils from bandits, persecutions by both Jews and Gentiles, opposition by believers who proved false, being hungry, cold, and without proper clothing — because of which, he says, he was "exposed to death again and again," but in which he gloried as a servant of Christ. C. H. Dodd's guess that it was a near-fatal illness at Troas is as good as any. But whatever it was, it seems to have caused Paul to contemplate his own death in a new way and to change his thinking about whether he himself would be alive or dead at the time of Christ's Parousia.

Central Features of Paul's Statements

Admittedly, the terms "death" *(thanatos)*, "resurrection" *(anastasis)*, "trans-formation" *(allagē;* cf. the verbs *allassō* and *metaschēmatizō)*, and "immor-tality" *(athanasia, aphthartos,* or *aphtharsia)* do not appear in 2 Cor 4:14–5:10. Nonetheless, the ideas represented by these terms are very much to the fore in this passage by the use of synonymous expressions. Certainly "wasting away outwardly" (4:16) and "the destruction of our earthly tent" (5:1) refer to death; while "he [God] will also raise us with Jesus" (4:14) and "we have [proleptically?] a building from God, an eternal house in heaven, not built by human hands" (5:1) have in mind the believer's res-urrection. And with almost as much confidence, it can be affirmed that "swallowed up" and "life" in the purpose clause "so that what is mortal may be swallowed up by life" (5:4) allude to the believer's transformation and immortality, respectively.

A number of scholars understand Paul in 2 Cor 5:1-10 to be primarily focused on death, rather than Christ's coming, and to be principally con-cerned with the state of believers in an interim period between death and the Parousia. They argue that under the catalyst of a Hellenistic anthro-pology, Paul here develops a view of the intermediate state wherein a believer's personal "self" acquires immortality at death and so gains at that time conscious fellowship "with Christ" (in line with Dodd's "realized" interpretation); yet they also argue (going beyond Dodd) that Paul in this passage visualizes believers as having to await final fulfillment "with Christ" at the Parousia, at which time they will then experience the resurrection of their bodies (cf., e.g., A. Plummer, *Second Epistle of St. Paul to the Corinthians* [1915] 160-61; J. Dupont, ΣΥΝ ΧΡΙΣΤΩΙ: *L'union avec le Christ suivant saint Paul* [1952] 135-91; L. Cerfaux, *The Christian in the Theology of St. Paul* [1967] 191-212, 223). But such statements as "he [God] will also raise us with Jesus" (4:14), "we have [proleptically] a building from God" (5:1), and the Spirit guarantees "what is to come" (5:5) suggest that Paul's focus throughout this passage — even though personally weighed down by an intense realization of his own mortality — is still firmly fixed on the resurrection of believers that will occur at Christ's Parousia.

There are, indeed, a number of exegetical issues in 2 Cor 4:14–5:10 that cry out for treatment if one were to attempt a full exegesis of these verses. Certainly such expressions as "at home in the body we are away from the Lord" and "away from the body [we are] at home with the Lord" (5:6-9) sound fairly Hellenistic. On the other hand, Paul's basic opposition to a Hellenistic anthropology is highlighted by his revulsion to being "found naked" or "unclothed" at death (5:3-4) — that is, to existing as some disembodied soul or spirit that only awaits a future embodiment.

Probably more important to note in this passage, however, is the sequence of ideas presented: (1) death ("wasting away outwardly"; the destruction of our "earthly tent"); (2) resurrection ("he [God] will also raise us with Jesus"; "we have a building from God"); (3) transformation (mortality "swallowed up"); and (4) immortality (postresurrection "life"). Such a sequence suggests how these concepts were related in Paul's own mind — both logically and chronologically — at the time when he wrote 2 Corinthians (or, at least when he wrote chaps. 1–7). And that sequence stands as a paradigm for how their relationships should be understood by us today.

In 1 Cor 15:50-54 Paul insisted that immortality is neither a quality inherent to human beings nor a condition bestowed on them by God at creation: "Flesh and blood (*sarx kai haima,* which is a locution for humanity in its finitude and frailty) cannot inherit the kingdom of God," for humans decay (are "perishable") and die (are "mortal"). "Only God is immortal" *(ho monos echōn athanasian),* as the doxology of 1 Tim 6:16 declares. Angels, of course, are also immortal, having been created as immortal beings by an immortal God. But no person is said elsewhere in the Pauline letters to be immortal, whether inherently, by creation, or at death. And 2 Cor 4:14–5:10 need not be interpreted as a shift in Paul's central focus — that is, from immortality as a result of resurrection and transformation at Christ's Parousia to immortality as gained by believers at death. Rather, though with an increased consciousness of his own mortality, the sequence of events in 2 Cor 4:14–5:10 continues to be: (1) death, (2) resurrection, (3) transformation, and then (4) immortality.

Discernible Shifts in Paul's Statements

Although there is no essential shift of focus in 2 Cor 4:14–5:10 — that is, from a focus on Christ's Parousia and the resurrection of believers to a principal interest in death and some type of soulish immortality at death — there yet remain two features that have been seen as subsidiary shifts in Paul's statements in this passage. These shifts have to do with (1) his descriptive language, and (2) his own expectation regarding how he himself would fit into the scenerio he envisages. For while the language of 1 Thess 4:13-18 and 1 Cor 15:12-58 is literal and highly apocalyptic, that of 2 Cor 4:14–5:10 is metaphorical — "a building from God," "an eternal house in heaven," "a house not made with hands," "not to be found naked," and "not to be unclothed but to be clothed [with our heavenly dwelling]" — and without apocalyptic imagery. And while in 1 Thess 4:15-17 Paul associates himself with those who will be alive at Christ's coming, throughout 2 Cor 4:14–5:10 he identifies himself with those who will die before the Parousia.

"It is clear," as William Baird points out, that in 2 Cor 4:14–5:10 "Paul's eschatological language has undergone change" — although that change, as Baird goes on to insist, should not be seen as "a gradual development out of Jewish into Hellenistic forms," for "major eschatological concepts have remained relatively constant" in the passage ("Pauline Eschatology," 327). Such a change may be posited to have come about because of Paul's "increasing concern for the past and the present" (ibid.). For although his earlier writings incorporate concerns regarding the present (e.g., Gal 5:1-12; 6:7-10; 2 Cor 10:3-4; 11:12-15), and his later letters reflect a continued interest in the future (e.g., Rom 8:19-25; Phil 1:10; 2:16; 3:10-11, 20-21; 4:5), Paul's principal concerns in writing 2 Corinthians 1–7 had to do with circumstances in the present — which had been motivated by the stinging rebukes of his Corinthian converts and some traumatic, near-death experience faced shortly before he wrote these chapters.

Paul's thought in 2 Corinthians 1–7 appears to have become "increasingly personal" and more realistic with respect to his own death (Baird). It is not, therefore, too surprising to see in 2 Cor 4:14–5:10 his identification with those who will die before the Parousia — that is, a change in his personal expectation as to how, exactly, he himself would be related to the Parousia. Yet, even with such a change of expectation, Paul's focus on Christ's coming and the resurrection of believers at that time seems to have remained constant.

6. Romans 8:19-25; 13:11-12

Paul's letter to believers at Rome, while in many ways the heartland of Christian theology and piety, has always been a difficult letter to analyze and interpret. In large measure, understanding Romans has been difficult because of uncertainties as to (1) the identity and situation of its addressees, (2) the "dual character" of its contents (i.e., the presence and distribution of both Jewish and Gentile features), and (3) the purpose of Paul in writing.

There is little doubt, however, regarding the letter's provenance. Rom 15:14-32, the "Apostolic Parousia" or travelogue section, sets out the details quite clearly: that it was written (1) at the close of Paul's mission in the eastern part of the Roman empire (vv. 19-23), (2) during his final, three-month stay at Corinth (v. 25; cf. Acts 20:2-3), and (3) just prior to returning to Jerusalem with a collection for the impoverished believers of that city (vv. 25-27, 30-31) — and that after his trip to Jerusalem, he planned to visit the Christians at Rome; and then, with their assistance, to continue his mission in the western part of the empire on to Spain (vv. 24, 28-29). The letter can, therefore, be dated sometime during the spring of A.D. 58 or 59, since Acts 20:6 tells us that Paul, traveling to Jerusalem by land through Macedonia, was again back at Philippi during Passover.

It would be somewhat pedantic to try to retain our pedagogical four-fold outline of "the circumstances," "the basis," "central features," and "discernible shifts" in discussing the eschatology of Romans. Some of these matters for Romans are hotly debated. Each of them would require an extensive discussion beyond the limits at our disposal for any proper treatment.

RICHARD N. LONGENECKER

It is only the last of the four, that regarding "discernible shifts in Paul's statements," that is of concern for our present purposes. Suffice it here to say that the notion that Paul made any substantial change in his eschatology from the time he wrote 1 Thessalonians or 1 Corinthians to when he wrote Romans (i.e., over the course of eight or nine years, from about A.D. 50-58/59) — in particular, any change in his central focus with respect to the resurrection of believers — is confounded by a comparison of his statements in Romans to those in 1 Thessalonians and 1 Corinthians.

Certainly the cosmic eschatology of Rom 8:19-22 puts an end to any theory that Paul shifted from a collective eschatology in his earlier letters to a personal, individual eschatology in his later letters. Similarly, references in Rom 8:23-25 to the "groaning," "eager waiting," and "hope" of believers for "our adoption as sons" — that is, "the redemption of our bodies" — oppose any view that Paul shifted his focus from resurrection and transformation at Christ's Parousia to simply death and subsequent immortality.

Likewise, it needs to be noted that the language of Rom 8:19-25 has a distinctly apocalyptic flavor, similar to the imagery of 1 Thess 4:13-18 and 1 Cor 15:12-58. Furthermore, the eschatological climax to the exhortations of Romans 12–13 that appears in 13:11-12 — "The hour has come for you to wake up from your slumber, because our salvation is nearer now than when we first believed. The night is nearly over; the day is almost here!" — puts an end to any theory that Paul shifted in his later letters from a sense of imminence regarding Christ's coming (as in 1 Thess 4:14-18) or from a sense of urgency regarding living for God in light of the nearness of the Parousia (as in 1 Thess 5:1-11; cf. also 1 Cor 7:29-31).

7. Philippians 1:21-26; 3:10-11, 20-21; 4:5

Philippians is a particularly difficult letter to evaluate in terms of a developmental hypothesis. Scholars in the past often took it to be a composite of two or three letters — for example, 4:10-23 being one letter, 1:1–3:1 plus 4:4-7 another letter, and 3:2–4:3 plus 4:8-9 another. On such a view, one must first determine the respective situations and relative chronologies of the various parts of the composite writing before attempting to trace out the development of any of its themes. But partition theories for Philippians are usually seen today as being, in the words of W. G. Kümmel, "totally unconvincing" (*Introduction to the New Testament*, rev. ed., trans.

198

H. C. Kee [Nashville: Abingdon, 1975] 333; see also 332-35), and deservedly so.

More serious is the question of the letter's provenance and date. While Phil 1:12-26 indicates quite clearly that it was written from prison, the question remains: Was it written from Ephesian imprisonment (sometime during A.D. 53-57), Caesarean imprisonment (about A.D. 58-59), or Roman imprisonment (about A.D. 60-62)? Issues regarding provenance usually have to do with (1) the number and nature of the journeys between Philippi and Rome reflected in the letter, and (2) the kinship of the contents and rhetoric of the letter to Paul's other letters, particularly to material in Galatians and 2 Corinthians. Cogent arguments can be mounted in support of each of these postulated situations and times of writing. And, obviously, whatever is accepted with respect to the provenance and date of Philippians has a profound effect on how one relates its themes, rhetoric, and language to the other Pauline letters.

Philippians 1:21-26, together with 2 Cor 5:1-10, has often been interpreted as evidencing a shift away from an apocalyptic mind-set, which focused on a corporate resurrection of believers at Christ's Parousia, to a more Hellenistic concern for the individual person, which focused on death and immortality. In Phil 1:21-23, for example, Paul writes: "For to me, to live is Christ and to die is gain. If I am to go on living in the body, this will mean fruitful labor for me. Yet, what shall I choose? I do not know! I am torn between the two: I desire to depart and be with Christ, which is better by far." But, as William Baird points out, "the shifts in eschatological language in II Cor. v and Phil. i do not primarily involve a change in Paul's idea of the time of the end, but a change in Paul's understanding of his own relationship to the end" ("Pauline Eschatology," 327).

Both 2 Corinthians 5 and Philippians 1 reflect Paul's ambiguity as he faces the prospect of his own death — that is, as he is anxious about certain traumatic, near-death experiences — and so he desires "to depart and be with Christ." His reactions are similar in the two passages, though the circumstances were probably different (i.e., a near-fatal illness in 2 Corinthians; a possible judicial sentence of death in Philippians). Indeed, such similar reactions may suggest a particular period in Paul's life when this type of reaction, for some reason, was more common. Or, conversely, they may reflect only a similarity in Paul's responses at different times in his ministry when he was faced with near-death situations. It is precarious to identify Paul's reactions to a potential judicial sentence of death as having taken place sometime shortly after his writing of 1 Corinthians 15 (as in the Ephesian imprisonment theory), or at a later time that was roughly coordinate with his writing of 2 Corinthians 5 (as in the Caesarean imprisonment theory), or sometime later still after the writing of Romans (as per a Roman imprisonment theory) — though, for reasons set out by Dodd ("Change and Development," 5-26), I personally favor the third option.

Nonetheless, however Phil 1:12-26 is evaluated, it cannot be said that Paul's hope for Christ's coming and the resurrection of believers that will take place at that time is in any way abated in Philippians. For in 3:10-11, in what is probably his most revealing autobiographical statement, he speaks of wanting "to know Christ and the power of his resurrection and the fellowship of sharing in his sufferings, becoming like him in his death, and so, somehow, to attain to the resurrection of the dead." And in 3:20-21 he says: "Our citizenship is in heaven. And we eagerly await a Savior from there, the Lord Jesus Christ, who, by the power that enables him to bring everything under his control, will transform (*metaschēmatisei*, "refashion" or "change the outward form of") our lowly bodies so that they will be like his glorious body." So while the ringing affirmation of 4:5, "The Lord is near!" *(ho kyrios eggus)*, has often been taken in a spatial manner (e.g., "Christ is always present among his people"), in context it should undoubtedly be understood primarily in temporal terms to mean: "The Parousia of Christ is imminent, and that fact should affect the believer's attitudes and actions!"

8. Conclusion

What, then, can be said in reply to our question "Is there development in Paul's resurrection thought?" A number of proposed shifts are unable to be validated. Particularly is this so with regard to claims that he shifted (1) from a Jewish anthropology in his earlier letters to a Hellenistic anthropology in his later letters, (2) from a world-renouncing mind-set to a world-affirming mind-set, (3) from a collective eschatology to a personal, individual eschatology, or (4) from a focus on Christ's Parousia and the resurrection of believers to a primary concern with his own death and subsequent immortality. Yet three shifts in Paul's thought about the resurrection of believers do seem to be evident in his letters.

200

The first has to do with what he himself identifies in 1 Cor 15:51 as an explication of an enigma or "mystery" — that is, that the resurrection of believers is not simply the revivification, resuscitation, or reanimation of dead persons, but has to do primarily with transformation. For, as he says twice in 1 Cor 15:51-52, "We shall [all] be transformed" *(allagēsometha);* and again in Phil 3:21, "He [i.e., the Lord Jesus Christ] will transform *(metaschēmatisei)* our lowly bodies so that they will be like his glorious body." Evidently, while contemplating Christ's own resurrection some time after writing 1 Thessalonians 4–5 and before writing 1 Corinthians 15, Paul came not only to understand Christ's resurrection as the basis for the actuality of a future resurrection of believers, Christ's Parousia as the time of that resurrection, and Christ as the agent of resurrection, but also to view Christ's resurrection as an eschatological revelation that clarified and set out the nature of a believer's resurrection.

Another shift also seems evident in the resurrection statements of Paul's letters in his use and nonuse of apocalyptic imagery. For while the language of 1 Thess 4:13-18 and 1 Cor 15:12-58 is highly apocalyptic in nature, that of 2 Cor 4:14–5:10 and Phil 1:12-26 is devoid of apocalyptic imagery. This might, of course, be only a matter of circumstances, for Paul in Rom 8:19-25 — which was certainly written after his letters to his Thessalonian and Corinthian converts — uses a number of apocalyptic expressions in his compacted, cosmic portrayal of the resurrection hope of both believers and all creation. Nonetheless, there does seem to be something of a reduction in Paul's apocalyptic imagery and expressions as we move from his earlier to his latter letters.

Likewise, there seems to be a shift in his letters regarding his own expectation vis-à-vis Christ's Parousia and the resurrection. For while in 1 Thess 4:15-17 he associates himself with those who will be alive at the Parousia, throughout 2 Cor 4:14–5:10 he identifies with those who will die before that event. And probably he so identifies himself, as well, in Rom 8:19-25, which is set in the context of "suffering" and "glory," and Phil 1:21-26, which reflects the possibility of a judicial death sentence.

Nonetheless, whatever shifts of thought, mood, or personal expectation might be postulated, it needs to be emphasized and enunciated clearly that the focus of Paul's teaching regarding the resurrection of believers was always on Christ's Parousia and the resurrection of believers that would then take place. And it is this resurrection message that remains constant in his teaching.

Selected Bibliography

Baird, William. "Pauline Eschatology in Hermeneutical Perspective." *New Testament Studies* 17 (1971) 314-27.

Barrett, C. K. "New Testament Eschatology." *Scottish Journal of Theology* 6 (1953) 136-55.

Benoit, Pierre, and Roland E. Murphy, eds. *Immortality and Resurrection.* New York: Herder, 1970.

Dodd, C. H. "The Mind of St. Paul: A Psychological Approach" and "The Mind of St. Paul: Change and Development." *Bulletin of the John Rylands Library* 17 (1933) 3-17 and 18 (1934) 3-44. Reprint, "The Mind of Paul: I" and "The Mind of Paul: II," in *New Testament Studies.* Manchester: Manchester University Press, 1953, 67-82 and 83-128.

Furnish, Victor Paul. "Development in Paul's Thought." *Journal of the American Academy of Religion* 38 (1970) 289-303.

Gaffin, Richard B., Jr. *The Centrality of the Resurrection: A Study in Paul's Soteriology.* Grand Rapids: Baker, 1978.

Harris, Murray J. *Raised Immortal: Resurrection and Immortality in the New Testament.* London: Marshall, Morgan & Scott, 1983; Grand Rapids: Eerdmans, 1985.

————. *From Grave to Glory: Resurrection in the New Testament.* Grand Rapids: Zondervan, 1990.

Hurd, John C., Jr. *The Origin of I Corinthians.* London: SPCK, 1965.

Lincoln, Andrew T. *Paradise Now and Not Yet: Studies in the Role of the Heavenly Dimension in Paul's Thought, with Special Reference to His Eschatology.* Cambridge: Cambridge University Press, 1981. Reprint, Grand Rapids: Baker, 1991.

Longenecker, Richard N. "The Nature of Paul's Early Eschatology." *New Testament Studies* 31 (1985) 85-95.

Moore, A. L. *The Parousia in the New Testament.* Leiden: Brill, 1966.

Perkins, Pheme. *Resurrection: New Testament Witness and Contemporary Reflection.* Garden City, N.Y.: Doubleday, 1984.

Plevnik, Joseph. *Paul and the Parousia: An Exegetical and Theological Investigation.* Peabody, Mass.: Hendrickson, 1997.

Schep, J. A. *The Nature of the Resurrection Body.* Grand Rapids: Eerdmans, 1964.

Stanley, David M. *Christ's Resurrection in Pauline Soteriology.* Rome: Pontifical Biblical Institute, 1961.

CHAPTER 9

Resurrection and the Christian Life in Paul's Letters

G. WALTER HANSEN

AN EPITAPH inscribed on a tombstone, which is now built into the wall of a house on the island of Cos in the south Aegean Sea, epitomizes the life of an eighty-three-year-old man who lived during the Roman imperial age and exhorts those who pass by as follows:

> One, Chrysogonus [. . .] lies here,
>   of nymphs an adorer,
> Saying to each passer-by,
>   "Drink, for you see the end."
>   (Deissmann, *Light from the Ancient East*, 294-95)

The tomb of Sardanapallus, the founder of Tarsus, obliquely offers similar advice. According to the Roman geographer Strabo (63 B.C.–A.D. 24), a stone statue was erected next to Sardanapallus' tomb with the fingers of the statue's right hand snapping together and an inscription reading:

> Eat, drink, play, because all else is not worth this!
>   (Strabo, *Geography* 14.5.9)

The meaning of the epigram, of course, is that all else is not worth a snap of the fingers.

Exhortations to "eat, drink, and be merry" in the face of approaching death were, as Adolf Deissmann has pointed out, "well-known formulae of

203

ancient popular morals (often, no doubt, of popular wit)" and "by no means rare in epitaphs" of the Greco-Roman world during the imperial period (cf. *Light from the Ancient East*, 295). Drinking was promoted by inscriptions on the brims of glasses and goblets that read:

Why are you here? Make merry!

Apparently, such an inscription meant that you should make merry as long as you are here — that is, as long as you are alive (cf. ibid., 129-31).

In 1 Cor 15:32, Paul, for the sake of his *ad hominem* argument, momentarily agrees with such maxims: "If the dead are not raised, let us eat and drink for tomorrow we die." His statement reflects the words of Isa 22:13b, "'Let us eat and drink,' you say, 'for tomorrow we die!'" More expressly, however, it echoes many of the popular slogans of Paul's day, which, in effect, declared: "If death is the end, then eat, drink and make merry. If the present moment is the only time we have to indulge the senses to the full, because there are no bodily pleasures beyond the grave, then let's party now, for party days will soon be over."

But as soon as these words are out of his mouth, Paul reacts to them with another cliché of his day. "Do not be deceived," he warns, for as the old adage goes: "Bad company ruins good morals" (1 Cor 15:33). The citation is from the Athenian comic poet Menander (ca. 342-291 B.C.), whose ethical maxims circulated in various collections and were known widely. The bad company described in this citation from Menander's *Thais* is the company of a prostitute who provides sexual favors in return for gifts. She loves no one but always makes a pretense. Such evil companionship corrupts good character.

From Paul's point of view, the Corinthian Christians were being corrupted by evil companions who promoted hedonism on the premise that there is no resurrection from the dead. "How can some of you say," Paul asks, that "'there is no resurrection of the dead'?" (1 Cor 15:12). Evidently, while none of Paul's Corinthian converts denied the resurrection of Christ, some of them were denying the bodily resurrection of believers in Christ. They seem to have bought into the prevailing philosophy of their culture, which was a version of Platonic dualism that argued (1) that the soul is of great value, but the body has no intrinsic value, (2) that the immortal soul is temporarily imprisoned in the body, (3) that the body will be discarded at death and thereafter have no further relationship with the soul, and (4) that, therefore, whatever is done in the body during one's earthly life doesn't much matter. The hedonistic philosophy of some (at least) of Paul's converts at Corinth is probably echoed in their slogan, "Food is for the stomach, and the stomach for food" — which also meant that "sex is for the body, and the body is for sex" (1 Cor 6:13). In other words, the only purpose of the body is to indulge the bodily appetites.

Christians at Corinth were evidently being invited to banquets that encouraged gluttony, drunkenness, and sexual indulgence (cf. Winter, "Gluttony and Immorality," 80-82). They may have rationalized their participation in the hedonistic lifestyle of their culture on the basis of the common slogan: "All things are permitted for me!" (6:12; 10:23). A number of first-century texts indicate that "it was the prerogative of those who possessed power who could afford to live by that maxim with relative impunity, whether as privileged citizens or rulers" (cf. Winter, "Elitist Ethics"). It seems, in fact, that the socially powerful in first-century Greco-Roman society, as well as those who considered themselves to be spiritually gifted in the Corinthian church, assumed that they had a right to such an elitist ethic, and so on that basis legitimized unlimited permissiveness. And it may be postulated that it was against such hedonistic ethics among his converts at Corinth that Paul developed his argument for the resurrection of the body in 1 Corinthians 15 (cf. ibid.).

The denial of the resurrection negated Paul's own arduous way of life. His argument in 1 Corinthians 15 is enclosed by two references to strenuous, self-sacrificing work. The first is at the very beginning, where he claims that by God's grace his own extraordinary work for the gospel was not in vain (v. 10); the second is at the end, where he calls on the Corinthian believers to excel in the work of the Lord because they know that their work is not in vain in the Lord (v. 58). Furthermore, in the middle of his argument he describes in more detail some aspects of his own apostolic mission: he faced danger every hour, died every day, and fought wild animals at Ephesus (vv. 30-32). Paul's life, in fact, was characterized by selfless sacrifice, not self-centered hedonism.

The whole presentation of 1 Corinthians 15, which is Paul's fullest treatment of the subject of the resurrection of believers, is designed to undergird his imperative call for believers at Corinth to stop following a self-indulgent way of life: "Come to a sober and right mind, and sin no more" (15:34). The reality of the resurrection demands the Christian way of life. The conviction that God raised Jesus from the dead — with its corollary that believers in Christ will also be raised — is, as Paul Achtemeier rightly points out, the "generative center" of Paul's theology and ethics ("Quest for Coherence," 138).

But is there no place for eating and drinking in the Christian life? Must every believer in the resurrection become an ascetic, face danger every hour, "die" every day, and fight with "wild beasts," as Paul did? No doubt Paul presents his life as a paradigm to be followed, but he also encourages eating and drinking in this same letter to converts at Corinth: "Whether you eat and drink or whatever you do, do all to the glory of God" (10:31). Eating and drinking, working and resting, sacrifice and pleasure all have their place in the Christian life, *if* their aim is the glory of God.

But what moral criteria are to be used to decide what actions will glorify God? How does the resurrection answer ethical questions? Our purpose in this chapter is to observe how Paul applies the ethical implications of the resurrection to guide moral decisions in Christian communities. In the discussion that follows we will trace out five links between resurrection and ethics. In so doing, we will argue that the resurrection of Christ in Paul's thought (1) establishes the *authority* of Jesus Christ as Lord, (2) gives *liberty* to believers to serve the Lord, (3) creates a new *community* where the love of Christ is expressed, (4) guarantees *accountability* before the judgment seat of Christ, and (5) points to *conformity* to the resurrection body of Christ.

1. The Authority of Christ

The ethics of Paul are based on the fundamental conviction that "Jesus is the risen Lord." This confession is applied by Paul to all of the ethical issues confronted by Christian believers in his churches. Two prominent examples may be here cited, one from Romans and one from Philippians.

The Exhortations of Romans 12:1–15:13

Since the whole of Romans is directed toward the problem of the relation of Jews and Gentiles — that is, their relation first to God and the gospel, and then to each other — we may safely assume that those whom Paul calls "the weak" were Jewish Christians who were concerned about observing dietary laws and Sabbath laws, whereas "the strong" were Gentile Christians who cared little for such ethnic regulations. Evidently, a crisis in the Roman church came about because of a clash between the different lifestyles of Jewish Christians and Gentile Christians. Paul answers this crisis by appealing to the resurrection.

The ethical standards used by the Jewish vegetarian Sabbatarians and the Gentile nonvegetarian non-Sabbatarians in their judgments of each other are all subordinated by Paul to the authority of Jesus Christ as Lord. What mattered in these disputes over food and days was not cultural traditions or religious rituals, but obedience to the Lord. For, writes Paul:

> If we live, we live to the Lord, and if we die, we die to the Lord; so then, whether we live or die, we are the Lord's. For to this end Christ died and lived again, so that he might be the Lord of both the dead and the living. (Rom 14:8-9)

Since Jesus lives as the Lord of both the dead and the living, no one can take his place by exercising absolute authority over the conduct of another believer. No Christian can turn his or her conduct into a law for someone else to follow. Only Christ has the right to demand such obedience, since he died and lives again to be the Lord of all.

Paul is promoting moral freedom, but not moral relativism. Freedom from the censorious dictates of fellow Christians is not freedom from obedience to the Lord. Both the weak group and the strong group are "not accountable to each other because neither is the other's lord," but both are accountable to the risen Lord (cf. Keck, "Accountable Self," 8). It is the Lord who establishes moral boundaries and direction for a Christian lifestyle.

At a number of points in the exhortations of Rom 12:1–15:13, Paul's words clearly echo words of Jesus that were later incorporated into the canonical Gospels:

1. Rom 12:14: "Bless those who persecute you; bless and do not curse them" (cf. Matt 5:44);
2. Rom 12:17, 21: "Do not repay anyone evil for evil. . . . Do not be overcome by evil, but overcome evil with good" (cf. Matt 5:39-42);
3. Rom 13:8, 9-10: "the one who loves another has fulfilled the law. . . . [the commandments] are summed up in this word, 'Love your neigh-

bor as yourself.' Love does no wrong to a neighbor; therefore, love is the fulfilling of the law" (cf. Mark 12:28-34; Matt 22:34-40; Luke 10:25-28);

4. Rom 14:10: "Why do you pass judgment on your brother or sister?" (cf. Matt 7:1);
5. Rom 14:13: "Let us therefore no longer pass judgment on one another, but resolve instead never to put a stumbling block or hindrance in the way of another" (cf. Mark 9:42; Matt 18:7; Luke 17:1-2);
6. Rom 14:14: "I know and am persuaded in the Lord Jesus that nothing is unclean in itself" (cf. Mark 7:15);
7. Rom 15:17: "The kingdom of God is not food and drink, but righteousness and peace and joy in the Holy Spirit" (cf. Jesus' teaching on the kingdom of God throughout the Gospels).

These parallels have often been noted. What is usually missed, however, is Paul's reason for accepting these words as authoritative. What gives these words their authoritative force is not that they were spoken by a great moral teacher of the past, but that they are the words of the one who is now risen and the believer's authoritative Lord. Paul's confidence in the teaching of Jesus that "nothing is unclean in itself," for example, is based on his own association with the risen Lord Jesus (cf. Rom 14:14: "I know and am persuaded in the Lord Jesus"). For Paul, therefore, the resurrection of Jesus Christ validates all the moral instruction of his earthly ministry and establishes that instruction as the external, propositional basis for Christian conduct.

Paul also appeals to the example of Jesus. His own teaching that "each of us must please our neighbor for the good purpose of building up the neighbor" is based on the fact that "Christ did not please himself; but, as it is written, 'The insults of those who insult you have fallen on me'" (Rom 15:2-3, quoting Ps 69:9). Christ's willingness to give up his own pleasure and to submit to the insults directed against God by the enemies of God (as referred to in Ps 69:9) provides the model for Christians to follow in their relationships with one another.

This example of Christ is given authoritative power by the believer's present association with the risen and exalted Christ. Paul goes on to exhort the members of the Roman church to "welcome one another, therefore, just as Christ has welcomed you, for the glory of God" (15:7). It is their own experience of the risen Lord's inclusive welcome that is to set the pattern for their generous acceptance of others. Only the risen Christ can be an authoritative pattern for believers to follow. His exemplary submission is validated by his exaltation.

The Christ Hymn of Philippians 2:6-11

This connection between the example of Christ and his exaltation is also the basis for Paul's ethical application of the Christ hymn in Philippians 2. Interpreters often debate whether the hymn of 2:6-11 sets forth an ethical ideal or a kerygmatic proclamation. Does the hymn call Christians to follow the example of Jesus, or does it call Christians to kneel before the risen, exalted Jesus and call him Lord?

Those who take the hymn as an ethical ideal point to the verbal parallels between the moral instruction both before and after the hymn, on the one hand, and the hymn itself, on the other. Believers are exhorted to "do nothing from selfish ambition or conceit, but in *humility regard* others as better than yourselves" (2:3) — just as Christ, in the words of the hymn, "did not *regard* equality with God as something to be exploited, but emptied himself . . . and being found in human form he *humbled* himself" (2:6-8). And, conversely, just as Christ in the words of the hymn "became *obedient* to the point of death" (2:8), so believers "have always *obeyed*" (2:12). The humility and obedience of Christ, therefore, serves as a paradigm for Christian humility and obedience.

Those who argue for a kerygmatic interpretation, however, insist that a paradigmatic interpretation misses the point of the hymn. The climax of the hymn is the proclamation of the universal lordship of Jesus Christ. By focusing only on the example of Christ's humiliation in verses 6-8, the ethical view, it is claimed, treats verses 9-11 as an irrelevant appendage, since the exaltation of Christ cannot be imitated by Christians. According to the kerygmatic interpretation, the hymn should be seen as being used in its present context to remind Christians of their baptismal confession that "Jesus Christ is Lord" (v. 11). The hymn does not hold up Christ as an example to be followed; rather, it announces the salvation that has been accomplished by Christ and is to be experienced in Christ. In this interpretation the phrase "in Christ," which introduces the hymn (v. 5), is taken in its usual Pauline sense as a reference to the Philippians' union with Christ. Thus, Paul derives Christian conduct from the gift of salvation in Christ, not from the example of Christ.

But is not the setting up of these two interpretations as opposing interpretations presenting a false dichotomy? Certainly Paul's ethical appeal to humble service and obedience is based on the example of Christ's self-emptying, self-humbling obedience — an obedience that was expressed even to the extent of death on a cross. Just as certainly, though, the authoritative power of Christ's example is based on God's exaltation of Christ to universal dominion. The objection that only naive ethical idealism would see the descent and exaltation of a divine being as an example for human conduct misses the dynamic correspondence that is set up in Paul's letters between the exalted Lord and humble Christian service. Christians are called to fashion their lives to correspond with the self-emptying action of the Lord whom they worship.

The Lord Jesus is not just the object of Christian imitation; he is the focus of Christian worship. If Christ only taught moral guidelines by his words and actions, then his moral authority would not be substantially different from any other great moral teacher, such as Confucius. But God declares in the resurrection of Jesus that the actions of the one who "took the form of a servant" are the actions of the Second Adam, the originator of a new humanity. Unlike the First Adam, this Second Adam did not grasp for equality with God, but emptied himself. In his exaltation, his self-emptying is validated by God as the embodiment of the moral order of the new creation. As George Caird has aptly said: "He has not left behind the character and methods of his earthly life in order to wield in heaven an autocracy which on earth he had renounced. . . . The renunciation of rights and dignity, the humble self-surrender which led Jesus to the cross, these God had declared to be the only greatness recognized in heaven" (Caird, *New Testament Theology,* 189). His exaltation to universal dominion was the result of his humiliation. By his self-emptying he regained the dominion over creation that Adam lost by his self-seeking.

So Paul appeals to the moral authority of Christ in both Rom 12:1–15:13 and Phil 2:6-11 by proclaiming the gospel of the death and resurrection of Christ. Moral authority is not exercised by imposing arbitrary commands. The authority of Christ is the authority of the narrative of his obedience. And his exaltation is the authority of his character as servant and Lord.

2. Liberty in Christ

If Christians were simply given a new moral standard established by God's vindication of his new and perfect humanity in the resurrection of Jesus Christ, that would hardly be good news. What humans need, being finite and imperfect, is also a moral transformation so that they will be able to participate in this new humanity. Only as new moral agents are we able to receive the new moral standard as good news (cf. O'Donovan, *Resurrection and Moral Order*, 101).

Moral Transformation by Participation in the Resurrection of Christ

Paul's exposition of the gospel offers precisely that kind of moral transformation by participation in the resurrection of Christ. Through baptism believers "in Christ" are united "with Christ" in his death and resurrection (Rom 6:3-11). This "narrative identification," as James McClendon calls it (*Ethics*, 257), means: "Christ was raised from the dead through the glory of the Father, that we too might walk in newness of life" (Rom 6:4).

In Rom 6:5 Paul uses the past tense to refer to union "with Christ" in his death ("if we have been united with him in a death like his") — but then shifts to the future tense to refer to union "with Christ" in his resurrection ("we will certainly be united with him in a resurrection like his"). This change from past to future tense has led some to suppose that Paul considered identification with Christ on the cross to be a past fact, which has already been accomplished, but participation with Christ in his resurrection to be a future hope, which has yet to be realized. George Caird, however, rightly calls this interpretation "a shallow travesty of Paul's argument, which turns from first to last on the style of life which the believer is to live here and now" (Caird, *New Testament Theology*, 188). For, as Caird goes on to point out, "Union with the crucified Jesus is no more a fact than union with the risen Christ; both are convictions about the inclusive nature of Jesus' own death and resurrection, and the second is logically entailed in the first" (ibid.).

Paul's whole argument, in fact, points to the new ethical conduct that believers are called to express as a result of being united with Christ in his resurrection. The purpose of union with Christ through baptism is that "we too might walk in newness of life" (6:4). "So you must consider yourselves dead to sin and alive to God in Christ Jesus" (6:11).

211

Ethical Living by Union with Christ in His Death and Resurrection

Paul continues his explanation of union with the risen Christ by drawing parallels with marriage in Rom 7:1-6. The Christian is like a woman who was bound by law to her first husband as long as he lived. But when he died, she was free to marry a second husband. Before believing in Christ, the Christian's first husband was the law. The law aroused sinful passions and children were born: "fruit for death." But then by dying with Christ, the Christian was set free from the binding obligation of the law and was married to the risen Christ. Union with him produces children: "fruit for God."

The purpose of freedom from slavery to the law is "that we might serve in the newness of the Spirit and not in the oldness of the letter" (7:6). In the remainder of Romans 7, Paul cries out in despair as he rehearses the painful tragedy of human experience under slavery to the law. Then in Romans 8 Paul claims the triumph of freedom in Christ empowered by the Spirit. The law only had the power to reveal human inability to respond to the righteous demands of God (8:3). But the indwelling Spirit who raised Jesus Christ from the dead gives believers the power to put to death addictive and self-destructive habits so that they can truly live out the risen life of Christ. "For if you live according to the flesh, you will die; but if by the Spirit you put to death the deeds of the body, you will live" (8:13).

This process of "putting to death" and "putting off" old sinful practices ("the old self") so that the new risen life of Christ ("the new self") can be "put on" is spelled out in detail in Col 3:1-17 and Eph 4:22-24. The lists of vices and virtues in these contexts depict the transformation of character that comes from union with Christ in his death and resurrection. Transformation of character is not accomplished by superhuman effort. The imperatives of these passages are easily turned into the basis of a new legalism if they are separated from Christ's death and resurrection. Separated from the narrative of Christ, the commands to put off anger, wrath, malice, slander, and abusive speech (Col 3:8) and to put on compassion, kindness, humility, meekness, and patience (Col 3:12) only expose human impotence more completely than the Mosaic law did. But when there is narrative identification with Christ in his death and resurrection, then there is an inner renewal of the image of God in righteousness, holiness, and knowledge (Col 3:10; Eph 4:23-24). True Christian freedom, therefore, is the experience of this subjective restoration of the image of God through union with Christ so that the objective revelation of God's holiness and righteousness in the person of Christ can be expressed in ethical conduct (cf. O'Donovan, *Resurrection and Moral Order,* 22-26).

This double emphasis on the revelation of the image of God *in Christ* and the restoration of the image of God *in Christ* may be the best way to interpret the *"in Christ"* phrase in Phil 2:5. As a reference to the revelation of a pattern of attitudes and actions in Christ that believers should follow, this verse could be translated, "Let this mind be in you that was in Christ Jesus" (NRSV). As a reference to the transformation of believers through their union with Christ, it could be translated, "Let your bearing towards one another arise out of your life in Christ Jesus" (NEB). Even if the "in Christ" formula is interpreted in its usual Pauline sense as a reference to believers' union with Christ, this interpretation does not negate the ethical force of the hymn. For it is in union with Christ that Christians, like Paul, "know Christ and the power of his resurrection and the sharing of his sufferings by becoming like him in his death" (Phil 3:10).

Union with Christ makes knowledge of Christ a transforming knowledge, not a condemning knowledge. This confidence in the inner transforming power of God as the basis for ethical conduct informs Paul's application of the Christ hymn in Phil 2:12-13. The indwelling power of God frees believers both to will and to work in accordance with God's good purpose. Participation in the death and exaltation of Christ proclaimed in the Christ hymn liberates Christians to follow his pattern of obedience in the form of a servant and to proclaim his universal victory as Lord.

3. Community in Christ

Participation in the resurrection of Christ transforms individuals by bringing them into a new community in Christ. Throughout his letters, Paul derives his ethics from the reality of this new community in Christ.

New Community Ethics in Galatians

In writing to believers in Galatia, Paul portrays his own identification with the death and resurrection of Christ as an experience of the end of the world and an entrance into a new creation: "But may it never be that I

213

should boast except in the cross of our Lord Jesus Christ, through which the world has been crucified to me and I to the world. For neither is circumcision anything, nor uncircumcision, but a new creation" (Gal 6:14-15). Here he describes his conversion in apocalyptic terms. It was the end of the world for him!

His apocalyptic metaphor of the crucifixion of the world, of course, does not mean an end of the world in a literal, cosmic sense. Rather, it means an end to the old world order. As Paul explains in 6:15, the crucifixion of the world means an end of the old world order structured by hostility, which is caused by ethnic distinctions. "For neither circumcision nor uncircumcision is anything, but a new creation is everything." After Paul's personal identification with the cross of Christ, he no longer identified himself on the basis of ethnic or social distinctions — such as Jew or Gentile, circumcision or uncircumcision, slave or free. For just as Paul's identification with the cross of Christ crucified the world to him, so his identification with the resurrection of Christ brought him into the reality of the new creation.

Paul reminds his Galatian converts that their baptism into Christ united them in a new community where the old ethnic, social, and gender hierarchies — which were so highly valued and rigorously defended in the ancient world — are all abolished in Christ. "For all of you who were baptized into Christ have clothed yourself with Christ. There is neither Jew nor Greek, there is neither slave nor free, there is neither male nor female; for you are all one in Christ Jesus" (Gal 3:27-28). The principles of unity and equality that are true of all believers in Christ are to guide them in their relationships with each other. So the racism, social elitism, and sexism that is so rampant and destructive in the world is to be abolished in the new creation, the new community in Christ.

New Community Ethics in 1 Corinthians

Even Paul's advice on sexual conduct in marriage is informed by his vision of equality in Christ. His response in 1 Corinthians 7 to questions about marriage emphasizes equality between the sexes in the marriage relationship: "Each man should have his own wife, and each woman her own husband. The husband should give to his wife her conjugal rights, and likewise the wife to her husband. For the wife does not have authority over her own body, but the husband does; likewise the husband does not have authority over his own body, but the wife does" (vv. 2-4). Paul's emphasis on the full mutuality of sexual relations in marriage cannot be derived from his Jewish or Hellenistic backgrounds. Rather, it reflects his understanding of the new creation in Christ (cf. Longenecker, *New Testament Social Ethics,* 78).

This equality of men and women in Christ also guides Paul's response in 1 Cor 11:2-16 to questions that arose within the Corinthian church regarding the role of women in worship. Whatever we make of Paul's cultural references and *ad hominem* arguments in this passage, we must not miss the fact that he affirms the equal right that women have to pray and prophesy in the public worship of the church (vv. 4-5). Furthermore, he asserts the interdependence of men and women "in the Lord": "Nevertheless, in the Lord woman is not independent of man or man independent of woman" (v. 11). On the basis of this new standing that women and men have "in the Lord," women are to participate fully and with authority in the worship of the church (cf. Longenecker, ibid., 82).

These two examples of practical counsel on relations between men and women in 1 Corinthians illustrate how Paul worked out the ethical implications of the new creation where "there is neither male nor female, for you are all one in Christ Jesus" (Gal 3:28).

New Community Ethics in 2 Corinthians

In 2 Corinthians 5 Paul points to the reconciliation of broken relationships on the basis of being a new creation in Christ. Again he focuses on identification with Christ's cross and resurrection: "He died for all, so that those who live might live no longer for themselves, but for him who died and was raised for them" (v. 15). Viewing all of life from the perspectives of the cross and the resurrection leads to a new view of others — "from now on we regard no one from a human point of view" (v. 16). Everyone in Christ is viewed as a member of the new community created by God in Christ, because now "if anyone is in Christ, there is a new creation: everything old has passed away; see, everything has become new" (v. 17, NRSV).

Too often 2 Cor 5:17 has been taken only as a reference to a person's individual, subjective experience of conversion. Some translations perpetuate this individualistic focus by rendering the Greek words *kainē ktisis* as "*he is* a new creature" (KJV, NKJV, NASB) or "*he is* a new creation" (RSV, NIV). Simply on the basis of grammar, of course, these translations are possible, since the lack of subject and verb may be supplied by reference to the individual "*he* [or, *that one*] *is*." Such individualism, however, obscures the scope of Paul's apocalyptic vision.

In the cross and resurrection of Christ, God has initiated the fulfillment of his ancient promise to bring "new heavens and a new earth" into being (cf. Isa 65:17-19). Whoever is in Christ, therefore, is already in this new creation and part of God's new community. The new creation is not just future. Paul calls the church to exhibit the reality of this new creation and so of his converts' membership in God's new community, through his ministry of reconciliation. "We entreat you on behalf of Christ," Paul says: "Be reconciled to God" (5:20).

No doubt this was the language that Paul used in evangelism. But in 2 Cor 5:20 he is addressing this appeal to Christians. God's reconciliation of the world to himself through Christ, Paul evidently means, is to be applied to broken relationships within the church. Thus relationships can be healed when Christians live out the reality of the new creation in the new community, as initiated by the reconciling act of God in Christ and as announced by the reconciling ministry of the apostles.

New Community Ethics in Philippians

Paul also applies the reality of the new community in Christ to strained relationships in the Philippian church by reminding them that they are "citizens of heaven" (3:20) and so should live as citizens of heaven "in a manner worthy of the gospel of Christ" (1:27). The gospel is what is to guide this new community — a community that is, in fact, a heavenly community of God's people on earth. Christ's humble obedience, which was expressed even to the extent of death, and his exalted lordship constitute the factors that provide the rule of life for all who are "in Christ" (2:5-11).

Life in union with the exalted Lord includes down-to-earth responsibilities. As members of a heavenly colony on earth, Christians are to "do all things without murmuring and arguing" so that they will "shine as stars in the world" (2:14-15). According to Paul, the church's influence in the world depends on Christians living as responsible citizens of heaven. By expressing their identity as a heavenly community through their humble service, they bear witness to their union with the risen Lord who "emptied himself by taking the form of a servant" (2:7).

4. Accountability before Christ

The resurrection of Christ guarantees the prospect of the future judgment of Christ, which extends even to the community of believers in Christ. Paul, in fact, frequently uses the expectation of a future judgment to motivate Christian conduct.

In 2 Corinthians, for example, he moves from reflections on his present, momentary afflictions vis-à-vis his hope for a future, "eternal weight of glory" (in 1:3–4:18) to a warning about the importance of pleasing God (5:1-8). In view of God's future judgment, Paul says: "So we make it our aim to please him. For all of us must appear before the judgment seat of Christ, so that each may receive recompense for what has been done in the body, whether good or evil" (2 Cor 5:9-10).

The key question in the interpretation of 2 Cor 5:10 is whether to take it as referring to an evaluation of Christians or to a separation between Christians and non-Christians. In favor of the first interpretation is Paul's use of "all of us" *(pantes hēmas)* here and elsewhere (e.g., 1 Cor 12:13; 2 Cor 3:18). If this text refers exclusively to the assessment of Christians resulting in different rewards and punishments according to the deeds done by Christians, then it is parallel to the final examination of Christian work by fire on the day of judgment described in 1 Corinthians 3: "The work of each builder will become visible, for the day will disclose it, because it will be revealed with fire, and the fire will test what sort of work has been done" (3:13). If the work is of the quality of gold, silver, and precious stones, it will survive the test and the worker will be rewarded (3:14). But if the work is of the quality of wood, hay, or straw, it will be burned up; the builder will suffer loss, yet "the builder will be saved, but only as through fire" (3:15). While Paul does not base salvation itself on the believer's work, he does indicate, both here and elsewhere in his letters, that the work of a Christian has value and will be evaluated. Work done in the present somehow affects future rewards or losses.

If, then, 2 Cor 5:10 is to be read from this perspective, the evaluation at the judgment seat of Christ will not concern the question of ultimate salvation or condemnation. Condemnation is out of the question, for only believers in Christ are evaluated in this judgment scene, and Paul is emphatic elsewhere that "there is no condemnation for those who are in Christ Jesus" (Rom 8:1). Nevertheless, believers are fully accountable for the quality of their work done in the body. The anticipation of facing Christ's assessment, therefore, motivates Christian service, as Paul says immediately following in 2 Cor 5:11: "Knowing the fear of the Lord, we try to persuade others."

Yet as plausible as it may be to interpret Paul's reference to the judgment seat of Christ in 2 Cor 5:10 as a description of the evaluation of Christians only, there are good reasons for understanding this judgment as a separation of believers and unbelievers (cf. Travis, *Christ and the Judgment of God,* 107-11). First, Paul's use of "all of us" does not preclude the possibility that he expects that true Christians will be separated from professing Christians. For Paul concludes 2 Corinthians with the following warning: "Examine yourselves to see whether you are living in the faith. Test yourselves. Do you not realize that Jesus Christ is in you? — unless you fail to meet the test" (13:5).

Paul was under no illusion that all of those who were participating in the life of the church were genuinely experiencing the life of Christ. Even those who had taken the sacraments of the church must be warned that there was no magical element in the sacraments themselves that guaranteed salvation. So he warns Christians at Corinth that even though "our ancestors were all under the cloud, and all passed through the sea, and all were baptized into Moses in the cloud and sea, and all ate the same spiritual food, and all drank the same spiritual drink, . . . nevertheless God was not pleased with most of them, and they were struck down in the wilderness" (1 Cor 10:1-5). Paul uses this lesson from Israelite history to warn those who professed to be Christians: "If you think you are standing, watch out that you do not fall" (10:12).

Falling out of God's grace looms as a dreadful prospect in Paul's warnings to Christians (cf., e.g., Gal 5:4). Therefore, his warning that "all of us must appear before the judgment seat of Christ" (2 Cor 5:10) may indicate that in the day of accountability before Christ the reality of salvation must be demonstrated by the quality of deeds done in the body. Genuine salvation will be evident in good deeds. Evil deeds point to lack of salvation.

A second reason for seeing this judgment scene as the separation of believers and nonbelievers is the good–evil *(agathon–phaulon)* antithesis of 2 Cor 5:10. This antithesis makes a radical distinction between moral good and reprehensible evil. To apply it only to differing qualities of Christian service ignores the strong moral sense of the word "evil" *(phaulon)* in biblical and first-century usage. For example, John's Gospel indicates that the one who does evil *(phaula)* is an unbeliever who hates the light (John 3:18-20). Furthermore, John promises the resurrection of life to those who do good, but the resurrection of condemnation to those who do evil *(ta phaula)* (5:29). According to Josephus, the Pharisees believed that the good are resurrected, but the souls "of the wicked" *(tōn phaulōn)* receive eternal punishment *(Jewish War* 2.163).

Even though Paul's word for evil in Rom 2:9 is *kakon* rather than *phaulon,* the judgment scene of Romans 2 should be viewed as a true parallel to the judgment of 2 Cor 5:10. For in Romans 2: "There will be anguish and distress for everyone who does evil *(to kakon),* the Jew first and also the Greek, but glory and honor and peace for everyone who does good *(to agathon),* the Jew first and also the Greek" (vv. 9-10). The universal judgment will demonstrate that "God shows no partiality" (v. 11).

Paul's teaching in Romans on a universal judgment based on doing good must be interpreted in the context of his entire letter, and so seen as an implicit reference to believers who demonstrate the reality of their faith in Christ by their righteous conduct (cf. Fitzmyer, *Romans,* 297). Judgment on the basis of doing evil should be viewed as a reference to those who do not have a transformation of their moral conduct. Even the immediate context already points in this direction. Those who do good are those who "seek for glory and honor and immortality." To such seekers God "will give eternal life" (2:7). On the other hand, judgment comes on those "who are self-seeking and who obey not the truth" (2:8). So good deeds or evil deeds are the evidence of what one is seeking. In the context of the rest of his letter to Christians at Rome, what Paul is saying here in 2:8 is that eternal life is given to those who seek Christ and judgment is on those who are self-seeking.

The judgment of 2 Cor 5:10 that separates believers and unbelievers, however, will be on the basis of character, and not just on the basis of individual deeds. The whole of life is seen as a unity by the way Paul refers to "what was done" with the aorist verb *epraxen.* Paul's shift to the singular in the phrase "whether it be good or evil" also indicates that the whole of life will be taken into consideration in this judgment. In other words, Paul is not painting a picture of scales weighing individual good deeds against

219

individual evil deeds. Rather, a person's whole direction of life will be assessed as to whether it was pleasing to God or not (5:9). The judgment will distinguish between two radically different kinds of people. As in Rom 2:5-11, Paul here in 2 Cor 5:10 is speaking of a universal judgment where the conduct of one's life, seen as a whole, is taken as evidence of character and relationship to God. It is on this basis that genuine believers will be separated from unbelievers (cf. Travis, *Christ and the Judgment of God,* 110).

The resurrection of Christ, therefore, means that a final evaluation before the judgment seat of Christ is universal and inescapable. The prospect of such a final evaluation is a strong motivation for Christian conduct. For this reason, Paul's prayers express the request that Christians be pure and blameless in the day of Christ (cf. Phil 1:10; see also 1 Cor 1:8; 1 Thess 3:13; 5:23). Paul is not under any illusion of sinless perfectionism; his letters give ample evidence that people called saints still struggle with sin in their lives. And his prayers teach that the way to purity of life is the way of growing in love: "my prayer is that your love may overflow more and more with knowledge and full insight to help you determine what is best, so that in the day of Christ you may be pure and blameless" (Phil 1:9-10). No matter how well Christians love one another, their love can still increase more and more (1 Thess 4:9-10). So the goal of purity is not attained by keeping a list of laws, but by expanding ever more and more in the capacity and expression of love.

Paul's own desire that he "may attain the resurrection from the dead" motivated him to "press on . . . straining forward to what lies ahead" (Phil 3:11-14). His conduct was motivated by the prospect of a final evaluation that would result in rewards or losses. So he ran hard to win the prize (Phil 3:14; 1 Cor 9:24-26), and he disciplined his body so as not to be disqualified (1 Cor 9:27).

Although it may be difficult to relate the themes of grace and judgment in Paul's letters, any account that omits this pervasive theme of God's universal judgment is misleading (cf. Hays, *Moral Vision,* 41). Romans begins with a reminder of the universal judgment of God: "God's righteous judgment will be revealed" (2:5). And it ends with a repetition of that theme again: "For we will all stand before the judgment seat of God. . . . So then, each of us will be accountable to God" (14:10-12). Paul's account of the gospel does not negate a message of judgment but demands it. The gospel proclaims that Christ is risen and exalted; therefore, every knee will bow before him and every tongue confess that he is the Lord (Rom 14:11; Phil 2:9-11).

5. Conformity to Christ

However awesome the prospect of a final evaluation by the risen Lord was for Paul, it certainly did not diminish his hope of total conformity to the glorious resurrection body of Christ. In fact, his eager expectation that the Lord "will transform the body of our humiliation that it may be conformed to the body of his glory, by the power that also enables him to make all things subject to himself" was for Paul the basis for his imperative to "stand firm in the Lord" (Phil 3:21–4:1).

In the Believer's Conduct

Even though there is a substantial difference between the "body of our humiliation" and "the body of his glory," Paul links Christian conduct in the present body to his expectation of a future resurrection body. So the believer's present bodily activity should be congruent with his or her expectations of a future bodily resurrection (cf. Scroggs, "Paul and the Eschatological Body," 29).

In his arguments against sexual promiscuity, for example, one of Paul's reasons for fleeing immorality is the resurrection: "The body is meant not for fornication but for the Lord, and the Lord for the body. And God raised the Lord and will also raise us by his power" (1 Cor 6:13-14). Paul's affirmation of the resurrection in the language of a traditional confession or creed refutes the Corinthian Christians' expectation of "redemption *from* the body" rather than "redemption *of* the body." Influenced by Platonic dualism that devalued the body, Christians at Corinth evidently thought that the body was only destined for destruction. On the contrary, asserts Paul, Christ's own bodily resurrection guarantees that the believer's body is not destined for destruction but for resurrection (cf. Fee, *First Epistle to the Corinthians*, 255-57). Since the Lord gave himself in his death and resurrection for the redemption of the body, the body is "for the Lord, and the Lord for the body" (1 Cor 6:13).

In the Restoration of All Creation

Likewise, Paul bases his hope for the restoration of all creation on the resurrection of Christ. The whole of creation, he says, is groaning and waiting to be set free from futility and bondage to decay and to be given the glorious freedom of the children of God (Rom 8:19-22). Believers who have the Spirit enter into this groaning of creation, waiting for the redemption of their bodies (8:23). The hope of all believers is that the resurrection of Christ guarantees their own bodily resurrection (8:11). And the hope for all creation is that the bodily resurrection of believers in Christ guarantees the renewal of all creation.

"In opposition to the basic tenets of Hellenistic philosophy," David Stanley observes, "Paul asserts that nothing in the material universe is excluded from the redemption" (*Christ's Resurrection in Pauline Soteriology*, 194). This promise of the restoration of the whole created order affirms the moral order inherent within God's creation. As Oliver O'Donovan aptly comments: "In the resurrection of Christ creation is restored and the kingdom of God dawns. Ethics which starts from this point may sometimes emphasize the newness, sometimes the primitiveness of the order that is there affirmed" (*Resurrection and Moral Order*, 15).

Paul's argument in Romans 1 from the order of creation ultimately finds its validation in his affirmation in Romans 8 that creation is restored in the resurrection of Christ. Since everyone lives within the objective reality of God's created order and finds within human nature itself a reflection of that order, Paul can apply his Christian ethics to all. Paul does not view Christian ethics as merely the result of believers' decisions to live by this or that set of values. Rather, Paul's ethical perspective poses a contrast to the perspective that views Christian ethics as relevant only to those who choose to live that way, but irrelevant to those who choose to go a different way (cf. O'Donovan, *Resurrection and Moral Order*, 16-17).

Conclusion

The restoration of all creation in the resurrection of Christ provides the reason for one of Paul's favorite imperatives, which is three times repeated in Philippians: "Rejoice in the Lord!" "Rejoice in the Lord!" "Rejoice in the Lord always!" (3:1; 4:4). The repetition of this command to rejoice in the Lord must be associated with the conclusion of his Christ-hymn in Phil 2:11 (cf. 2:12-18), which announces the universal worship of all creation of Jesus as Lord. The culture of the Greco-Roman world that surrounded Paul and his churches called on everyone to make merry because death was the end of creation. Paul, however, exhorted his churches to rejoice — because the resurrection of Jesus was the beginning of the new creation.

Selected Bibliography

Achtemeier, Paul J. "The Continuing Quest for Coherence in St. Paul: An Experiment in Thought." In *Theology and Ethics in Paul and His Interpreters: Essays in Honor of Victor Paul Furnish,* edited by E. H. Lovering, Jr., and J. L. Sumney. Nashville: Abingdon, 1996, 132-45.

Caird, George B. *New Testament Theology.* Edited by L. D. Hurst. Oxford: Clarendon, 1994.

Deissmann, Adolf. *Light from the Ancient East: The New Testament Illustrated by Recently Discovered Texts of the Graeco-Roman World.* Translated by L. R. M. Strachan. Rev. ed. London: Hodder & Stoughton, 1927. Reprint, Grand Rapids: Baker, 1978.

Fee, Gordon D. *The First Epistle to the Corinthians.* Grand Rapids: Eerdmans, 1987.

Fitzmyer, Joseph A. *Romans: A New Translation with Introduction and Commentary.* New York: Doubleday, 1993.

Hays, Richard B. *The Moral Vision of the New Testament.* San Francisco: Harper, 1996.

Keck, Leander E. "The Accountable Self." In *Theology and Ethics in Paul and His Interpreters: Essays in Honor of Victor Paul Furnish,* edited by E. H. Lovering, Jr., and J. L. Sumney. Nashville: Abingdon, 1996, 1-13.

Longenecker, Richard N. *New Testament Social Ethics for Today.* Grand Rapids: Eerdmans, 1984.

McClendon, James W., Jr. *Systematic Theology: Ethics.* Nashville: Abingdon, 1986.

O'Donovan, Oliver. *Resurrection and Moral Order: An Outline for Evangelical Ethics.* 2d ed. Grand Rapids: Eerdmans, 1994.

Schrage, Wolfgang, *The Ethics of the New Testament.* Translated by D. E. Green. Philadelphia: Fortress, 1982.

Scroggs, Robin. "Paul and the Eschatological Body." In *Theology and Ethics in Paul and His Interpreters: Essays in Honor of Victor Paul Furnish,* edited by E. H. Lovering, Jr., and J. L. Sumney. Nashville: Abingdon, 1996, 14-29.

Stanley, David M. *Christ's Resurrection in Pauline Soteriology.* Analecta Biblica 13. Rome: Pontificio Instituto Biblico, 1961.

Travis, Stephen H. *Christ and the Judgment of God: Divine Retribution in the New Testament.* London: Marshall, 1986.

Winter, Bruce. "Gluttony and Immorality at Elitist Banquets: The Background to 1 Corinthians 6:12-20." *JIAN DOW* 7 (1997) 77-90.

————. "Elitist Ethics and Christian Permissiveness." In *After Paul Left Corinth: The Impact of Secular Ethics and Social Change.* Grand Rapids: Eerdmans, forthcoming.

IV. Experiences of the Early Church

CHAPTER 10

"Witnesses of His Resurrection": Resurrection, Salvation, Discipleship, and Mission in the Acts of the Apostles

JOEL B. GREEN

THE RESURRECTION of Jesus by God is the central affirmation of the Christian message in the Acts of the Apostles. Paul's proclamation among the Athenians, for example, is summarized as "good news about Jesus and the resurrection" (17:18), while much earlier in the narrative Peter and John come under investigation by the Jerusalem authorities on account of their message that "in Jesus there is the resurrection of the dead" (4:2). Indeed, the portfolio assigned to Jesus' followers according to Acts 1:8 is that they serve as "witnesses" from Jerusalem to the end of the earth. And we need not wait long to discover more precisely the substance of their testimony: they are to be "witnesses of his resurrection" (1:22). The chord thus struck is sounded repeatedly in the subsequent narrative, as Jesus' disciples disclose their roles as witnesses to God's having raised Jesus from the dead.

The importance of the resurrection for Luke is rivaled only by the significance of the death of the Messiah within the divine purpose, alongside which it often appears. Luke wants his readers always to keep in view the nexus between Jesus' death and his resurrection. It is also true, however, that the Book of Acts is especially concerned with the latter — that is, with Jesus' resurrection and its redemptive implications. Furthermore, one may without hyperbole go on to say that Acts is not only *a narrative about* the propagation of the testimony to Jesus having been raised up by God but is also itself *a witness to* the resurrection and its significance for the realization of the ancient plan of God.

Our study of Acts here is concerned not so much to demonstrate *that* this is the case as it is to show *how* Luke has constructed his "second volume" to function as such a witness. Two provisos, however, must initially be registered. The first is that, although our assumption is that the Gospel of Luke and the Acts of the Apostles together constitute one continuous narrative with a single theological outlook, our primary focus will be on part two of Luke's writing, that is, the Acts of the Apostles. The second proviso is that, because we will be attempting to sketch out matters having to do with the significance of Luke's theology of resurrection, it is important to recognize the inherent artificiality of the task before us. In order to accomplish our aim, we must turn Luke's narrative art into a more systematic presentation of its perspective than Luke has himself provided. Narrative is better suited to inviting reflection, provoking contemplation, raising questions. An analysis such as we will be undertaking in this chapter, however, is more oriented toward explanation and assertion.

With these two caveats, we may turn to discuss (1) Luke's understanding of the "truth" of the resurrection; (2) the pivotal role of resurrection within the more encompassing Lukan theme of salvation; (3) the relationship between the resurrection message and Luke's Christology; (4) the relationship between the resurrection message and Luke's emphases on discipleship and mission; and (5) the resurrection message as both hope and scandal. An analysis of Luke's theology of resurrection along these lines will take us far toward grasping in what sense it is appropriate to describe his narrative as providing a witness to the resurrection.

1. "To This We Are Witnesses": The "Truth" of the Resurrection

What does it mean to be "a witness of his resurrection" (1:22)? Insofar as this phrase accurately depicts Luke's understanding of those who continue and extend the ministry of Jesus, it is critical that we understand its meaning (as in 2:32; 3:15; 4:33; 5:32; 10:39-41; 13:30-31; 22:15; 26:16; see also Luke 24:48; cf. Maddox, *Purpose of Luke-Acts,* 74-76; Trites, *Concept of Witness,* 128-53; Kee, *Good News,* 95-107). On this point, Luke is remarkably forthcoming.

Luke is interested, at least at the outset of Acts, in the *that* of the resurrection. He principally wants to certify the truth of *its status* as an event, though he is also concerned with *its nature* as an event. The question of the character of the resurrection is important on account of the variety of ways in which "the afterlife" could have been understood within Greco-Roman and Hellenistic Jewish traditions of that day (see Nickelsburg, *Resurrection, Immortality, and Eternal Life*).

Earlier in his Gospel (Luke 24:36-43), the evangelist addressed this matter by recounting how Jesus offered proof of his own materiality as evidence of his resurrected existence (cf. Green, *Luke,* 851-59). Luke's portrayal negates two possible categories, among many, for conceptualizing the afterlife — the one barbaric, the other more sophisticated: first, by showing that Jesus' disciples did not mistake him for a resuscitated corpse; then, by certifying that Jesus' resurrected life is not that of an "immortal soul" freed from bodily existence. Jesus is represented in Luke's Gospel as being alive beyond the grave as a fully embodied person. Jesus' affirmation is emphatic — "It is I myself! Touch me and see!" (v. 39), or, more colloquially, "It is really me!" — intimating continuity between the phases of Jesus' life before crucifixion and after resurrection. He demonstrates this declaration, first, with reference to his hands and feet, flesh and bones, and second, by his capacity to eat food. Repeated references to "seeing" and the important notation that Jesus ate "in their presence" signify that the *apologia* being provided here is for the sake of the authentic witness that the disciples would subsequently be called to give.

Luke's account of Jesus' appearance at the close of the Third Gospel, then, indicates that Luke was not working with such anthropological dualisms as advocated by some Greek philosophers (like Plato) or some Hellenistic Jews (like Philo) (cf. Martin, *Corinthian Body*, 3-37). Rather, Luke lays stress on Jesus' embodied existence beyond the grave, highlighting the radical continuity between the humiliated, crucified Jesus of Nazareth and the resurrected, exalted Messiah and Lord (cf. Schneider, *Apostelgeschichte*, 1:219).

This emphasis on the status of Jesus' resurrection as an event is continued in Acts, first with reference to the "many convincing proofs" *(pollois tekmēriois)* with which "Jesus presented himself alive" to his followers (1:1-3). The Greek term *tekmērion* appears nowhere else in the New Testament and only three times in the LXX (cf. esp. Wis 5:11; 3 Macc 3:24, where it is used for "convincing evidence"; see also Josephus, *Jewish Antiquities* 5.39; 17.128). Aristotle designated evidence of this nature as irrefutable, proven, and conclusive (*Rhetoric* 1.12.16-17 [1357b]), and here in Acts 1:3 it has the similar force of "credible proof." This concern with the *that* of Jesus' resurrection — and particularly its corporeal nature — is also marked in Acts with references to Jesus' eating with his disciples (1:4; 10:41). In a different way, it comes to the fore by an interest in Jesus' capacity to avoid physical deterioration in the tomb (2:25-28; 13:35-37, with reference to Ps 16:10).

Data available in the speeches in Acts indicate that, from the Lukan perspective, confirmation of Jesus' resurrection was not to be limited to evidence of the material nature of Jesus' resurrected body (cf. Buckwalter, *Luke's Christology,* 115-16). As if these "convincing proofs" were somehow insufficient, it is further noted by Luke that the Holy Spirit witnesses to Jesus' exaltation (5:32). In the account of Peter's defense before the Jerusalem council, Peter's logic seems to be that the gift of the Spirit to those who obey God is itself a sign of the reality of the resurrection. His logic depends on his earlier assessment of the Spirit-empowered phenomena under scrutiny in 2:1-13 — namely, that God's having raised Jesus from the dead was a necessary precondition to the general outpouring of the Spirit (2:32-33). Thus if the Spirit has been poured out, Jesus must have been raised from the dead.

Additional testimony for the resurrection of Jesus is drawn in Acts from the Scriptures — for example, in 2:22-36, where Pss 16:8-11 and 110:1 are read as proofs of Jesus' resurrection; similarly, in 13:26-37 with the use of Ps 2:7, Isa 55:3, and Ps 16:10. In these two ways — the witness of the Spirit and the witness of Scripture — the divine performance and the divine voice are also brought to bear in the resurrection apologetic of Acts.

In drawing attention to Luke's interest in the nature of Jesus' resurrection as an event, our discussion has already begun to spill over into another way of putting the question of the meaning of Luke's phrase "a witness of his resurrection" in Acts 1:22. Read against the backdrop of Luke's narrative-theological concerns, the claim that the resurrection of Jesus actually took place is not nearly so interesting or important as is its significance. This is because the resurrection of Jesus is precisely the raising to life by God of one who had been utterly rejected both by the Jewish leaders — that is, by persons whose own legitimacy was tied up in their status as interpreters of the will of God — and by the Roman leadership — that is, by persons whose elevated social and political positions were maintained and broadcast by their carefully scripted attention to issues of honor and status. The exaltation of one who had thus suffered what in the Roman

230

world would have been the ultimate humiliation, being publicly executed naked on a cross, constitutes a profound irony that calls into question the existing world order as that order was conceived and practiced by the Jewish and Roman elite alike. And here we have, graphically put, the paradox of Luke's vision of salvation and discipleship.

2. "God Exalted Him . . . as Leader and Savior": Resurrection and Salvation

Although Luke does not oppose the attribution of atoning significance to Jesus' death (e.g., Luke 22:19-20; Acts 20:28), the cross does not figure prominently as the basis of his soteriology. This is not because Luke has no "theology of the cross." Rather, it is because he places the primary importance of the cross elsewhere than on a theory of the atonement. What Luke does, in fact, is to present the resurrection of Jesus, together with his ascension, as the basis for the offer of salvation (cf., e.g., Marshall, "Resurrection in the Acts"; George, "Mort de Jesus pour Luc").

Luke sets forth the logic of his soteriology early in Acts, in his portrayal of Peter's Pentecost sermon in Acts 2:14-40. The citation of Joel 2:28-32 (LXX) in verses 17-21 is particularly important, for it contains at its beginning and end two central aspects of the Lukan soteriology: at its beginning, the universalistic outreach of salvation, which is identified as the reception of the Spirit (vv. 17-18); at its end, the identification of "the Lord" as the agent of salvation (v. 21). This accent on "the Lord" anticipates the christological climax of Peter's sermon in verse 36: "Therefore let the entire house of Israel surely know that God has made him both Lord and Messiah, this Jesus whom you crucified." As Lord, Jesus is the one on whom people are to call for salvation.

How did Jesus come to be regarded as Lord? The exegesis represented in Peter's use of Psalms 16 and 110 is crucial, for it demonstrates that it is because of his exaltation to God's right hand that Jesus is Lord (vv. 29-35). What is more, verse 33 makes it plain that the phenomena under question are only the aftermath of the outpouring of the Spirit, which is itself the consequence of Jesus' exaltation. That is, a corollary of Jesus' having been raised up from the dead by God is that he now administers the promise of the Father (cf. Luke 11:13; 24:49; Acts 1:4), which is the gift of the Spirit.

Having established the connection between the phrase "the name of

231

the Lord," Jesus' exaltation, and divine salvation, Luke builds on this understanding in various ways. For example, in 3:1-26 the "complete health" of a man born lame is attributed to the efficacy of "the name" (v. 16), the conclusion being reached by means of a rehearsal of the significance of Jesus' having been "glorified" (v. 13) and "raised from the dead" (v. 15). And later in 4:10-12, a statement regarding God's vindication of Jesus (v. 11) — which is stated as having been accomplished through resurrection (v. 10) — leads in verse 12 to a declaration of the universal significance of Jesus' name for salvation (cf. Jervell, *Theology of the Acts*, 97-98).

It needs to be noted, however, that Luke's development of the soteriological importance of Jesus' resurrection lacks precision at this point. Sometimes he appears to give salvific meaning to his resurrection and at other times to his ascension. This is because, though separated temporally by forty days (cf. 1:3), the resurrection and ascension of Jesus share for Luke a single theological interpretation. In fact, in 2:31-34 Luke moves easily from resurrection to ascension, referring to both as Jesus' "exaltation at the right hand of God." And in 5:30-31 he parallels Jesus' resurrection and his ascension, with both having God as their subject and both being interpreted as God having "raised up" (v. 30) or "exalted" (v. 31) Jesus to the position of disseminating beneficently on God's behalf the blessings of salvation.

Perhaps the clearest affirmation in Acts of the soteriological significance of Jesus' exaltation comes in 5:30-31 (the passage just alluded to): "The God of our ancestors raised up Jesus. . . . God exalted him at his right hand as Leader and Savior, to give repentance to Israel and the forgiveness of sins." This is a straightforward claim that Jesus' confirmation as Savior — that is, as the one who "gives" repentance and forgiveness — is grounded in both his resurrection and his ascension.

Already in Luke 2:11, of course, Jesus was designated as "Lord" and "Savior." And throughout his portrayal of Jesus' public ministry in his Gospel, Luke has presented Jesus as engaged in a ministry that conveyed repentance and forgiveness to Israel. Hence, it would be inaccurate to suggest that only with his exaltation did Jesus *become* Lord, Leader, and Savior. Rather, as Robert Tannehill has helpfully observed: "Just as there are several important stages in the life of a king, from birth as heir to the throne to the anointing . . . , to actual assumption of the throne, so in the life of Jesus according to Luke" (*Narrative Unity*, 39). Nonetheless, now as the enthroned one (i.e., Messiah) and benefactor of the people (i.e., Lord), the exalted Jesus reigns as Savior, pouring out the benefits of God's salvation.

3. "But God Raised Him Up":
Resurrection, the Paradox of Salvation, and Christology

The story of Jesus is woven into the narrative of Acts in sometimes subtle ways that demonstrate how Luke's understanding of God's salvific purpose is both grounded in his portrait of Christ and manifest in the experience of those being saved. In particular, it needs to be observed how the paradox of Jesus' career — stretching, as it does, from utter dishonor to divine vindication and exaltation — portends the Lukan notion of salvation as status reversal and transposition. This is witnessed early on in Luke's Gospel in the reversal of fortune experienced by the childless Elizabeth (Luke 1:24-25), and it is documented in prophetic terms in Mary's Song (1:52-53). As an exemplar of this Lukan theme within the Book of Acts, the account of the Ethiopian eunuch in 8:26-40 bears careful scrutiny.

The Three Intertwined Stories of Acts 8:26-40

In the narrative section of 8:26-40, Luke introduces his readers to three stories. Each of the three stories is intertwined with the others around a common configuration of motifs, which can be related to social status and acceptance in the socio-religious life of the ancient Mediterranean world. The first story is about an Ethiopian eunuch.

In the agonistic world of Luke, where people were generally concerned with the exotic and with social rank, the Ethiopian eunuch is presented initially as a man of acclaim. He is a person of enviable power in his native land, being in charge of his country's treasury. He merits a chariot (i.e., a wagon), which undoubtedly came with a driver and attendants. He is able, it seems, to read the unconventional Greek of the Old Testament Septuagint (LXX). Even his appearance was probably alluring, with his dark skin making him an object of wonder and admiration among people of the Greek and Roman worlds.

Among the people of God, however, with whom the eunuch wanted to identify (cf. v. 27c: "he had come to Jerusalem in order to worship"), he was an outcast. His black skin may have made him seem somewhat exotic, but it also differentiated him from others. Moreover, as a castrated male, while he could appreciate the beauty of the Jerusalem temple, he could never have full access to it or its rituals (cf. Deut 23:1). He lived religiously, in Jewish eyes, at the edge of the world — one might say at "the end of the earth," as some ancient geographers referred to Ethiopia. Scholars continue to debate whether he was also a Gentile. But in some ways, given the many other strikes against him, the ethnic question is not key. For having just visited the temple, he had been again reminded that he could never be a full participant in the temple cult or a full member of the people of God — that for all his devotion, he would always be to Jews an outsider or, in sociological terms, a "marginalized" person.

The second character in the narrative of 8:26-40 is Philip, and his story is also a mixed one. He is hardly known to us, being only first introduced into the narrative of Acts at 6:1-7 because of problems related to food relief. There he is cast as a Greek-speaking Jewish Christian — that is, one from among a minority group within the Christian community at Jerusalem — who was appointed to serve in that community. His position does not seem, at first, to have been one of prominence. Yet the reader of Acts quickly comes to realize that Luke has portrayed Philip as a significant leader and prophet in the early church.

Philip's significance is highlighted by Luke in a number of ways. First, the role he is given, as one who serves at table, has already been recast by Jesus as being one of leadership among the people of God — a leadership, in fact, like that of Jesus himself (cf. Luke 12:37; 22:24-27; Acts 6:2). Second, he is characterized as a person of "good standing," who was "full of the Spirit and of wisdom" (6:3). Third, in the immediately preceding account of 8:4-25, Philip proclaims Jesus Christ in Samaria, thereby fulfilling Jesus' instructions to his followers in 1:8. And finally, in the present narrative of 8:26-40, he shows himself to be one who listens to the voice of God, follows the prompting of God's Spirit, and interprets the Scriptures correctly. The story of Philip, therefore, is the story of one whose status as a relative outsider among the people of God was overturned so that his role in the realization of God's plan would be a prominent one. Might his status reversal portend hope for the Ethiopian eunuch?

At the climax of the dialogue between the eunuch and Philip, we hear the story of Jesus, which also is presented as a mixed story. From one perspective, Jesus is the humiliated one, who had been denied justice according to the words of Isa 53:7-8 that were being read by the eunuch. Indeed, Jesus' crucifixion is depicted in Luke's Gospel as a heinous act in which Jesus suffered the extremes of debasement. Yet Jesus is also portrayed as God's Anointed One, whom God raised up, exalting him as Lord and

Savior. This reversal is documented in Luke 22–24. It is also summarized repeatedly in the speeches in Acts — particularly as Peter and the others declare, "You killed the author of life, but God raised him from the dead" (e.g., 3:15). And in 8:33, as the eunuch cites Isaiah 53, we hear a comparable transition from somber tones to celebration: The one who has suffered humiliation — who can describe his family? It is so numerous, for he has been raised up from the earth!

Having read from Isaiah, the eunuch inquires, "About whom does the prophet speak?" This is an important query, because it underscores the importance for Luke of a proper interpretation — both of Scripture and of the events that he recounts. It is also important because the eunuch thus points to the scope of possible referents for the text he has read. Who will experience the reversal Isaiah describes? Does Isaiah write about himself or about someone else? Does he write, perhaps, about the eunuch? What of the many persons who help to make up the Lukan narrative — such as the demon-possessed, the leprous, the crippled, the diseased, the poor — regarding whom Mary's Song in the Lukan infancy narrative portends that they have been lifted up (1:52)? Is there hope for persons like the eunuch, the outcast, the marginal? About whom did Isaiah speak?

Philip's answer is clear: Isaiah wrote of Jesus. As important to Luke's understanding of the good news as this particular identification may be, its wider implications should not be overlooked. In Luke's account, what is true of Jesus has the further consequence that, though the eunuch is a socio-religious outcast, he has not been forgotten by God. Jesus' humiliation on the cross has led to his being exalted by God. And in his being raised up he has made possible and opened the way for others, too, to experience this salvation-as-reversal. Indeed, Philip's proclamation of the good news of Jesus, in which the preaching of "good news to the poor" (Luke 4:18-19) as well as the story of Jesus' own death and resurrection must have been paramount, has as its effect the reversal of the eunuch's marginal status. He embraces the good news and is baptized — that is, he is embraced within the community of God's people.

These three stories, which focus respectively on an Ethiopian eunuch, a Greek-speaking disciple, and Jesus — with each sharing a common configuration of motifs — together form a single tapestry in this narrative of Acts. The effect of Luke's presentation is to exhibit, in a way that is unique to narrative, that Jesus' resurrection, when understood as exaltation, portends the nature of salvation for others.

Resurrection and Christology

This reading of Acts 8:26-40 points to a number of important affirmations regarding Jesus' person and his message that are developed throughout the Acts of the Apostles. Perhaps the most important of these affirmations is that the resurrection of Jesus was God's own act (2:22, 32; 3:15, 26; 4:10; 5:30; 10:41; 13:33-34; 17:3, 31; 26:8; see also Luke 9:22; 24:34; cf. Jervell, *Theology of the Acts*, 31-32). This is consistent with the overwhelmingly *theo*logical orientation of Luke-Acts, where always and everywhere it is God's own purposes that are being worked out — first in the story of Israel, then in the life and ministry of Jesus, and now in the collective life of those who follow him. In contrast to this act of God, Luke sets the acts of human agents, especially those of the Jerusalem elite, who have pronounced their verdict against Jesus. The resurrection of Jesus, therefore, is God's renunciation of all human verdicts against Jesus, as Peter and the other apostles are depicted as saying in 5:30: "The God of our ancestors raised up Jesus, whom you had killed by hanging him on a tree" (see also 2:23-24; 3:13-15; 4:10; 10:39-40; 13:27-31; cf. Harrison, "Resurrection of Jesus Christ," 223).

By this vindication of Jesus and his message, Luke declares the continuity between Jesus of Nazareth and Jesus the exalted Lord. This is important within the Lukan narrative precisely because the identity of Jesus as God's Son was not universally recognized nor his message universally embraced. It was important for Luke's audience, too, as they struggled with their own questions concerning the authenticity of their faith. Luke's readers, it seems, were faced with the question: In following Jesus as Lord and Messiah, have we truly aligned ourselves with the ancient purpose of the God of Israel? Angelic and divine voices notwithstanding (cf. Luke 1:32, 35; 3:21-22), the legitimacy of Jesus' authority is presented as being perpetually in the dock in Luke's Gospel — with scribes sometimes joined by Pharisees in an attempt to monitor Jesus' practices in order to ascertain whether they cohered with conventional understandings of the divine will. Jesus' endeavor to wrestle the temple away from the Jerusalem leaders and to restore it to its role within God's purpose (Luke 19:45-48) served only to exacerbate their hostility against him.

In effect, Israel was left with only two choices — either to follow their tried-and-true leaders at Jerusalem, or to adopt the way of Jesus the Galilean. At the eleventh hour, when Jesus most needed their backing, the people of Israel (*ho laos*, "the people"; often also *hoi ochloi*, "the crowds" or "multitude") repealed their support of him and joined their leaders in calling for his execution (Luke 23:13-25). Repudiated by the Jewish leaders, who drew their authorization from their key roles in relation to God's temple, how could Jesus be seen as one who spoke on God's behalf? Suffering disgrace at their hands, how could Jesus be accepted as having the divine imprimatur, as being God's own son?

Luke's answer is grounded in a profound irony: those who opposed Jesus, though they believed they were serving God, were unwittingly serving a diabolic purpose. This is evidenced by God's response to the execution of Jesus. In raising him from the dead, God demonstrated in a quite tangible fashion that it was Jesus, and not his opponents, who rightly comprehended and fully embodied the divine purpose.

God's exaltation of one so thoroughly spurned by Israel's leaders had the further effect of vindicating Jesus' message concerning the nature of God's kingdom. Jesus had represented the coming of the kingdom as the coming of God's reign of justice, which means the deconstruction of worldly powers and worldly systems of valuation. In raising Jesus from the dead, God verified the truth of Jesus' message. Now status within the people of God would not be calculated according to socially determined norms, such as Abrahamic lineage, family heritage, economic resources, gender, religious purity, and the like. Rather, it would be determined, most fundamentally, by the beneficence of God, and then by one's comportment vis-à-vis God's redemptive purpose. Jesus taught that the coming of the kingdom had transposed the world order, so as to accord privilege in the divine economy to the poor, the hungry, those who weep, the reviled, and the excluded (cf. Luke 4:18-19; 6:20-26). His rejection, sealed in the ignominy of his death, might have been understood as the negation of his message. Instead, Jesus' message found its definitive vindication in his having been raised by God from the dead.

Resurrection is not for Luke, then, simply a matter of speculative affirmation. Rather, it is intimately associated with his Christology and his understanding of the means and nature of salvation. In the resurrection, God has provided for Jesus' ministry an unassailable sanction, so that Jesus' message of salvation-as-reversal and his career as the one whose humiliation has been overturned in exaltation might become paradigmatic for the redemptive experience of those who follow him. In his being raised up, so are the least, the last, the lost, and the left out raised up — not so that they might bask in their newly found experience of status among the people of God, but so that they might embody and witness to his message of reversal.

4. "But God Raised Him Up": Resurrection, Discipleship, and Mission

Our examination of the Lukan account of the Ethiopian eunuch and Philip in Acts 8:26-40 also suggests that Christian discipleship and Christian mission are to be understood as being based on and determined by Jesus' resurrection. This means that the power of God manifested in Jesus' ministry and on full display in his resurrection is to be folded into the daily life of the believing community. The very existence of believers, in fact, is to be one that matches the story of Jesus — a movement in life that incorporates both suffering and glory.

The first healing recorded in Acts — in 3:1-26, with its aftermath then depicted in a trial before the Jewish leaders in 4:1-22 — is appropriately picturesque. A man over forty years old, who had been crippled from birth, is "raised up" by Peter and John, who were proclaiming the "raising up" of Jesus (cf. 3:7, 15; 4:2). In so doing, the apostles establish themselves as "witnesses of the resurrection." Furthermore, in Luke's portrayal of this healing there is the suggestion that the power of the divine presence is also to be manifest in the lives and through the ministries of those who derive their identity "from the ongoing life and reality of the One who lived, died, and was raised" (Lorenzen, *Resurrection and Discipleship*, 212; cf. Dupont, *Salvation of the Gentiles*, 72-76).

The nexus between Jesus' resurrection and the mission of the apostles (and that of all subsequent believers) runs deeper still. For Jesus' resurrection, as Luke presents it, is the necessary precursor to the mission of the disciples. Notwithstanding the two accounts of Jesus sending out his followers for mission in Luke 9:1-6 and 10:1-20, the primary characterization of the disciples in Luke's Gospel is as persons who are "with" Jesus (e.g., 6:17; 7:11; 8:1, 22; 9:10; 22:11, 14, 28, 39). Though being "with" Jesus entailed companionship with him — sharing in his successes and failures, in his acceptance and rejection — the disciples initiated little and seem often to have understood even less. Their role throughout Luke's Gospel is surprisingly undeveloped. Indeed, toward the end of the lengthy journey from Galilee to Jerusalem, which constitutes the central section of the Gospel (9:51–19:48), the disciples almost disappear from view altogether. Nor do they play an active role during the Lukan narrative of Jesus' teaching in the temple but seem instead to have faded into the crowds (cf. 20:1–21:38). Their ongoing lack of perception of Jesus' identity is typified by the witness of the two disciples on the road to Emmaus, whose hopes for redemption were dashed by Jesus' crucifixion (so 24:19-21).

Whatever skepticism about the disciples we may bring from Luke's first volume is almost immediately countered by their overwhelmingly positive characterization in his second volume. The source of this transformation is not difficult to discern. Having been encountered by the Holy Spirit at Pentecost and subsequently, they hear the voice of the Spirit, follow the leadership of the Spirit, and are empowered by this same Spirit. So they speak boldly in mission and defense. Yet, as we have seen, in the Lukan formulation Jesus' capacity to disseminate the Spirit derives from his exaltation — that is, from his resurrection and ascension. Without the resurrection, therefore, there is no outpoured Spirit, and without the outpoured Spirit there is no divine mission.

The transformation experienced by Jesus' followers is also evident in Luke's writing in a second way. At the root of the disciples' lack of comprehension in Luke's Gospel is their incapacity to correlate Jesus' messianic status with the prospect of his cruel and shameful death (cf., e.g., Luke 9:44-45; 18:31-34). Misunderstanding at this fundamental level, however, has as its corollary an even more pervasive problem — the disciples' ineptitude in grasping the overall nature of God's redemptive work in its focus on the elevation of those of lowest status in society (e.g., Luke 18:15-17; 22:24-27; cf. 1:46-55). Against this backdrop, it is easy to understand why the disciples would experience the resurrection of Jesus as the validation of his topsy-turvy message.

God does indeed raise up the disgraced! What is more, following his resurrection, Jesus opens up both his disciples' minds and the Scriptures in order that his disciples might fathom anew the shape of his ministry together with the whole of the history of God's people (Luke 24:25-27, 44-47; Acts 1:1-3). The light of the resurrection, therefore, casts its "backshadow" on previous events — that is, the resurrection serves as the hermeneutical key by which the past is interpreted as having contained signs pointing to what has now begun to unfold. The present, understood as the future of the past, is seen to have been immanent in the outworking of God's purpose in the past (cf. Morson, *Narrative and Freedom*, 234).

With the resurrection itself as proof of Jesus' interpretation of the Scriptures and of God's purpose, the disciples were well equipped to engage in mission. Certainty at this level was necessary, since their message was one that could only have attracted opposition — both because of the nature of its religious claims, which were extraordinary within the Roman empire, and because of its departure from conventional understandings of Scripture within contemporary Judaism.

Likewise in Acts, it is Jesus' own humiliation and resurrection that prepare for and legitimize the experience of those involved in Christian mission as being persons who themselves experience rejection. One of the most transparent illustrations of the parallelism between Jesus and his followers on this point is recounted in 14:19-20, where Paul, having been trailed by Jews from one city to the next, finally becomes their victim at Lystra. His Jewish opponents win over the crowds, and together they stone Paul and drag him out of the city — where he is left for dead. But "when the disciples surrounded him, he arose and went into the city," and then continued on in his missionary journey. So Paul recapitulates in his mission the career of Jesus, from death to life. And as Paul himself interpreted the experience, "It is through many trials that we must enter the kingdom of God" (Acts 14:22).

In a different way, the stoning of Stephen had earlier validated Stephen's character and message. Rejected by the Jewish council at Jerusalem just as Jesus had been, he nonetheless had a vision of the glory of God (Acts 7:54-56). Seeing the Son of Man at God's right hand, he was therefore a witness of the resurrection in a most literal way. And having been granted such a vision, he is portrayed as one who had extraordinary access to God — and this in spite of his rejection by those whose self-identity was as the official interpreters and spokespersons of God.

The account of Peter and John raising up the crippled man at the gate of the temple also suggests that the power exercised in Christian mission is none other than the power that raised Jesus from the dead. It would be too much to say, of course, that Jesus' followers called people into a full realization of resurrected life. After all, a handful of texts in Acts point to a future resurrection and a resultant future life (see Section 5 below). Nevertheless, the Lukan eschatology is focused primarily on "today," and therefore on the invitation to participate in a new existence in the present. Luke has multiple ways of speaking about the concept of salvation — for example, by the use of such expressions as "healing," "rescuing," and "forgiving." But all of these expressions are oriented toward human restoration. The engine of a restoration of this magnitude can only be the divine power that is focused on the raising up of Jesus in resurrection.

With respect to manifestations of resurrection power in the Christian mission, Luke sets forth an important interpretive symbiosis: miracles done at the hands of Jesus' disciples are possible only because Jesus has been raised from the dead, but also these selfsame miracles verify that Jesus has been raised up by God. As recipients of the outpouring of the Spirit, Jesus' witnesses are able to perform "signs and wonders" in a way consistent with the Lukan portrait of Jesus as the Savior who made available through his presence and ministry the beneficent, miraculous power of God (e.g., Acts 2:22, 43; 4:30; 5:12; 6:8; 8:6, 13; 14:3; 15:12). As Luke summarizes: "With great power [i.e., through 'signs and wonders'] the apostles gave their testimony to the resurrection of the Lord Jesus" (4:33). Manifestations of apostolic power, therefore, verify that Jesus has been raised from the dead and indicate the continuing presence of divine power through his disciples.

The text just cited, Acts 4:33, is significant in an additional way. Situated within the heading of one of the notable Lukan summaries of the life of the early community of believers, this reference to the apostles' "testimony to the resurrection" is also important for what it suggests about the connection between Jesus' resurrection and the nature of the life of the community. The summary in Acts 4 begins as follows:

> Now the whole group of those who believed were of one heart and soul, and no one claimed private ownership of any possessions, but everything they owned was held in common. With great power the apostles gave their testimony to the resurrection of the Lord Jesus, and great grace was upon them all. There was not a needy person among them. . . . (vv. 32-34a, NRSV)

It is possible, of course, to read this dual emphasis on economic *koinōnia* ("fellowship, sharing") and the proclamation of the resurrection as simply two consequences of the disciples having been filled with the Spirit following their prayer in 4:23-31. In this case, one would understand the text to be saying that the empowering of the Spirit was visible in both the common life of the community and the resurrection witness of the apostles. Undoubtedly, this is at least part of what Luke wants to affirm. We should not, however, overlook the fact that the apostles' testimony to the resurrection in verse 33 is not given in list form as merely one of two such effects but, rather, is situated between two references to economic sharing within the community in verses 32 and 34. Thus Luke's construction of this summary suggests some sort of interpretive relationship between the proclamation of the resurrection and care for the needy in the community.

Such a correlation is supported by the many times in Luke-Acts that resurrection and hunger/nourishment are held in tandem. For example, Jesus raises a little girl from the dead and then commands that she be given something to eat (Luke 8:49-56). Another example is when the gracious father says of his lost-but-found son, "This son of mine was dead and has come back to life" — with this rationale then used to justify the preparation of a feast (Luke 15:11-32). Likewise, the resurrected Jesus shares table fellowship with the Emmaus travelers (Luke 24:13-35); and Peter notes that, following the resurrection, Jesus ate and drank with his followers (Acts 10:41). Even the eschaton itself is portrayed as a banquet (e.g., Luke 13:29; 14:15), and other examples could be cited. In this way, Jesus' resurrection is intertwined with the Lukan motif of table fellowship and such quintessentially Lukan themes as nourishment for the hungry, inclusion of those who are needy and outcast, redemptive fellowship, and the negation of conventional concerns with honor and status. The community of goods envisioned by Luke, with its care for the needy, is itself, therefore, a tangible demonstration and substantiation of the resurrection of Jesus from the dead.

Again, resurrection is not for Luke a matter of speculative affirmation. Rather, it is intimately associated — as was also his Christology and his understanding of the means and nature of salvation — with Christian discipleship, the Christian's mission, and the life of the believing community. The continuation of "signs and wonders" and care for those in need are but two prominent features on the landscape of Luke's narrative portrayal of the significance of the resurrection for the lives of the believing community.

5. "Why Is It Thought Incredible by Any of You That God Raises the Dead?": Resurrection as Hope and Scandal

We have seen that the narrator of Acts is transparently concerned not only with the actuality and nature of the resurrection, but also with its wider ramifications for the experience of salvation and the character of Christian community and mission. We may explore in yet one more way how God's raising Jesus from the dead relates to the overarching plan of God. This has to do with a future resurrection of the dead, which is affirmed by the apostles in Acts even in the face of controversy.

Paul, for example, is portrayed as asserting before his interlocutors that he had been indicted for holding to the message of "the resurrection of the dead" (23:6; 24:21), just as Peter and John had been taken into custody by the Jerusalem elite on account of their proclamation that "in Jesus there is the resurrection of the dead" (4:2). Clearly for Luke, the resurrection of Jesus, although a past event, portends the future resurrection of all humanity to face judgment. The resurrection of Jesus, therefore, constitutes God's promise of a future resurrection of humans. And this places humanity in a new situation in the present (cf. 10:42; 17:31; 23:6; 24:15, 21; 26:6-8; see Harrison, "Resurrection of Jesus Christ," 224-25; Dupont, *Salvation of the Gentiles,* 76).

On the subject of the resurrection, Jesus' followers and the Pharisees were in agreement — so much so that Paul could articulate the nucleus of his message as "the hope of the resurrection of the dead" and expect to gain a favorable hearing before many of the Jewish leaders at his trials (cf. 23:6-8; see also 26:6-8). Resurrection, therefore, is not only the center of the Christian message in Luke-Acts; it also functions as the distinguishing mark of faithful Israel. Those among Israel's "twelve tribes" who "worship earnestly day and night" have this hope, and so they look forward to attaining the promise that God made to their forebears — "that God raises the dead" (26:6-8). In their proclamation of a future resurrection, then, Jesus' witnesses in the Acts of the Apostles testify that God's ancient promises have been fulfilled in Jesus' resurrection, and that those who embrace this viewpoint also share in Israel's hope.

At the outset of Luke's Gospel, Simeon predicts the divisive role that Jesus will have within Israel: "This child is destined for the falling and the rising of many in Israel, and to be a sign that will be opposed so that the inner thoughts of many will be revealed" (Luke 2:34-35a). This divisive role is played out in graphic terms in the Third Gospel, leading finally to the cross. Yet even Jesus' heinous death does not signal the ultimate expression of his role as the one over whom Israel will divide. Division continues in Acts, as energized especially by the opposing views people take toward Jesus' resurrection. The division will culminate in "the resurrection of both the righteous and the unrighteous" (24:15) — that is, in the final judgment, an event still future that finds its guarantee in Jesus' own resurrection (17:30-31).

Jesus' resurrection, as noted above, *makes available* repentance and the benefits of salvation. To this, however, may now be added that Jesus'

JOEL B. GREEN

resurrection *invites* repentance; it summons people to reorient their lives toward the purpose of the God who raised Jesus from the dead. This summons constitutes the call to response that is enunciated in the early Christian mission. In Acts, the summons to repentance is grounded in Jesus' resurrection in two ways. First, his resurrection pledges the advent of a future judgment of all people, which ought to provide the impetus necessary for repentance on their part. Second, his resurrection points emphatically and incontrovertibly to the fact that God's purpose has been made manifest in the ministry of Jesus and in the ministries of those who serve in his name. Those who resist Jesus and his witnesses, therefore, together with those who have been ignorant of God's purpose for the world, have proof in the resurrection of Jesus that they have erred in their allegiances and behaviors, and so need to repent.

The logic of the resurrection message as Luke portrays it pivots on the actuality of the resurrection of Jesus, and this explains the care with which he organizes diverse witnesses to it. This also explains why Jesus' followers in Acts continue to attract hostility. Not everyone embraces the idea of resurrection (e.g., 17:32; 23:8), and among those who do, not everyone is prepared to grant that Jesus has been raised from the dead. Because of the way that Luke presents the centrality of the resurrection for Israel's own life, a decision on this point becomes all the more crucial. Those who oppose the resurrection message segregate themselves from the genuine people of God (cf. Jervell, *Theology of the Acts,* 90-91).

Conclusion

The signal importance of the resurrection message for Luke is marked, above all, by his decision to continue his first volume with a second that takes as its immediate cause and point of departure the resurrection of Jesus — which, together with his ascension, is interpreted as his exaltation as Lord and Christ. On the basis of Jesus' resurrection, Luke can affirm the ongoing, dynamic activity of God among Jesus' followers and emphasize that their resurrection message is nothing less than the realization of Israel's hope. In this way, the resurrection message serves Luke's larger aim to tie the story of the early church into the story of Jesus, and the story of Jesus into the story of Israel — with these three stories together constituting the one story of the outworking of God's redemptive purpose.

244

In Luke's hands the resurrection (and ascension) becomes decisive for his portrayal of Jesus. God's having raised Jesus from the dead is viewed as the definitive sanctioning of Jesus and the character of his mission, as well as the divine affirmation of Jesus' status — regardless of alternative, less sanguine interpretations that might accrue to Jesus on account of his opposition to the Jerusalem leadership and his shameful execution. What is more, not only is Jesus installed as Lord, Leader, and Savior on the basis of his being raised up, but the resurrection itself — this "being raised up" — helps to define the substance of Luke's soteriology. For although "salvation" takes many forms in the Lukan narratives — such as healing, forgiveness of sins, restoration, the gift of the Spirit, and so on — all of these forms represent ways in which the metaphor of "raising up" comes to concrete expression. Jesus is lifted up! And with him so also are those who, for whatever reason, live on the margins of God's people.

The christological and soteriological focus of Luke's perspective on the resurrection of Jesus also undergirds his depiction of the community of Jesus' followers and the mission that they undertake. Jesus' resurrection serves as the centerpiece of their proclamation. At the same time it provides unassailable confirmation of the veracity of the early Christians' understanding of God's purpose and of their interpretation of Scripture. Furthermore, the signs and wonders that accompany the mission of Jesus' followers provide evidence that Jesus has been raised by God, just as they demonstrate the ongoing presence of the resurrection power of God within and through the Spirit-led mission. Thus Luke in his Gospel and his Acts affirms the "truth" of Jesus' resurrection — both its actuality as an event in history and its significance within the divine plan.

Selected Bibliography

Buckwalter, H. Douglas. *The Character and Purpose of Luke's Christology.* Cambridge: Cambridge University Press, 1996.

Dupont, Jacques. *The Salvation of the Gentiles: Studies in the Acts of the Apostles.* New York: Paulist, 1979.

George, Augustin. "Le sens de la mort de Jesus pour Luc." *Revue Biblique* 80 (1973) 186-217.

Green, Joel B. *The Gospel of Luke.* Grand Rapids: Eerdmans, 1997.

———. "'Salvation to the End of the Earth' (Acts 13:47): God as Savior in the Acts of the Apostles." In *The Book of Acts and Its Theology,* edited by I. H. Marshall and D. Peterson. Grand Rapids: Eerdmans, 1997, 83-106.

Harrison, Everett F. "The Resurrection of Jesus Christ in the Book of Acts and in Early Christian Literature." In *Understanding the Sacred Text: Essays in Honor of Morton S. Enslin on the Hebrew Bible and Christian Beginnings*, edited by J. Reumann. Valley Forge, Penn.: Judson, 1972, 217-31.

Jervell, Jacob. *The Theology of the Acts of the Apostles.* Cambridge: Cambridge University Press, 1996.

Kee, Howard Clark. *Good News to the Ends of the Earth: The Theology of Acts.* London: SCM; Philadelphia: Trinity Press International, 1990.

Lorenzen, Thorwald. *Resurrection and Discipleship: Interpretive Models, Biblical Reflections, Theological Consequences.* Maryknoll, N.Y.: Orbis, 1995.

Maddox, Robert. *The Purpose of Luke-Acts.* Edinburgh: T. & T. Clark, 1982.

Martin, Dale B. *The Corinthian Body.* New Haven: Yale University Press, 1995.

Marshall, I. Howard. "The Resurrection in the Acts of the Apostles." In *Apostolic History and the Gospel: Biblical and Historical Essays Presented to F. F. Bruce on His 60th Birthday*, edited by W. W. Gasque and R. P. Martin. Grand Rapids: Eerdmans, 1970, 92-107.

Morson, Gary Saul. *Narrative and Freedom: The Shadows of Time.* New Haven: Yale University Press, 1994.

Nickelsburg, George W. E., Jr. *Resurrection, Immortality, and Eternal Life in Intertestamental Judaism.* Cambridge: Harvard University Press, 1972.

Schneider, Gerhard. *Die Apostelgeschichte.* 2 vols. Freiburg: Herder, 1980.

Tannehill, Robert C. *The Narrative Unity of Luke-Acts: A Literary Interpretation.* Volume 2: *The Acts of the Apostles.* Minneapolis: Fortress, 1990.

Trites, Allison A. *The New Testament Concept of Witness.* Cambridge: Cambridge University Press, 1977.

CHAPTER 11

Living a Life of Faith in the Face of Death: The Witness of Hebrews

WILLIAM L. LANE

THE WRITER of Hebrews addressed a congregation of Christians that was experiencing a crisis of faith and a failure of nerve. He knew these men and women personally (cf. 13:19, "that I might be *restored* to you") and classed himself among their leaders (13:17-19). The community had become apathetic toward the gospel tradition they had received (2:1-4) and had lost some of their members through defection (10:25). Those who remained seem to have regressed to a level of immaturity (5:11-14). There had been a serious erosion of faith and hope. The members of the community appear to have thought that they could push back the hands of the clock and deny the extent of their experience as Christians.

These men and women had been believers in Jesus for some time and so should have been mature in their faith. The writer could not permit them to pretend otherwise. He was, however, fully aware that their social climate had grown hostile against them. Feeling socially alienated, they had become lax in their response to Christian commitment. They had become a church at risk.

The writer of Hebrews desired to be with his friends in order to strengthen them in their time of crisis. Unable to travel at this time, he crafted a "word of exhortation" for them as a substitute for a visit until he could come (13:19, 22-23). The Letter to the Hebrews, therefore, is a sermon on the cost of discipleship that seeks to call the church to endurance, certainty, and renewed hope.

1. Crisis and Community Response

The crisis to which Hebrews is a response seems to have been precipitated by an imminent threat of renewed persecution. The social history of the community addressed can be sketched out in terms of its response to humiliation and public abuse. From the beginning, suffering had been a constituent part of their Christian experience. In fact, in 10:32-34 the writer is able to make his addressees' own past stance of firm commitment to Christ and to one another — even under the pressure of abusive treatment and the loss of property — a paradigm for an appropriate response to a new peril that was facing them. It may have been the memory of past sufferings that accounts for the earlier desertion of some members of the community, which is frankly acknowledged in 10:25, and for an inclination to avoid contact with outsiders on the part of those who remained, which seems to be alluded to in 5:11-14.

If the members of the community had begun to respond to their present crisis by withdrawal and concealment, they had scriptural warrant for such reactions. The prophet in Isa 26:20, in an apocalyptic passage of great significance, had exhorted his people: "Go, my people, into your rooms and shut the door behind you; hide yourselves for a little while until his wrath has passed." The writer of Hebrews alludes briefly to Isaiah's exhortation in 10:37, acknowledging its eschatological importance and his addressees' comparable situation ("In a little while, the one who is coming will come and will not delay"). But he goes on to qualify this statement in 10:38-39 by the citation of Hab 2:3-4: "But the righteous will live by faith; my soul takes no pleasure in anyone who shrinks back" — a text that calls the community of God to sustained faithfulness in a difficult situation. In so doing, the writer is explicit in warning the community that God's displeasure rests on those who withdraw from the public arena through defection or concealment (cf. T. W. Lewis, "'. . . And If He Shrinks Back' [Heb X.38b]").

The sharp admonition of 10:35, "Do not throw away your boldness, seeing that it has a great reward," indicates that those addressed had regressed from the valiant stance that they had displayed at the beginning of their life together. It is reasonable to infer that they looked on the current threat as being more ominous than the earlier occasion recalled in 10:32-34. And while they may not have been under actual persecution at the time, the perception of persecution can be just as shaking to a community as persecution itself.

248

The community appears to have believed that what was now at stake was not merely the loss of property, but also the loss of human life. This suggestion finds a measure of support in 11:35b-38, which celebrates the faithfulness of men and women who were exposed not only to humiliation and persecution, but also to execution — and who were not delivered by divine intervention. The catalogue of martyrs in chapter 11 is crowned by the reference in 12:2 to Jesus, who was crucified, disregarding the disgrace and shame associated with a Roman cross. Jesus' endurance of unwarranted hostility, shame, and sadism is then used by the writer in 12:4 to provide perspective on the sufferings that were being actually endured by the community: "You have not yet resisted *(oupō antikatestēte)* to the point of bloodshed while struggling *(antagōnizomenoi)* against sin."

The agonistic ("competitive," "combative") vocabulary of this caustic comment of 12:4 is undoubtedly deliberate. The verbs "resist" *(antikathistēmi)* and "struggle" *(antagōnizomai)* occur only here in the New Testament. Furthermore, while these terms are appropriate to the athletic metaphor of 12:1, the imagery in 12:4 is decidedly more combative than that in 12:1. It is no longer a footrace that is in view, but the boxing arena — which involved bloodshed and even death. The sudden change in metaphor, together with the shift in focus from Christ to the community, signals the introduction of a new unit of thought in 12:4-11, where the writer seeks to clarify the meaning and purpose of disciplinary sufferings in the experience of the new people of God.

The pointed observation of 12:4, "You have not yet resisted to the point of bloodshed," could be understood figuratively to mean, "You still have not done your utmost." The expression is drawn from the Greek games, where the most dangerous contest was the armed boxing match. It can be understood entirely within the confines of an athletic metaphor, for boxing was the supreme test in the pentathlon ("five events") of those ancient games, and bloody wounds were commonplace. According to Seneca "the Younger" (ca. 4 B.C.–A.D. 65), the Stoic philosopher who was a contemporary of the writer of Hebrews, the true athlete was the man who "saw his own blood" (Letter 13 in *L. Annaei Senecae ad Lucillum epistula moral*, ed. O. Heuse [Leipzig: Teubner, 1914] 24). The allusion in 12:4, of course, is to the violent death of Jesus, who endured crucifixion, the point being that Jesus had to suffer far more degrading shame and deeper hostility than anything yet experienced by the community. On this athletic imagery understanding, the writer's intention was to say that the members of the community had not yet given the fullest measure in their struggle against sin. The sustaining of the athletic metaphor in 12:1-4 lends support to this interpretation.

An alternative proposal, however, is to find in 12:4 a reference to an anticipated bloody persecution of the community. The declaration "You have not yet resisted to the point of bloodshed" would then amount to a statement of fact: although members of the community had endured persecution in the form of insults, imprisonment, banishment, and the loss of property (10:32-34), they had not yet been exposed to martyrdom. As one community of believers within a larger network of believers (13:17, 24), they had escaped, to date, an ordeal involving bloodshed. No one had yet died the martyr's death.

The strongest argument in favor of this alternative explanation is the parallel use of the expression "to resist to the point of death" in the Maccabean accounts of those who endured torture and death under the Seleucids. The expression appears in those accounts with clear reference to martyrdom (cf. 2 Macc 13:14, "to contend to the point of death"; *4 Maccabees* 17:9-10, "they avenged their race by looking to God, and by enduring tortures, even to the point of death"). The suggestions of a potential, personal antagonist and of a conflict involving bloodshed in Heb 12:4 call to mind the extensive use of athletic imagery in *4 Maccabees* to portray the Jewish martyrs as athletes who were exemplars of endurance in the contest of faith (cf. *4 Maccabees* 11:20; 13:15; 15:29; 16:16; 17:11, 13). That the writer of Hebrews commonly compares the situation of his audience with that of Christ strongly favors this second interpretation.

The concluding phrase of 12:4, "while struggling against sin," suggests a conflict with a hostile power that stands in opposition to the community. In 12:1 the writer had referred to "the sin that so easily distracts" as a hindrance to the Christian life. In that context, "sin" suggests the weariness that overtakes a distance runner and subverts his determination to complete the race. Likewise, the primary reference in 12:1 is to a subjective, inward struggle against sin. With the change of imagery in 12:4, however, there is also a change of nuance in referring to "sin." The personification of sin as an enemy who must be overcome, even by bloodshed, shows that the reference is more objective. The distinctive nuance of "sin" in 12:4 is determined by the reference to "sinners" in 12:3, where the term refers to those who were hostile to Christ in the concrete situation of Golgotha and the cause of his sufferings. The expression "sin" in 12:4, therefore, is a periphrasis for "sinners" in 12:3, and so refers objectively to any source of hostile opposition to the church.

In the light of the context established by 12:2-3, the writer's observation in 12:4 has a shaming function. The sufferings of the community were insignificant in comparison with those endured by Jesus. His sufferings were both quantitatively and qualitatively greater than theirs. Yet the members of the community appear to have been on the verge of becoming weary and disheartened (12:3). They had become a community at risk. So they are summoned to a firm resolve to contend valiantly for faith, regardless of the cost.

Believers in Jesus are, to a certain extent, engaged in the same struggle that Jesus was. They must not regard themselves as exempt from the ordeal of faith endured by the attested witnesses who preceded them (11:35b-38; 12:1) and by Jesus himself (12:2-3). This is the emotionally charged setting in which it is proper to inquire about living a life of faith in the face of death in Hebrews.

2. Pastoral Strategy of the Writer

The Oral Substructure of His Writing

The writer of Hebrews would have preferred to have spoken directly to his friends (cf. 13:19, 23). He knew that in the realm of oral speech a speaker and his audience become bound together in a dynamic relationship within a world of sound. But geographical distance and the urgency of the situation made writing necessary. Nonetheless, the writer never forgot the power of oral communication. So his exhortation to his friends was crafted to communicate its point as much aurally as logically, with its appeal being as much to the ear as to the eye and mind.

In the event of communication, aural considerations often prove to be the decisive ones. The writer clearly understood speech as agonistic, and he used it effectively in the service of mission. He was prepared to commit the power of speech to the written text as a tool of advocacy. In Hebrews the voice of the text is an intentional response to other voices, which were distracting the members of the community from a proper devotion to God, to the gospel, and to one another in the assembly.

The writer's purpose was not to craft a piece of oratory, but to communicate a convincing message to those in danger of forfeiting the grace of God (cf. 3:12-15; 4:1-2, 11; 6:4-8; 10:26-31; 12:15-17, 25-29). He drew creatively on the Scriptures, which already had exercised a formative influence on the life of the community. Likewise, he drew on the Jewish synagogue tradition of homiletical midrash, which was designed to bring a past word of Scripture into the present experience of a congregation; on the gospel tradition, which was the legacy of their former leaders (2:3-4; 13:7-8); and on the power of persuasion. The writer was not just a skilled rhetorician, though; he was also a caring pastor who understood human frailty and the potential for moral failure in the face of the threat of violent death (cf. 2:14-15; 5:13). So using a number of effective pastoral strategies, he balanced instruction, exhortation, reminder, encouragement, and warning — alternating confrontation with affirmation — to stabilize the community and to move them beyond a lack of nerve to a fresh commitment to Christ and the gospel (see further Lane, "Hebrews as Pastoral Response").

A Call to Bear the Cross and Shame of Jesus — Even to the Extent of Martyrdom

A clarion call to commitment is sounded throughout Hebrews (cf. 2:1-4; 3:6, 14; 4:1, 11, 14-16; 6:11-12; 10:19-25, 35-39; 12:1-4, 7, 12-13, 14, 25-29; see also Lane, *Hebrews: A Call to Commitment,* passim), but it is crystallized in the exhortation to costly discipleship in 13:13: "So then, let us go out to him outside the camp, bearing the disgrace he bore." The immediate context of this verse directs attention to Jesus who "suffered death outside the city gate" (13:12). The implied reference is to the historical event of Jesus' death on Golgotha outside the city of Jerusalem (cf. John 19:17, 20; Mark 15:20). The factual basis of the gospel tradition finds expression in the phrases "outside the city gate" and "he suffered death."

It was Roman practice to perform executions beyond the inhabited area of a city (cf. Plautus, *Soldier* 359-60; Artemidorus Daldianus, *Dreams* 2.53). Execution "outside the gate" *(extra portem)* entailed, for Jesus, the shame of exclusion from the sacred precincts of Jerusalem (cf. Heb 12:2, "despising the shame" [of crucifixion]). The juxtaposition of "outside the city gate" with "he suffered death" brings out an element of shame in 13:12 that is not in the verb "suffered" itself. The fact that Jesus died as one who was rejected by his own people gives added poignancy to his death, for he was repudiated by the people, and his death appeared to seal his rejection as final. Jesus, in fact, offered his sacrifice to God as an outcast.

The exhortation of Heb 13:13 to leave the camp, identifying fully with Jesus, introduces a distinct understanding of discipleship, for Jesus' action in going "outside the city gate" (13:12) set a precedent for others to follow. Discipleship in Hebrews, therefore, is to emulate Jesus, leaving behind security, congeniality, and respectability — in effect, risking the reproach that fell on him. Christian identity is a matter of "going out" to him. It entails costly commitment to follow Jesus resolutely, even in the face of death.

In the context of the allusion to Golgotha in 13:12, this summons to discipleship implies following Jesus on the way to the cross. The writer appears to have been thoroughly familiar with the primitive tradition that associates the "going out" of Jesus with the bearing of his cross (cf. John 19:17; Mark 15:20-21). In fact, since the cross is explicitly associated with "shame" in 12:2, the exhortation of 13:13 should probably be seen as a parenetic adaptation of the familiar call to discipleship in terms of cross-bearing that appears in the Synoptic Gospels (cf. Mark 8:34; Matt 10:38; 16:24; Luke 14:27).

As enunciated by Jesus, the call to discipleship is a call to martyrdom. The conditions of discipleship in Mark 8:34 and parallels — "deny one's self" (but not Jesus!) and "take up the cross" — are parallel. In the pre-synoptic tradition, the summons to discipleship is linked both with the concept of shame (Mark 8:34-38 par.) and with the severance of social ties (Matt 10:37-38; Luke 14:26-27). The synoptic evangelists appear to have understood the requirement of self-denial as synonymous with the bearing of shame (Mark 8:34, 38; Matt 16:24; Luke 9:23-26), just as they linked cross-bearing with confession (Mark 8:38 par.). The distinctive understanding of discipleship that comes to expression in Heb 13:13 appears to be informed by this presynoptic strand of the early Jesus tradition.

Discipleship in this context means being directed by the course of Jesus' life, with such a discipleship being affirmed in the acceptance of reproach for Jesus' sake. The qualifying phrase in 13:13b, "bearing his shame," is motivated through the allusion to Jesus' humiliation in 13:12b, "outside the city gate . . . by his own blood." What the writer of Hebrews calls for is a "shared" reproach — that is, bearing the same stigma that Jesus bore. He perceived that there is a form of intimate sharing that unites Jesus and his followers in the common experience of repudiation and disgrace.

Readiness to bear Jesus' shame is an integral part of discipleship. In an earlier experience of public abuse, the community had learned experientially that the price of communal intimacy was shared suffering (10:33). They are now urged once more to emulate their own bold example, fully recognizing that identification with the crucified Jesus will invite the same contempt with which he was treated. Those who have been consecrated to the service of God through Jesus' blood (13:12) have only two options: they can gain *everything* together with Jesus, or they can lose *everything* without him. For this reason the writer urges the community to "go out to him" in a display of courageous faith in the face of death.

3. Belief in the Resurrection of the Dead

The writer of Hebrews remained optimistic about the community because it had been established on a firm foundation. He refers to that foundation in 6:1-2 but shows no inclination to review with his auditors the foundational features of the Christian faith. He regarded the members of the community as those who should have been mature. So he encouraged them to be "carried forward by God to the goal of spiritual maturity" (6:1), for they were capable of receiving solid food, and their faculties had been exercised through the making of responsible decisions (5:13-14).

The Elementary Christian Teaching

Elaborating on the elementary Christian instruction on which the community had been founded, the writer mentions for the first time in 6:1-2 belief in "the resurrection of the dead." My understanding of this important text is reflected in my translation, as follows:

> So then, let us leave standing the elementary Christian teaching, and let us be carried forward [by God] to the goal of spiritual maturity, not laying again a foundation consisting of repentance from works that lead to death and of faith in God, the catechetical instruction concerning cleansing rites and laying on of hands, the resurrection of the dead and eternal judgment.

Certain key elements in the above translation require comment.

The text refers to the foundational teaching that the community acquired years ago (5:12) in the form of catechetical instruction. When the writer urges his friends to "leave standing" *(aphentes)* the elementary Christian teaching, he is affirming its enduring value. He regarded the foundational instruction as so firmly established that the urgent need was for only a fuller appreciation and application of that teaching. The foundation is solid. It need not — indeed, cannot — be laid again (6:1-4). The extended exhortation to the community in 6:1-12 is precisely a reminder of that foundation.

The second clause in 6:1, "not laying again a foundation," clarifies in a negative fashion the meaning of the positive injunction: "Let us leave standing the elementary Christian teaching and be carried forward [by God] to the goal of spiritual maturity." In context, spiritual maturity implies (1) surrender to God's active influence within the community (6:1), (2) receptivity and responsiveness to the received tradition (5:11-14), (3) an earnest concern for the full realization of hope (6:11), and (4) unwavering faith and steadfast endurance (6:12). The metaphor of the foundation describes the elementary Christian teaching positively as the basis for the Christian life.

This conclusion has been called into question on the ground that none of the six items listed in 6:1-2 refers to anything specifically Christian. Each of the six articles, however, is related to the high-priestly Christology that is developed in the subsequent section of 7:1–10:18, which makes explicit the christological structure of the foundation. "Repentance from dead works" and "faith in God" are reviewed in 9:14 from the standpoint of the redemptive accomplishment of Jesus. There "dead works" are defined as the external regulations associated with the Levitical priesthood in the earthly sanctuary (9:10). Likewise, discrimination between useless "cleansing rites," on the one hand, and purification by the blood of Jesus, on the other (9:9-10, 19; 10:22) — or between priests appointed by "the laying on of hands" according to the law, which in its weakness could not achieve the maturation of the people of God, and the high priest appointed by the oath of God and the power of an indestructible life (5:1-6; 7:5, 15-28) — demonstrates the relationship between the foundational teaching and the advanced instruction provided in 7:1–10:18. Accordingly, in 6:1-2 the writer is not asking the community to discard one aspect of Christian instruction for another, but to build on the solid foundation already laid for them.

The translation I have offered for Hebrews 6:1-2 reflects a textual variant. I accept in verse 2 the accusative case of the Greek term for "teaching" (i.e., *didachēn*), which is supported by P[46], B, the Old Latin *d*, and the Syriac Peshitta, rather than the genitive form (i.e., *didachēs*), which enjoys strong support from good representatives of all the major types of text (ℵ A C D I K P 33 81 614 1739 Byzantine Lectionaries it vg sy[h] cop arm). Although the support for the accusative is relatively slight, it is early and weighty. It is probable that the surrounding genitives led to the alteration of an original accusative reading to the genitive in the remainder of the manuscript tradition. I take it, therefore, that the reference is to "catechetical instruction."

Reading the text in this manner clarifies the character of the foundation. On such a reading, the phrase "catechetical instruction concerning cleansing rites and laying on of hands, the resurrection of the dead and eternal judgment" stands in apposition to "the foundation" of repentance from dead works and of faith in God. This means that the laying of the foundation consisted in the provision of catechetical instruction. This reading therefore suggests that repentance and faith were prompted, at least in part, by teaching that developed a distinctly Christian perspective on the articles of faith enumerated in 6:2 — including "the resurrection from the dead" and "eternal judgment."

The Foundational Nature of the Resurrection

Certainly the community addressed by the writer of Hebrews had been instructed in the central features of the Christian message when it was founded. This instruction must have been not only in the common biblical and Jewish belief in the resurrection at the end of the age, but also in the factual basis for that hope in the resurrection of Jesus from the dead. This is an important deduction that may explain why there is so little direct appeal to the fact of Jesus' resurrection in Hebrews.

Also to be noted in the witness of Hebrews to Jesus is that the writer subsumes Jesus' resurrection within a dominant pattern of reference to Jesus' death and exaltation. This pattern is evident already in the confessional summary at the opening of the homily: "This Son . . . made purification for sins and then sat down at the right hand of the divine Majesty on high, having been exalted as far above the angels as the name which he has inherited is superior to theirs" (1:3-4). The writer could adopt this mode of speaking because instruction regarding the resurrection of Jesus — which was integral to the foundational teaching they had received — had already been given to the members of the community. So his appeal to that foundational teaching in 6:1-2 implicitly called to mind among his addressees the basis of Christian hope in the event of Jesus' resurrection (cf. 6:11, ". . . with regard to the realization of your hope until the end").

Some of the biblical and historical roots of the community's foundational belief in the resurrection of the dead are exposed in the catalogue of the triumphs of persevering by faith in 11:1-40. The most distinctive aspect of that exposition is the development of the relation of faith to suffering and martyrdom. It is striking that the individuals mentioned in this celebrated digest of the history of Israel exercised faith in the face of death. Almost without exception, the context links the exemplars of faith in some way or other to death — either their own death or that of one of their family (see vv. 4, 5, 7, 11-12, 13, 17-19, 20, 21, 22, 23, 25-26, 29, 30, 31, 33-34, 35-38). Even those for whom death is not specified in the chapter were exposed to severe trial or peril for fidelity to God.

This capacity to endure suffering and death presupposes a relationship to the unseen, heavenly world. Likewise, this recital of faith in action displays the practical and pastoral orientation of the catalogue. Chapter 11 has been carefully crafted to address a crisis of faith in the life of the Christian community, whose members had earlier experienced adversity, humiliation, loss of property, and imprisonment (10:32-34). In its listing of men and women of faith who were the addressees' forebearers, the chapter was designed to strengthen the men and women of the community in their resolve to be faithful to God — even in the event of martyrdom (cf. 12:1-4).

The "Offering of Isaac" and Belief in the Resurrection

The writer refers explicitly to the community's belief in the resurrection of the dead when he refers to the dramatic trial of Abraham's faith that took place when God commanded him to offer in sacrifice his son Isaac (11:17-19; cf. Gen 22:1-18). When Abraham obeyed God's mandate to leave Ur, he simply gave up his past. But when he was summoned to Mount Moriah to deliver his own son to God, he was asked to surrender his future as well, for fulfillment of the promise of an innumerable posterity was tied securely to the life of Isaac.

The demand for the life of Isaac was, undoubtedly, a fierce challenge to the faith of Abraham. It threatened the integrity of the promise of God. It also seemed to contradict both the character of God and the depth of human affection. But Abraham accepted what he could not understand on the basis of his own rich experience with God. He appears to have understood intuitively that the obedience of faith called for an allegiance to God that extended beyond even the most intimate of family ties.

Abraham was prepared to comply with the terrifying command because "he considered that God was able to raise up even the dead." The writer adds by way of commentary, "because of this conviction also, in a foreshadowing, he did receive him back" (11:19). It may actually have been the promise in Gen 21:12, which is quoted in Heb 11:18 ("It is through Isaac that your descendants will be reckoned"), that motivated Abraham to offer his son as a gift to God. Abraham believed against all natural probability that God would be able to accomplish his promise of descendants through Isaac, despite the seemingly contradictory command to sacrifice his life as a burnt offering. This seems to be the connection between the biblical quotation and the deduction that immediately follows in 11:19a: "he considered that God was able to raise up even the dead."

When the writer states that Abraham "considered' (logisamenos) that God was able to raise the dead, he uses a term that denotes inward conviction or persuasion, not simply a considered opinion. The aorist tense of the participle suggests that Abraham's conclusion was made once and finally. Thus the writer may be saying that Abraham was so certain that God could perform what he had promised that, by faith, he was prepared to offer Isaac in the conviction that God would revive the dead.

On the other hand, the thematic connection between 11:11-12 and 17-19 may indicate that in the writer's view Abraham was influenced by his experience of being empowered to become a father to Isaac (11:11-12). That is, as a direct result of his experience of the power of God to overcome death with respect to his own body (11:12a), he considered that God was able to vanquish death in the case of his son. An antecedent to this line of reasoning can be found in 2 Macc 7:22-23, where the mother of the seven martyrs reasons from the power of God in producing life in the womb to the ability of God to restore life to the dead.

Whatever his rationale, Abraham placed his full confidence in the power of God, before which even death cannot erect a barrier. The reference to God as able to revive the dead is confessional in form; it may, therefore, have as its source a primitive Christian formulation.

The writer's commentary on this event in 11:19b affirms that the direct result of Abraham's firm conviction concerning God's ability to raise the dead was that he received Isaac back "in a foreshadowing." The restoring of Isaac by such an unanticipated reprieve, and at the last moment, is depicted as a specific instance of God's power to raise up his own from the dead. The sacrifice is seen as a gift that God returns, thereby guaranteeing the reception of what was promised according to Gen 21:12. Thus when Abraham received Isaac back from the altar of sacrifice, there was a foreshadowing of the future resurrection of the dead.

This understanding appreciates the causal relationship between the inference drawn in 11:19b and the reference to the resurrection in 11:19a. The "foreshadowing" was a veiled event. It is not necessary to believe that Abraham recognized the connection between the receiving back of Isaac from the altar and the resurrection of the dead. But the Christian community *is* capable, the writer believes, of recognizing the deeper significance of that event.

It is natural to read 11:19b in the light of the conceptual background shared by the writer and his addressees because of their common heritage in the synagogues of the Jewish Diaspora. The recitation of the first three of the Eighteen Benedictions (the *Shemoneh Esreh*) was an integral part of the synagogue liturgy by the first century. The second of these prayers pronounces a blessing on God "who makes the dead alive." In the Jewish midrashic tradition this blessing was linked with the *Aqedah,* or the biblical account of "the offering of Isaac" (Gen 22:1-18). According to the tradition, when Isaac was restored to Abraham, he exclaimed together with his father, "Blessed be God who raises the dead!" (*Pirqe R. Eliezer* 31 [16b]; cf. *4 Maccabees* 7:19; 13:17; *Palestinian Targum* to Lev 22:27). In drawing a connection between the resurrection and the offering of Isaac in 11:19, the writer of Hebrews may therefore have drawn on this Jewish tradition, with which the members of the community he addressed may also have been familiar (cf. Rom 4:17).

In presenting Abraham's "offering of Isaac" as the prototypical example of faith in "God who raises the dead," the intention of the writer of Hebrews was to call his addressees from apathy and despair to a fresh experience of faith in the power of God. It is that power that stands behind God's solemn pledge to fulfill his unalterable word of promise to them.

259

And it is the faithfulness of God to his promise that is the primary thrust of the writer in 11:17-19. For it is the divine faithfulness, the writer holds, that is the basis for exercising faith in the face of death.

"That They Might Obtain a Better Resurrection"

With the statement "And what more shall I say?" of 11:32a, the catalogue of exemplary persons and events in 11:4-31 — each introduced by the ana-phoric "by faith" — gives place to an enumeration of names in rapid succession (11:32b), which is followed by an abstract of the accomplishments of faith by nameless persons that extends the historical survey into the post-biblical period (11:33-38). This eloquent abstract of the acts of triumphant faith provides an effective conclusion to the whole discourse of chapter 11. What needs to be noted, however, is that in 11:33-35a of that conclusion the recital progresses from one glorious achievement or deliverance to another, each attained "through faith," whereas in 11:35b-38 the tone changes as attention is focused on those who exercised faith in the face of death — but who were granted no immunity from humiliation, suffering, and death.

The reference to women who "received their dead by resurrection" (11:35a) belongs to the initial series as a final proof of the benefits of faith in the face of death. The allusions are to the widow of Zarephath of Sidon, who received back from God, as a result of the dynamic faith of Elijah, her son who had died (1 Kings 17:17-24; cf. Sirach 48:5; *Lives of the Prophets* 10.5-6 [ed. C. C. Torrey, 27, 42]), and to the Shunammite woman, whose son was restored to her as a result of the indomitable faith of Elisha (2 Kings 4:18-37). In the latter case, the mother's haste in going to Elisha on Mount Carmel despite her deep distress, and her quiet response "Everything is all right" in answer to her husband's inquiry (2 Kings 4:22-26), were expressions of her own firm faith that she would, indeed, receive her son back from the dead "by resurrection." But the catalogue of those who enjoyed the rich benefits of faith after difficult trials (11:32-35a) then gives way to a recital of the experience of others for whom deliverance came ultimately only through suffering and martyrdom (11:35b-38). The transition is effected by a change of subject in 11:35b-36 ("but others . . . and others . . ."), which is followed by a frank acknowledgment that the demonstration of invincible faith did not imply immunity from persecution, humiliation, and violent death.

260

The statement that "they were tortured after refusing to accept release" (11:35b) evokes a graphic impression of suffering without relief. The main verb *tympanizō* signifies "to beat to death," and so generally "to torture" (cf. Plutarch, *Moralia* 60A). The cognate noun *tympanon* denotes the "rack" or stake to which those who were beaten were fastened (cf. 2 Macc 6:19, 28), or the cudgel with which the beating was administered (cf. Aristophanes, *Plutus* 476). The reference in 11:35b may be to a form of torture in which a person was stretched out on a rack and his taut stomach beaten as one beats a drum, until the muscle walls collapsed and death occurred from internal injuries. From this practice the verb came to mean "to break on the wheel" (cf. *3 Maccabees* 3:27; Josephus, *Against Apion* 1.20, 148; Plutarch, *Dio* 28.2; for reference to the "wheel," see *4 Maccabees* 5:32; 8:13; 9:12, 17, 19, 20; 10:7; 11:10, 17; 15:22; Philo, *Against Flaccus* 10, 85). On the other hand, the reference may be to death by brutal scourging (cf. *4 Maccabees* 5:32; 6:3-6, 10; Tacitus, *Annals of Rome* 2.35.5; Suetonius, *Nero* 49; *Claudius* 34).

The experience of such savagery was one of recent memory for the Jewish community at Alexandria. As Philo tells us, there the Roman prefect Flaccus (appointed A.D. 32) arranged a spectacle in a theater that consisted of Jews "being scourged, hung up, bound to a wheel, brutally mauled and hauled off for their death march through the middle of the orchestra" (*Against Flaccus* 85). Those who were tortured in this manner had refused the opportunity to gain their freedom at the cost of renouncing their faith. They could have avoided torture and death had they been prepared to comply with the demands of their tormentors, but they resolutely refused to do so. They had been compelled to express their faith in the face of death.

The writer's statement in 11:35b is amply illustrated by the behavior of Eleazar, the ninety-year-old biblical scholar, who refused the pretense of renouncing commitment to God so that he might "be released from death" (2 Macc 6:22). He willingly chose the rack and endured a brutal beating. And, "when he was about to die under the blows, he groaned aloud and said: 'It is clear to the Lord in his holy knowledge that, though I might have been released from death, I am enduring terrible sufferings in my body through this beating, but in my soul I am glad to suffer these things because I fear him'" (2 Macc 6:30; cf. also 7:24).

The writer of Hebrews calls on the community to recognize that the resoluteness expressed by the ancient people of faith in their refusal of release was purposeful — "in order that they might obtain a better resurrection" (11:35b). The restoration of those who had died "by resurrection"

(11:35a) refers to a temporary gift of life, as sons were restored to their mothers. The vanquishing of death was only anticipated in their experience. It was not definitive; they would experience mortality again. It is, however, the final defeat of death in the experience of the eschatological resurrection that is contemplated in the phrase "the better resurrection" (11:35b), where the adjective "better" expresses a qualitative distinction. The contrast implied is between a temporary return to mortal life after coming so close to death and the experience of authentic, endless life — or, between resuscitation (11:35a) and final resurrection to life (11:35b).

The reference to the refusal of release and the enduring of torment in the context of a firm expectation of attaining the resurrection shows unmistakably that 11:35b alludes to 2 Macc 6:18–7:42. The Jewish historian recounts the martyrdom of Eleazar and of a mother and her seven sons at the hands of Antiochus IV Epiphanes and his officers. Specific reference is made to the hope of the resurrection in the account of the sufferings endured by three of the seven brothers, as well as in the encouragement offered to them by their mother (cf. 2 Macc 7:9, 11, 14, 22-23, 29). The defiant words of the fourth brother to Antiochus capture the spirit in which they all met their death: "One cannot but choose to die at the hands of men and to cherish the hope that God gives of being raised again by him. But for you there will be no resurrection to life!" (2 Macc 7:14).

The example of the Maccabean martyrs demonstrated the ability of faith to sustain a resilient spirit even in the face of dehumanizing abuse. Unwavering faith in God and firm belief in the resurrection proved to be the sources of enduring excruciating suffering and of moral courage in the face of death. And it was this aspect of the truth that the writer wanted the members of the Christian community that he addresses to grasp from his recital of those who clung to a foundational belief in the resurrection of the dead.

4. The Resurrection of Jesus from the Dead in Hebrews

Jesus' Solidarity with the Human Family

The writer of Hebrews makes much of Jesus' solidarity with the human family (2:5-18). This is affirmed especially in a meditation on Psalm 8 in 2:5-9, which speaks of the transcendent Son of God having made the human condition — particularly its liability to death — his own in order to achieve for humanity the glorious destiny designed by God. The incarnation set in motion a sequence of events in which abasement and humiliation were followed by exaltation. Jesus' full, authentic humanity had direct relevance for the community. His coronation and investiture with priestly glory and honor provided assurance that the power of sin and death had been nullified. The vision of the psalmist will yet be realized. In Jesus, therefore, the community of faith is to find the pledge of their own entrance into the imperial destiny intended by God for them.

Elaborating on his meditation, the writer asserts that what Jesus experienced was consistent with God's known character and purpose (2:10). It was congruous with the divine intention celebrated in Psalm 8 that God should graciously decree that his Son identify himself with humanity and rescue them through his own humiliation and death. The sufferings that Jesus endured were appropriate to the goal to be attained and were experienced in accordance with God's fixed purpose. Jesus' qualification to come before God in priestly action through the suffering of death opened the way for others to participate in the glory that he attained. It achieved deliverance from enslavement to the devil and the removal of a paralyzing fear of death (2:10-15).

A string of three quotations from the Old Testament in 2:12-13 illustrates that Jesus did not blush to identify himself with the people of God. The second quotation, taken from Isa 8:17 (cf. 2 Sam 22:3; Isa 12:2), is striking: "He also says, 'I will trust him'" (2:13a). In the context of his reference to suffering in 2:10, the writer here insists that Jesus had to exercise faith in the face of death. The citation had immediate relevance for the community addressed. The fact that Jesus' confidence was fully vindicated after he had experienced a shameful death assured the members of the community that they could also trust God in difficult circumstances.

Jesus as the Exemplar of Faith in the Face of Death

The portrait of Jesus as the perfect exemplar of faith in the face of death is sustained throughout Hebrews (cf., e.g., 5:7-8). In particular, it is brought before the community again in 12:2: "fixing our eyes upon Jesus, the champion in the exercise of faith and the one who brought faith to complete expression, who . . . endured a cross, disregarding the disgrace. . . ." The text is unusually dense and resists facile translation. Nonetheless, it calls for clarification in the light of the larger development in Hebrews.

In the context of 11:1-40, the term "faith" must be understood absolutely, as the believing response to God demonstrated by the host of witnesses and preeminently by Jesus himself. The poignant expression in 12:2 points to Jesus as the perfect embodiment of faith, who exercised faith heroically. By bringing faith to complete expression, he enabled others to follow his example. The description of Jesus reiterates and makes explicit what was affirmed with a biblical quotation in 2:13, that Jesus in his earthly life was the perfect exemplar of trust in God in the face of death.

In the light of the essential need for the community to exercise faith in the face of death, the almost total absence of a direct appeal to Jesus' resurrection is, at least initially, certainly surprising. An appeal to vindication through resurrection would have constituted a powerful argument for perseverance in faith and hope. In Hebrews, however, the emphasis is placed on Jesus' sacrifice and exaltation. This is evident already in the confessional formula invoked in the opening lines of the homily, "[This Son] made purification for sins and then sat down at the right hand of the divine Majesty on high" (1:3c). Thus the earthly ministry of the Son is described from the first in cultic categories. The brief, unadorned reference to "the purification of sins" is slanted in the direction of the later discussion of Jesus' priesthood and sacrifice. The exaltation of the Son to a position at God's right hand conveyed an impression of his royal power and unparalleled glory.

Implicit References to the Resurrection of Jesus

Early Christians were familiar with the notion of the Son's enthronement at God's right hand from their creedal confessions and hymns. They would recognize immediately the allusion to Ps 110:1 and the reference to the Son's exaltation after his resurrection. In 1:3, as well as elsewhere in Hebrews, the allusion to enthronement at God's right hand serves as an inclusive reference to Jesus' resurrection, ascension, and continuing reign. That the Son has been exalted to God's right hand, therefore, means that he lives and rules with the authority and power of God himself. In this understanding, a reference to Jesus' resurrection is implied.

The kerygmatic summary of Jesus' earthly life in 5:7, of course, contains no reference to Jesus' resurrection. It merely provides content to the assurance that he entered fully into the human condition. Jesus' solidarity with the human family wrung from him his prayers and entreaties, cries and tears. The writer of Hebrews appears to have been more sensitive to this dimension in the Jesus tradition than any other writer in the New Testament.

The assurance that when Jesus offered his prayers and entreaties to God "he was heard because of his godly fear" has frequently been considered in relationship to the description of God as "the one who could save him from death." That approach has led naturally to such questions as: "In what sense, then, was Jesus heard?" — for he was certainly not rescued from impending death; and, "Is this another implicit reference to the resurrection of Jesus?" — the assumption being that "hearing" could consist only in Jesus' deliverance from death.

It is preferable, however, to interpret "he was heard" with reference to the context that speaks of the offering of sacrifice (5:1, 3), and to recognize that "the one who was able to save him from death" is simply a traditional circumlocution for God (cf. Hos 13:14; Ps 32:19 LXX [Ps 33:19 MT]; James 4:12). It defines not the content of Jesus' prayers but the character of God as the Lord of life who acts for the accomplishment of redemption.

But while denying that a reference to Jesus' resurrection is to be found in 5:7, we may still recognize an implicit allusion to the resurrection of Jesus in 7:16, where the writer affirms that to be a priest like Melchizedek is to be a priest "by the power of an indestructible life" *(kata dynamin zōēs akatalytou)*. The context develops the writer's argument that Jesus is an eternal priest like Melchizedek, and that the quality of his priesthood is superior to that of the Aaronic priesthood, which was based on a physical line of descent (7:11-25).

The adjective "indestructible" *(akatalyton)*, which occurs elsewhere in Jewish Greek writings only in *4 Maccabees* 10:11, appears to have been carefully chosen. It was well suited to assert that, although Jesus' human life was exposed to destruction through crucifixion, his life was not destroyed by the death that he suffered on a Roman cross. The phrase "the power of an indestructible life" describes the quality of life with which Jesus has been endowed by virtue of his resurrection and exaltation to the heavenly world, where he was formally installed in his office as high priest. The reference is to an objective event, rather than to a quality of life that belonged to Jesus inherently. The power of life that the resurrection conferred on Jesus demonstrated that his priesthood is not limited by the temporal character of the old Aaronic priesthood based on physical descent. Rather, it is undergirded by a power that overcame mortality and corruption, and consequently is beyond the reach of death. The acknowledgment that Jesus is a priest "like Melchizedek," therefore, implies that he is priest by virtue of his resurrection.

Explicit Reference to the Resurrection of Jesus

The only direct reference in Hebrews to the resurrection of Jesus is found in the fervent prayer-wish of 13:20-21, which serves to summarize the concerns of the previous section and to provide formal closure to the sermon as a whole. What is only implicit elsewhere (e.g., in 1:3; 7:16, 24) is here made explicit.

The prayer consists of an invocation of God, followed by two strophes of four lines each, both of which end with the name of Jesus, and a concluding doxology, which is directed to God (cf. Jewett, "Form and Function of the Homiletical Benediction," 20-25). The two strophes of the prayer provide a kerygmatic recital of divine activity as the ground of the writer's confidence in God's ability and willingness to mature his work within the Christian community, enabling them to do his will in an acceptable manner. The prayer-wish is attached to its setting by the connective "and" (which ought to be translated), which shows that it is intrinsically related to the preceding unit of discourse. The fact that the prayer-wish takes up central themes from the homily indicates that the formulation was not simply taken over from some preformed liturgical expression, but is to be seen as being organically related to the development of the sermon.

The invocation of "the God of peace" is expanded through a participial clause that points to the objective reality of God's saving action:

> And may the God of peace, who led out from the dead the great Shepherd of the sheep, by virtue of the blood of the eternal covenant, our Lord Jesus, make you complete with everything good to do his will, accomplishing in us what is pleasing to him through Jesus Christ. To him be glory forever. Amen.

The formulation indicates that the writer had been reflecting on Isa 63:11-14 LXX:

> Heb 13:20 — "who led out from the dead the great shepherd of the sheep"
>
> Isa 63:11-14 — "who brought up out of the land the shepherd of the sheep. . . . He who led forth . . . Moses. . . . He led them. . . . Thus you led your people to make for yourself a glorious name."

The reference in Isa 63:11-14 (LXX) is to God's appointment of Moses as the leader of Israel in the deliverance from Egypt. Moses, the shepherd of Midian (Exod 3:1), is the model for "the great shepherd" Jesus. According to Isa 63:11-14, Moses was "led forth as the shepherd of the flock." The entire people are specified as the object of God's leading.

This is also true of Jesus, who was led forth from the realm of the dead. Through him God has begun to lead his flock in order to make a glorious name for himself. That action will be completed when the flock of God is brought to an experience of celebratory rest (cf. Isa 63:14 LXX; Heb 2:10; 4:9). Appointment to the office of "shepherd" is the goal of the leading forth of Jesus from among the dead. The resurrection of Jesus, therefore, demonstrates God's decisive intervention by which he acknowledged and ratified Jesus' death on the cross as the means of the redemption of the human family.

The writer's choice of the compound verb "to lead out" or "bring up" to express the powerful intervention of God is consistent with the use of the cognate verb "to lead" in Isa 63:12-14 LXX. The work of "leading out" is the fundamental redemptive activity of God under both the old and new covenants. On it are based the exclusive claim of God to his people's allegiance as well as the ground for trust in God's power and readiness to sustain his covenant people in adversity. The intervention of God in leading his people out from Egypt in the Torah (e.g., Exod 6:7; 20:1-2; Lev 19:36; 25:38; 26:13; Num 5:31; Deut 5:6) and in the Prophets (e.g., Isa 64:11-14) and out from the realm of the dead in the Psalter (e.g., Ps 30:3; 71:20; 86:13) prefigured his decisive action in raising Jesus from the dead.

Jeremiah had prophesied that the old formula that spoke of "leading out" would be replaced by a new one (Jer 16:14-15; 23:7-8), which would belong integrally to the new covenant (Jer 31:31-34 MT; 38:31-34 LXX). The comment on Jer 31:31-34 and the full citation of the text in Heb 8:6-13 is recalled in 13:20 with the reference to "the eternal covenant." The formulation in 13:20 is, therefore, grounded in the conviction that God has established a new covenant with his people through the "leading out" of Jesus from the realm of the dead. This leading forth of Jesus is, for the new and eternal covenant, the fundamental action of God, which has replaced the foundational acts of salvation under the old covenant. It provides the ground of the obligation to obey God in a manner "pleasing to him" (13:21). And it is the basis for the writer's confidence that God will hear and respond favorably to his prayer for the community.

The presence of this homiletical benediction in 13:20-21 indicates the writer's awareness that his homily will be read aloud as the members of the community gather for worship. The prayer-wish brings the sermon to its conclusion on the note of a pastoral prayer for the men and women of the community. They are to find in the resurrection of Jesus the factual basis for Christian faith and hope. And they are to recognize in the decisive intervention of God in leading forth Jesus from the realm of the dead as the great Shepherd of the flock that God has an exclusive claim on their allegiance and that they may trust God for their future — even as Jesus trusted God, particularly in the face of death.

Selected Bibliography

Attridge, Harold W. *A Commentary on the Epistle to the Hebrews*. Philadelphia: Fortress, 1989.

Bruce, F. F. *The Epistle to the Hebrews*. Rev. ed. Grand Rapids: Eerdmans, 1990.

deSilva, D. A. *Despising Shame: Honor Discourse and Community Maintenance in the Epistle to the Hebrews*. Atlanta: Scholars Press, 1995.

Ellingworth, P. *Commentary on Hebrews*. Grand Rapids: Eerdmans, 1993.

Hay, David M. *Glory at the Right Hand: Psalm 110 in Early Christianity*. Nashville: Abingdon, 1973.

Hurst, Lincoln D. *The Epistle to the Hebrews: Its Background of Thought*. Cambridge: Cambridge University Press, 1990.

Jewett, Robert. "The Form and Function of the Homiletical Benediction." *Anglican Theological Review* 51 (1969) 18-34.

Lane, William L. *Hebrews: A Call to Commitment*. Peabody, Mass.: Hendrickson, 1987.

————. *Hebrews*. 2 vols. Dallas: Word, 1991.

————. "Preaching and Exegesis in the First Century: Hebrews." In *Sharing Heaven's Music: The Heart of Christian Preaching. Essays in Honor of James Earl Massey*, edited by B. L. Callen. Nashville: Abingdon, 1995, 83-94.

————. "Hebrews as Pastoral Response." In *Newell Lectureships*, vol. 3, edited by T. Dwyer. Anderson, Ind.: Warner, 1996, 103-201.

————. "Standing Before the Moral Claim of God: Discipleship in Hebrews." In *Patterns of Discipleship in the New Testament*, edited by R. N. Longenecker. Grand Rapids: Eerdmans, 1996, 203-24.

Lewis, T. W. "'. . . And If He Shrinks Back' (Heb. X.38b)." *New Testament Studies* 22 (1975) 88-94.

Swetnam, James. *Jesus and Isaac: A Study of the Epistle to the Hebrews in the Light of the Aqedah*. Rome: Biblical Institute Press, 1981.

CHAPTER 12

Witness and the Resurrection
in the Apocalypse of John

ALLISON A. TRITES

CHRISTIANS HAVE often faced situations that have resulted in personal and social opposition, emotional trauma, physical suffering, and even death. History records numerous cases of believers in Jesus being persecuted and martyred for their faith. There are reports from many sources that such activities against Christians continue today in various parts of the world.

What does the resurrection message of the New Testament have to say to believers facing such oppression? How are Christians to live their lives in the face of persecution and death — whether present reality or future threat; whether real or perceived; whether official or unofficial? The Apocalypse of John, or Book of Revelation, offers a presentation of the Christian life in the face of hostility and opposition that is both challenging and encouraging. It is a revelatory word from God that has been given for the guidance of God's people both past and present.

1. Introduction

The Circumstances

The circumstances giving rise to the writing of the Johannine apocalypse have traditionally been associated with the persecutions of the Roman emperor Domitian (A.D. 81-96), which were mounted at various times during his reign against Jews and others, but in his later years were directed also against Christians. Eusebius of Caesarea, the fourth-century bishop and church historian, explicitly makes this association in his *Ecclesiastical History:*

> Domitian, indeed, having exercised his cruelty against many, and unjustly slain no small number of noble and illustrious men at Rome, and having, without cause, punished vast numbers of honorable men with exile and the confiscation of their property, at length established himself as the successor of Nero, in his hatred and hostility to God. He was the second that raised a persecution against us, although his father Vespasian had attempted nothing to our prejudice. (3.17; cf. 3.18-20; 4.26.5-11)

This view of the Johannine apocalypse vis-à-vis Domitian's persecution was held by many early Church Fathers — for example, Irenaeus (*Against Heresies* 5.30.3, written sometime during A.D. 182-188) and Tertullian (*Apology* 5, written sometime during A.D. 193-216).

Lately, however, it has been argued that much of Domitian's negative reputation was undeserved and that no persecution was sponsored by him against Christians, either officially or unofficially (cf., e.g., T. D. Barnes, "Legislation against the Christians," *Journal of Roman Studies* 58 [1968] 32-50; L. F. Janssen, "'Superstitio' and the Persecution of Christians," *Vigiliae Christianae* 33 [1979] 131-59; P. Keresztes, "The Imperial Roman Government and the Christian Church," in *Aufstieg und Niedergang der römischen Welt* II.23.2 [1980] 247-315; R. MacMullen, *Christianizing the Roman Empire* [New Haven: Yale University Press, 1984]; B. W. Jones, *The Emperor Domitian* [London: Routledge, 1993]). Thus it is often proposed today that the Johannine apocalypse is responding either (1) to a perceived persecution that did not actually exist at the time, but which the writer viewed as imminent, or (2) to some local opposition against Christians, such as broke out sporadically at various places in the Roman empire, but which the seer of the Apocalypse viewed as being paradigmatic of Roman persecution generally.

In any event, John had been deported to Patmos, an island in the south Aegean Sea just off the coast of Asia Minor and west of Miletus and Ephesus. There he was imprisoned "because of the word of God and the testimony of Jesus" (1:9). Furthermore, Antipas, who is the only Christian martyr mentioned in the Apocalypse of John, had been killed in the city of Pergamum because of his "faithful witness" (2:13). Together, if nothing else, these events could well have triggered the perception of an imminent, widespread and officially sanctioned persecution. And in any event, the Apocalypse of John speaks to issues of how one lives out one's Christian life when facing persecution and the peril of death — whether that threat was then actually occurring or only perceived as being either imminent or possible.

The Major Characters

Believers in Jesus who were seen to be facing persecution are, of course, the addressees of the Johannine apocalypse. It is their situation — whether real, anticipated, or perceived — that is symbolically described in the writing. And it is to them that the words of this apocalypse must be understood as having primary relevance, even though it also has significance for all Christians who would later suffer hostility and opposition.

The oppressors of God's people are portrayed in various ways. A great whore is depicted in chapter 17, who corresponds to the city of Babylon in chapter 18. She is described as "the woman" who "was drunk with the blood of the saints and the blood of the witnesses to Jesus" (17:6). Furthermore, she is spoken of as sitting on seven hills (17:9) — a broad hint that Rome is in view, for the center of the empire was located there, and the seven kings mentioned fit the historical situation of the late first century A.D. Also in chapter 17 there is introduced a "beast," who stands as the archetypal symbol of the persecution of the church. The beast "goes to destruction" (17:11), and the fall of the great city "Babylon" (i.e., Rome) is the cause of profound rejoicing by the vindicated people of God (18:20). It is, therefore, the imperial persecutors of the church who are evidently being singled out.

Of greatest significance, however, is the presence of God. It is the person of God in the Apocalypse who must be reckoned with as the divine judge (note the use of the noun *krima*, "judgment," in 17:1 and 18:20, and the verb *krinein*, "to judge," in 16:5; 18:8, 20; and 19:2). Likewise, a major feature in John's presentation is his Christology. For Jesus is portrayed by John as the suffering Savior and victorious Lord who is worthy to be praised in worship: "For you were slaughtered and by your blood you ransomed for God saints from every tribe and language and people and nation" (5:9).

Jesus is presented in the Apocalypse as the model of conduct in the face of suffering, persecution, and death (note the references to the "blood" of Jesus in 1:5; 5:9; 7:14; 12:11, and to Jesus being "dead" in 1:18; 2:8). He is the true paradigm for the saints, because he endured all of these experiences and came through with flying colors — a point abundantly demonstrated by his resurrection. Jesus, therefore, is depicted as "the faithful and true witness" (3:14), and genuine believers are called to follow him through thick and thin, for he has "the keys of Death and of Hades" (1:18).

The Call for Faithfulness

John's message was intended to bolster loyalty to Christ in a time of testing and suffering. It was written to remind Christians that they are responsible to God for their stewardship of the gospel. Just as Jesus is referred to as being "called," "chosen," and "faithful" in the canonical Gospels, so also Christians are described as "his called, chosen and faithful followers" (17:14).

A tremendous emphasis is placed in the Johannine apocalypse on believers in Christ being "faithful" *(pistos)*, with this call for faithfulness being presented against the backdrop of both Christ's death and the death of those loyal martyrs who have followed in his train. Christ himself, who is described as "the firstborn of the dead," is depicted as totally faithful (1:5), and the seer's addressees are told to act in the same way in the letter to Smyrna (2:10). Antipas was faithful to his Lord, and for that faithfulness was "killed" (2:13). And those who support the Lamb in his war against the beast are praised as "called, chosen and faithful" (17:14).

As their spiritual "brother" *(adelphos;* see 1:9; 6:11; 12:10; 19:10; 22:9) and "fellow servant" *(syndoulos;* see 19:10; 22:9), John had a bond of kinship with Christians in these Asian churches who were struggling to "hold fast" their Christian faith (cf. the use of *krateō* in 2:13, 25; 3:11). Thus he addressed them with sympathy, but also challenge. He was a spokesman for God who had a much needed message to deliver, and he attempted to carry out his mandate with fidelity. The words directed to the church at Smyrna may be taken as typical of the ringing call to commitment he laid before all the churches he was addressing: "Do not fear what you are about to suffer. Beware, the devil is about to throw some of you into prison so that you may be tested, and . . . you will have affliction. Be faithful unto death, and I [the risen, conquering Christ] will give you the crown of life" (2:10).

273

John's prophetic words were designed to produce "conquerors" — people who would prove absolutely loyal to Christ in the face of suffering and persecution. Indeed, each Christian community was offered wonderful divine promises for those who would conquer in the times of testing that confronted them (cf. 2:7, 11, 17, 26; 3:5, 12, 21). They were to bear their witness as Christ had borne his. And they were to suffer for their convictions out of sheer faithfulness to his cause: "If you are to be taken captive, into captivity you go; if you kill with the sword you must be killed. Here is a call for the endurance and faith of the saints" (13:10). In such circumstances "perseverance" was a much needed virtue (cf. the use of *hypomonē* in 1:9; 2:2, 3, 19; 3:10; 13:10; 14:12).

Against such a threatening prospect, the concept of "witness" (*martyria*, from which our word "martyr" is derived) is clearly prominent in the Apocalypse. Christian people were being called to bear witness for Christ. But with the prospect of persecution, they faced the real temptation to soft-pedal their convictions or even to deny their faith (the verb *apokteinō* is used to describe believers who were "killed" in 2:13; 6:11; 11:7; 13:15). John himself had suffered for his faith in Christ and was therefore speaking to his addressees out of his own pain and distress. He was not only a "brother" and "fellow servant," but also a "partner" (*synkoinōnos*, 1:9) in the Christian enterprise, with all of the anguish that such a relationship entailed in times of persecution.

2. "The Testimony of Jesus"

The Background of the Testimony

In the Fourth Gospel, Jesus offers his testimony in the court of Pontius Pilate, the Roman governor, and challenges his enemies to testify against him if they are able to do so (cf. John 18:23, 37). None of his opponents, however, is able to prove him guilty of any sin. Pilate, in fact, repeatedly declares Jesus to be innocent of the charges laid against him (John 18:38; 19:4, 6; cf. Luke 23:4, 14, 22).

This same controversy — or lawsuit — regarding the claims of Christ reappears in the Book of Revelation, where persecuted followers of Christ will be required to stand in Roman courts and to acknowledge their faith in Christ before pagan judges. In such unfriendly, adverse situations they will be called to offer faithful witness for their Lord — being conscious always that their evidence is also being heard in the heavenly court, where judgments that are just and true issue from the divine throne (20:11-15).

The letters to the seven churches in chapters 2 and 3 are particularly instructive at this point. In the message to the church at Sardis, for example, Christ promises to acknowledge or "confess" the faithful Christian witness before God the Father in the heavenly court (so 3:5, using the significant verb *homologeō*, "confess"). This passage reminds one of the similar promise of Christ recorded in logia (or "Q") material of the Gospel tradition: "Everyone therefore who acknowledges me before others, I also will acknowledge before my Father in heaven" (Matt 10:32; Luke 12:8). Here the witness theme is of paramount importance, as it is in a similar passage in Paul (cf. Rom 10:9-10).

The converse is also stated: "But whoever denies me before others, I also will deny before my Father in heaven" (Matt 10:33; Luke 12:9). Refusal to bear witness for Christ was viewed as a serious matter having significant consequences. Thus the message to the church at Philadelphia commends believers who have not "denied" Christ's name (3:8; *arneomai* is used here, as in the Gospels, to indicate the opposite of witnessing; cf. Matt 26:70, 72; Mark 14:68, 70; Luke 22:57; John 13:38; 18:25, 27). Similarly, the message to the church at Pergamum takes special note of the fact that believers there have not "denied" their faith in Christ (2:13). It was vitally important to "keep" Christ's word (observe the repeated use of *tēreō* in 3:8, 10, as well as in 1:3; 2:26; 3:3; 12:17; 14:12; 22:7, 9).

Plainly, these were difficult days to serve God. But Christian witness was of vital importance if Christianity was to survive. Though they might be hauled into court and compelled to offer testimony under hostile circumstances, God was still actively seeking to speak to them through the Holy Spirit (cf. 2:7, 11, 17, 29; 3:6, 13, 22). The predictions of Jesus about future persecution were coming true: "They will hand you over to councils and flog you . . . and you will be dragged before governors and kings because of me, as a testimony to them and the Gentiles" (Matt 10:17). They were at those times also, however, to be the recipients of the promised Holy Spirit: "When they bring you before the synagogues, the rulers, and the authorities, do not worry about how you are to defend yourselves or what you are to say; for the Holy Spirit will teach you at that very hour what you ought to say" (Luke 12:11-12). These promises were now being realized as God gave "the saints" (*hoi hagioi*, which is one of the seer's favorite terms for believers; cf. 11:18; 13:7, 10; 14:12; 16:6; 18:20) the power to endure. The "prayers of the saints" were helpful in this connection (5:8; 8:3-4) — in fact, highly significant in the spiritual battle that was being waged.

In such a period of testing, John was acutely aware that "perilous times" (cf. 2 Tim 3:1, KJV) were facing the church. He knew that the Roman proconsul in the province of Asia had real legal power over Christians, for, as Paul said, "the authority does not bear the sword in vain!" (Rom 13:4). Still, he knew that ultimate judicial power rested in Christ's hands. So his focus was appropriately christocentric, directing attention to the one who possessed "the sharp, two-edged sword" (1:16; 2:12). And he attempted to reinforce in his addressees' consciousness the realization that it was the living Christ, and not Caesar's minion, who possessed final authority, and that this Christ was indeed "King of kings and Lord of lords" (19:16; cf. 1:5; 17:14).

John was a Christian prophet (22:9) and repeatedly calls his book a "prophecy" (*prophēteia*, 1:3; 22:7, 10, 18, 19). It was perfectly clear that followers of Christ would soon be hauled into Roman courts of law and sentenced to die if they maintained a faithful Christian witness (6:9; 13:10; cf. Matt 10:18; Luke 21:12). Antipas had suffered martyrdom for his faithful testimony (2:13). Other loyal Christians might well be expected to suffer in a similar way if they held "the testimony of Jesus."

The Intended Meaning and Response

But what did John understand by the phrase "the testimony of Jesus"? And what kind of a response was he looking for when he spoke to his fellow believers in such distressing times?

It is necessary, first of all, to consider the special nature of this phrase. "The testimony of Jesus" is not found in either the Fourth Gospel or the Johannine letters. Nonetheless, it appears prominently in the Apocalypse. Likewise, it is necessary to ask how the phrase should be understood, for it has been interpreted in several ways. From the standpoint of Greek grammar, it can mean either "the testimony offered by Jesus" (a subjective genitive interpretation) or "the testimony given about Jesus" by his followers (an objective genitive interpretation). Only a detailed study of the actual passages where this phrase is used will enable us to decide which interpretation is the more credible.

The first passage where the phrase is used is 1:2: "Who [John] testifies to everything he saw — that is, the word of God and the testimony of Jesus Christ." Here either meaning is possible, but the subjective genitive interpretation seems preferable in view of the phrase that precedes it. Thus "the testimony of Jesus" probably should be taken to mean "the witness that Christ imparts." Similarly 1:9, "the word of God and the testimony of Jesus," makes excellent sense when viewed as using subjective genitive constructions — thereby referring to "the word spoken by God and the testimony borne by Jesus"; as does also 12:17, "the commandments of God and the testimony of Jesus," when taken in this manner — thereby meaning "the commandments given by God and the testimony borne by Jesus." This interpretation receives additional support from the comment of the seer in 19:10: "For the testimony offered by Jesus is the spirit that inspires the prophets."

The other references to "testimony" point in the same direction. Thus John can speak of the souls of those who had been slain "for the word of God and for the testimony they had given" (6:9). Clearly there is a reminder here of the testimony of Jesus mentioned in 1:2 and 9, but the words "of Jesus" are missing. Still, the meaning must point in that direction. Thus the "word" here is the word provided by God, and the "testimony" is the testimony offered by Jesus. An objective genitive interpretation, in fact, is impossible in this passage, for the phrase "which they held" plainly "demands a witness that had previously been delivered to them by Christ and which they have loyally kept and maintained. For this testimony offered by Christ they were prepared to sacrifice their lives as martyrs" (Trites, *New Testament Witness in Today's World*, 121).

Two other passages in the Apocalypse support this view. The first is 11:7, where the reader is told that the two witnesses are killed "when they have finished their testimony"; the second is 12:11, where the Christian witnesses are said to have "conquered" Satan, their accuser, "by the blood of the Lamb and by the word of their testimony." In each of these cases "their testimony" refers to "the testimony which they gave." The reference is plainly to witness offered in extremely trying circumstances.

Thus all of the references to the testimony of Jesus in the Apocalypse can be consistently interpreted as references to the testimony given by him, rather than as the testimony about him (as many commentators have suggested). It is this wonderful testimony by Christ himself that has been committed to his people, the church. It is their solemn duty to preserve it and maintain it, however costly this may prove. Ultimately, of course, Jesus is "the Word of God" (19:13), so the testimony that he bears has a distinctly christocentric character. As in John's Gospel, the message to which Jesus bears witness in the long run concerns himself as the only completely true and faithful witness of God the Father (1:5; 3:14; cf. John 7:16-18; 18:37). His witness is unmarred by duplicity or sinfulness of any kind. So it must be respected and preserved at any cost by those who are his true disciples.

The Faithful and True Witness

How, then, does Jesus bear witness to the redemptive purpose of God? At the very beginning of his apocalypse, John has provided a significant clue. For in 1:4-5 he notes that the divine blessing comes not only from God and the Holy Spirit (in apocalyptic language, "the seven spirits who are before his throne"), but also from "Jesus Christ, the faithful witness, the firstborn of the dead, and the ruler of the kings of the earth." In this remarkable statement the seer uses three significant titles to describe Christ.

First he depicts him as the "faithful witness," recalling such Old Testament passages as Ps 89:37; Prov 14:5, 25; and Isa 8:2. Then he uses two messianic titles taken from Ps 89:27 that speak of "the firstborn, the highest of the kings of the earth." Putting these three titles together chronologically, he highlights Jesus' earthly life, his ministry, and his passion — when he bore "faithful witness," when he conquered death by his resurrection, and when in both the present and the future he exercises lordship over the potentates of the world. Here the resurrection and exaltation of Christ are placed against the somber background of his death. In this way, the costliness of Jesus bearing witness and laying down his life is underscored.

In his earthly life — and preeminently in his passion — Jesus had come to grips with the opposition of ungodly people. This was supremely true when he made "the good confession" before Pontius Pilate (cf. 1 Tim 6:13). He had borne witness to the truth (cf. John 18:37) and therefore could justly be described as "the faithful witness" (Rev 1:5; 3:14). The truthfulness and self-giving nature of Jesus' witness were beyond dispute. So the song of the myriads in heaven is altogether appropriate: "Worthy is the Lamb that was slaughtered to receive power and wealth and wisdom and might and honor and glory and blessing!" (5:12).

Christ is presented in the Apocalypse as the powerful one who by his sacrifice has won the victory over the forces of evil. This is the point suggested apocalyptically in the picture of the rider on the white horse who is called Faithful and True:

> He [Christ] is clothed in a robe dipped in blood, and his name is called "The Word of God." And the armies of heaven, wearing fine linen, white and pure, were following him on white horses. . . . On his robe and on his thigh he has a name inscribed, "King of kings and Lord of lords." (19:11-16)

Here is portrayed no "gentle Jesus, meek and mild." Here, rather, is the conquering hero who leads the forces of godliness to a glorious conquest over the demonic forces ranged against him and his people.

The campaign waged by Jesus had been a difficult one. That point is emphatically made in the Apocalypse in a number of ways. First of all, the seer acknowledges the historical reality of Jesus' death. Jesus had truly died (cf. the use of *nekros* in 1:18; 2:8). Furthermore, using sacrificial language, John says that Christ had been "slaughtered" (cf. the verb *sphazō* in 5:6, 9, 12; 13:8). However, he had subsequently "come to life" (*ezēsen*, 2:8), and so is designated "the living One" (*ho zōn*, 1:18). Now by virtue of his conquest of death he can justly be described as "the firstborn of the dead" (*ho prōtotokos tōn nekrōn*, 1:5; cf. Col 1:15, 18). In addition, he is spoken of as "the Alpha and the Omega, the first and the last," using language reserved elsewhere for God alone (cf. 1:17; 21:6; 22:13; see also 1:8 and Isa 41:4; 44:6; 48:12).

Jesus had to cope with false witnesses, rejection, and death. He had truly suffered, leaving believers in him an example that they should "follow" (cf. the use of *akoloutheō* with respect to the 144,000 in 14:4 and the armies of heaven in 19:14; see also 1 Pet 2:21). Because he had "conquered," he made victory possible for those who would come after him and face the same hostile conditions: "To the one who conquers I will give a place with me on my throne, just as I myself conquered and sat down with my Father on his throne" (3:21). A shared battle results in a shared victory. Thus, "John set the Lord before his persecuted followers as the ideal witness, who suffered and died but remained true to the end. . . . By remembering their crucified Lord, who is now 'ruler of the kings of the world' . . . they are to take fresh courage as they steel themselves for possible martyrdom" (Trites, *New Testament Witness in Today's World*, 123).

279

ALLISON A. TRITES

3. The Testimony of Christians

What kind of witness did John expect his fellow Christians to offer in such difficult times? The testimony of faithful Christians was to be in keeping with that of their Lord. It involved utter loyalty to the gospel. But believers in Jesus were to take encouragement from the fact that the living Christ had traveled the same road before them. He knew what they were going through (cf. the repeated use of *oida*, "I know," in the letters to the seven churches in 2:2, 9, 13, 19; 3:1, 8, 15). More than that, he was "walking" with them now (cf. the use of *peripateō* in 2:1 and 3:4; see also Gen 3:8; 5:22; Deut 23:14). Truly the exalted Christ was "in the midst of" the churches, which are symbolically referred to as the "seven golden lampstands" (1:12, 20; 2:1).

Christ had "conquered" the forces of evil by remaining faithful even unto death (5:5), and they were to conquer in the same costly way: "They conquered him [the devil] by the blood of the Lamb and by the word of their testimony, for they did not cling to life even in the face of death" (12:11; note the prominence of the verb *nikaō*, "conquer": 2:7, 11, 17, 26; 3:5, 12, 21; 6:2; 11:7; 13:7; 15:2; 17:14; 21:7). This meant that they must not flinch in the face of virulent opposition but be willing to suffer and die for Christ if necessary. Their instructions were clearly given and unmistakable: "Be faithful until death, and I will give you the crown of life" (2:10). Complete faithfulness and absolute commitment were required and demanded. The prophet was quite uncompromising in stating his expectations of believers in the face of the impending crisis.

When God fails to intervene as quickly as expected, the pain of unresolved suffering becomes intense. John the seer faced this issue head-on. Thus when the fifth seal is opened, he sees under the altar the "souls of those who had been slaughtered for the word of God and for the testimony they had given" (6:9). Their cries call out for vindication by a just God: "Sovereign Lord (*ho despotēs;* cf. Acts 4:24-30), holy and true, how long will it be before you judge and avenge our blood on the inhabitants of the earth?" (6:10). They are given white robes, which are symbolic of their ultimate victory, and told to wait until the full complement of their "fellow servants" has been killed — with an implied assurance that divine intervention would then come (6:11).

The sealing of the 144,000 follows in chapter 7, which reminds the servants of God of their divine protection. Despite appearances, God was in charge. The seer of Patmos saw the ancient promise of the psalmist being truly fulfilled: "He will command his angels concerning you to guard you in all your ways" (Ps 91:11). Divine sovereignty, in fact, is repeatedly asserted throughout the Apocalypse (note the frequent use of the divine passive "it was given," *edothē,* in 6:2, 4, 8, 11; 7:2; 8:3; 9:1, 3, 5; 13:5, 7, 14, 15; 16:8). God had not forgotten his people in the midst of their suffering and pain. Apocalyptic writers looked for a speedy divine intervention on behalf of God's suffering people. And the use of "soon" *(tachy)* in 3:11; 22:7, 12, and 20 — in answer to the burning question "How long?" of 6:10 — indicates that John was no exception.

4. The Testimony of the Resurrection

The testimony of Christians in the Apocalypse of John is predicated on the resurrection of Christ. Without his personal conquest of the grave, there would be no message of hope and no inspiration for martyrs to give their lives. John shares the perspective voiced by Paul in 1 Cor 15:19: "If in this life only we have hope in Christ, we are of all people most to be pitied." That is, if death had destroyed Jesus, there would be no word of encouragement to offer those who have placed their trust in him as Savior of the world and Lord of history.

The Resurrection Victory of Christ over Death

It is not surprising, therefore, that the Book of Revelation places a tremendous emphasis on the victory of Christ over death that was expressed so decisively in his resurrection. It was of the utmost practical importance for John to remind suffering Christians that Jesus Christ had conquered death, and that therefore they could expect to share in his eternal victory over sin and death if they remained faithful. As J. Denny Weaver observes concerning the celebratory note that is sounded in the Apocalypse — as, for example, in 5:9-10 and 12:

> The celebration concerns the fact that the confrontation has already ended in a victory for the forces representing God, namely the church. That victory occurs with the resurrection of Jesus . . . [and involves] a

281

specific historical confrontation (between church and empire). . . . [Thus the resurrection] is the beginning of a working out in history of the victory of church over world. At the same time, the existence of suffering in the world and the reality of the ongoing confrontation underscore that the culmination of the victory is future, and the motif of victory is not interpreted as triumphalism. (Weaver, "Atonement," 312-13)

The victory of Christ was won through suffering, self-giving love. It involved both words and deeds, and it demands complete commitment. The servants of God are summoned to win their victory over the forces ranged against them in the same way. Like the readers of Hebrews, they are challenged to "run with perseverance the race" that was set before them, "looking to Jesus the pioneer and perfecter" of their faith (cf. Heb 12:2). This is why they must leave their tormentors in the hands of God. For the judge of all the earth will do right (cf. Gen 18:25); God is both holy and just (Rev 16:5), and his judgments are "just" and "true" (*dikaioi* and *alēthinai*, which are two key words in John's vocabulary; cf. 15:3; 16:7; 19:2). Though divine intervention may be delayed, it will come at the appointed "time" *(kairos)*, for God's promised deliverance is "near" (1:3; 22:10), and his people will be vindicated as surely as Christ was vindicated. On the other hand, God has determined the exact "day" *(hēmera)* and "hour" *(hōra)* when he will punish the enemies of his servants (9:15; cf. 11:13; 14:7, 15; 18:10, 17, 19).

The great assurance suffering servants of God have been given is the resurrection of Jesus, "the firstborn from the dead" (1:5). In the opening vision the seer of Patmos has an apocalyptic vision of Christ, who encourages him with the words "I am . . . the living one. I was dead, and see, I am alive forever and ever; and I have the keys of Death and of Hades. Now write what you have seen, what is, and what is to take place after this" (1:17-19). In other words, it is because of the victory of Christ over death that John is able to offer a message of hope and encouragement to his Christian compatriots in the face of persecution and martyrdom. The eternal God whom they serve is presented as "Almighty," the one "who is and who was and who is to come"; he is also described as "the Alpha and the Omega" (1:8), titles used of Christ in the following vision and elsewhere in the book (cf. 1:17; 2:8; 22:13). It is by virtue of the Lord's victory over death that he can properly be described with the attributes of deity.

Thus the letters to the seven churches are seen as coming from the risen Lord, the mighty victor over death who is alive, walking among the churches — as highlighted particularly in 3:20: "I am now standing at the door and knocking" (Williams' translation) — and possessing complete omnipotence and omniscience in dealing with their respective situations. He is the one who "knows" absolutely their moral and spiritual condition, and he has total power both to execute judgment and to bring help to his struggling people. It is this resurrection message that John offered to his fellow believers in symbolic form — a message intended to bring blessing to those who read it aloud and heed its call to repentance, faith, and tenacious loyalty to Christ.

The prophecy announced by the seer is of great importance for the spiritual health of every Christian community and every individual believer. Each must answer personally the call to faithfulness: "Let everyone who has an ear listen to what the Spirit is saying to the churches" (2:7, 11, 17, 29; 3:6, 13, 22; cf. the similar instruction given by Jesus in the parable of the sower in Matt 13:9; Mark 4:9; Luke 8:8). The very repetition of the summons to hear is meant as a reminder of the urgent importance of the prophecy. God is giving his people definite instruction for a critical time in their experience, and they must pay careful attention to receive it with due thoughtfulness and humility.

Repentance, therefore, is frequently called for in the Apocalypse (note the frequency of the verb "repent," *metanoeō*, in 2:5 [twice], 16, 21, 22; 3:3, 19; 9:20, 21; 16:9, 11). It is one of the tragic features of the book that unregenerate people, who are often described as "the inhabitants of the earth" (cf. 3:10; 6:10; 8:13; 11:10 [twice]; 13:8, 12, 14 [twice]; 17:2, 8), fail to repent and so must experience the terrible punitive judgments of God. These judgments are spelled out by the seven seals (6:1-17), the seven trumpets (8:6–9:21), the seven plagues (15:1-8), and the seven bowls of wrath (16:1-21). On the other hand, the conquest of Christ gives occasion for songs of deepest praise (e.g., 19:1-10).

"The First Resurrection"

Some attention must now be given to the theme of "the first resurrection" *(hē anastasis hē prōtē)*, an expression that appears only in 20:5-6 (twice). This designation appears in the context of the portrayals of the binding of Satan and the millennium in 20:1-10. The millennium is, of course, a highly controversial topic (for helpful discussions, see Erickson, *Contemporary Options,* and Grenz, *Millennial Maze*). Whatever position one takes, it must not be used as a litmus test for orthodoxy.

At the outset, several observations are in order. First, these ten verses of 20:1-10 contain all the specific teaching in the Bible on the thousand-year reign of Christ and are found in a writing that often uses numbers in a symbolic way. For example, the number seven appears some fifty-two times in the Apocalypse to signal the idea of completeness. Such a symbolic use of numbers suggests that great care needs to be taken in the interpretation of the millennium and in one's understanding of the use of numbers elsewhere in the Apocalypse. With respect to the thousand-year period of 20:1-10, Bruce M. Metzger's words are appropriate: "As other numerals in this book are to be understood symbolically, and not literally, so this period of a thousand years represents the perfection and completion of the martyrs' reign with Christ, untroubled by Satan's wiles" (*The New Oxford Annotated Bible, New Testament,* 385).

Second, the details that John gives are sparse. Satan will be bound during the millennium. Faithful Christians who have been martyred will be restored to life at the beginning of Christ's reign. They will occupy thrones and participate in Christ's reign. And their condition will be one of blessing, for fear of the second death will be banished and they will function as priests of God and Christ.

Third, the millennial idea actually has only a secondary role in the whole passage. In the first section the emphasis lies on the seizure and confinement of Satan (20:1-3). In the second, the stress is on the resurrection of the martyrs and their reigning with Christ (20:4-6). And in the third, the main theme is Satan's release and subsequent banishment (20:7-10). We must, therefore, be careful to do justice to the whole context, which stresses the blessing associated with "the first resurrection" and the joy of the martyrs who share in it — in contrast to the ultimate doom of their satanic enemy, who is cast out and punished.

Fourth, the passage underscores the theme of divine control and sovereignty. Satan is seized, bound, confined, and eventually thrown out and punished. But untold blessing comes to those who have been totally faithful and have paid for their faithfulness with their lives.

The historical situation is grim, for the seer is speaking about those who have been or will be "beheaded for their testimony to Jesus and for the word of God" (20:4). He refers to these martyrs as those who "had not worshiped the beast or his image," a statement that recalls 13:16-17 and 16:2, where reference is made to those who had the mark of the beast. John's prophecy envisions those who suffered under oppressive Caesars as those "reigning" with Christ (note the use of *basileō* in 5:10; 20:4, 6; 22:5). John seems to be making the point that only the martyrs will be resurrected when he declares that "the rest of the dead" will not be raised until after the thousand years. Some commentators, however, have suggested that faithful believers who had resisted emperor worship but were not martyred may also be included, since these were later termed "confessors" in church history. In any case, "no other biblical evidence supports the idea that martyrs will be raised separately or prior to others" (M. Ashcroft, "Revelation," *Broadman Bible Commentary*, ed. C. J. Allen [Nashville: Broadman, 1972] 12:348). In principle, one might apply the prophecy spiritually to all believers through the centuries who have remained faithful to Christ. The point is made clearly in the words of 2 Tim 2:12, which are pertinent to all Christians who are called to deal with suffering and persecution in any form: "If we endure, we will also reign with him" (cf. Rom 8:17).

What, then, can be said about "the first resurrection" in 20:5-6? The expression includes specifically only those put to death as martyrs. Their lives had literally been "axed" (note the use of the graphic verb *pelekizō*, "behead" [i.e., with a *pelekys* or "ax"], which appears only here in the New Testament). This resurrection, however, must not be confused with the general resurrection spoken about in 20:12-13, in which John depicts multitudes "standing before the throne" to be judged when the books are opened.

The mention of "thrones" and the role of risen martyrs as "priests of God and of Christ" point us back to the visions of Daniel 7. In addition, there are clear echoes of Exod 19:6, with the status of Israel as priests and kings being applied by John the seer to suffering Christians as members of the people of God. In Daniel's vision it was the "saints of the Most High" who were to be given "an everlasting kingdom" (7:27), and so to be closely associated with "one like a son of man" (7:13-14). The kingdom in Daniel is one in which God's people will share God's reign by sitting on thrones. In the Apocalypse of John, of course, this is all given a profoundly christocentric interpretation and introduced to comfort Christians who were facing oppression and possible martyrdom. In sum, therefore, the message of the Apocalypse is that God will make good his promises to his people and give them the blessings of the kingdom.

In John's view there is a special blessing attached to those who are utterly faithful to Christ and who give their lives for his sake. Such people pay the supreme price. Thus the thrust of the presentation in 20:1-10 is a message of reassurance to God's suffering servants who may be facing similar prospects that the resurrection message of the Christian gospel is particularly relevant to them — the cries of the martyrs, so poignantly described in 6:9-11, have indeed been heard by a loving and gracious God.

5. Conclusion

The Apocalypse of John is plainly a "tract for tough times." The seer of Patmos was convinced that he had received a message from God to comfort, inspire, and encourage Christians who were facing difficult times (cf. 1:3, 10-20). John believed that God was the "living" God (cf. 4:9-10; 7:2; 10:6; 15:7), and that those who opposed God's purposes would ultimately be called to account (note his graphic description of the judgment of the dead in 20:11-15). Despite threats of persecution, God must be recognized as the divine judge who has the final word: "Anyone whose name was not found written in the book of life was thrown into the lake of fire" (20:15).

It was important for John's addressees to know that God was still on the "throne" and in charge of affairs (cf. Pss 45:6; 47:8; 89:14; 93:2; 103:19). It is not surprising, therefore, that he mentions this fact again and again (cf. 3:21; 4:2-10; 5:13; 6:16; 7:10, 15; 19:4; 20:11; 21:5). They needed to be reminded that the final outcome was not in doubt. From heaven's perspective, in fact, the victory could already be celebrated. Thus the seventh angel blows his trumpet and the voices of heaven declare: "The kingdom of the world has become the kingdom of our Lord and of his Messiah, and he will reign forever and ever" (11:15).

The ultimate victory is assured, for God is "Almighty" (*pantokratōr*) — which is one of John's favorite expressions for God (cf. 1:8; 4:8; 11:17; 15:3; 16:7, 14; 19:6, 15; 21:22). Accordingly, the Apocalypse is filled with the triumphs of God and of the Lamb over the forces of evil (note particularly chapters 4, 5 and 7; also the numerous hymns incorporated throughout the book). Thus John describes the heavenly worship of the twenty-four elders, who praise God in celebration of his victory and who proclaim that the time of "your [God's] wrath has come — the time for judging the dead and for rewarding your servants, the prophets and saints and all who fear your name, both small and great" (11:18). God will have the final word, and those witnesses who loyally hold the testimony of Jesus will be vindicated.

The great assurance of this grand finale is the fact that God has raised Jesus from the dead. Jesus in his earthly life, ministry, and suffering bore "faithful witness" to the divine purpose, leaving his followers an unblemished model of devotion and courage. More than that, he has conquered death by his resurrection and is now exercising lordship over the potentates of the world (1:4-5). This is the risen Lord whom the seer praises in 1:5b-6:

> To him who loves us and has freed us from our sins by his blood, and has made us to be a kingdom and priests to serve his God and Father — to him be glory and power for ever and ever! Amen.

This is the exalted Lord whose coming again in power and glory is anticipated at the climax of history (1:7) — which, by faith, the seer declares is imminent (cf. the repeated declaration: "See, I am coming soon!" of 22:7, 12; see also 2:16; 3:11; 22:20). In view of the victory that has been accomplished in the resurrection of Jesus from the dead, John declares his unshakable conviction that God, the righteous and omnipotent judge, will take care of all those who are faithful in the face of opposition and persecution — especially those who are faithful to the extent of martyrdom. They will, he proclaims, participate in God's eternal kingdom and so share in the glorious reign of the resurrected, glorified Christ.

Selected Bibliography

Bauckham, Richard J. *The Theology of the Book of Revelation.* Cambridge: Cambridge University Press, 1993.

Beasley-Murray, George R. *The Book of Revelation.* Grand Rapids: Eerdmans, 1981.

Boring, M. Eugene. "The Theology of Revelation." *Interpretation* 40 (1986) 257-69.

Caird, George B. *A Commentary on the Revelation of St. John the Divine.* New York: Harper & Row, 1967.

Erickson, Millard J. *Contemporary Options in Eschatology.* Grand Rapids: Baker, 1985.

Grenz, Stanley J. *The Millennial Maze.* Downers Grove, Ill.: InterVarsity Press, 1992.

Guthrie, Donald. *The Relevance of John's Apocalypse.* Grand Rapids: Eerdmans, 1987.

Kooy, Vernon K. "The Apocalypse and Worship — Some Preliminary Observations." *Reformed Review* 30 (1977) 198-209.

Ladd, George E. *A Commentary on the Revelation of John.* Grand Rapids: Eerdmans, 1972.

Laws, Sophie. *In the Light of the Lamb: Imagery, Parody, and Theology in the Apocalypse of John.* Wilmington, Del.: Michael Glazier, 1988.

Mounce, Robert H. *The Book of Revelation.* 2d ed. Grand Rapids: Eerdmans, 1997.

Thompson, Marianne Meye. "Worship in the Book of Revelation." *Ex Auditu* 8 (1992) 45-54.

Trites, Allison A. *The New Testament Concept of Witness.* New York: Cambridge University Press, 1977.

————. *New Testament Witness in Today's World.* Valley Forge, Penn.: Judson, 1983.

Wall, Robert E. *Revelation.* Peabody, Mass.: Hendrickson, 1991.

Weaver, J. Denny. "Atonement for the Nonconstantinian Church." *Modern Theology* 6 (1990) 307-23.

Index of Subjects

Abaddon, "Place of Destruction," 9, 43
Adam, First and Second, 154-55, 188, 210
Anatman (Anatta), state of "non-self," 4-5
Anthropology,
  dualistic, 6-7, 30, 36, 40, 80, 87, 90, 195, 204-5, 221, 229
  holistic, 42-43, 80-81, 87, 186, 190, 195
Apocalyptic Language/Imagery, 183-84, 190, 196, 198, 201, 214, 278
Apotheosis of the Soul, 70-72, 75, 77
Aqedah Isaac ("Binding/Offering of Isaac"), 257-59
Ascension
  of believers, 157
  of Jesus, 104, 117-19, 130-31, 157, 232, 239, 244-45, 264
Astral Imagery, 92-93, 107
Atman, the eternal "soul," 3

"Beloved Disciple," 130, 132-33, 137-38, 141
Book of the Dead, 23-26, 28
Buddhism, 4-5, 14, 15

Christian Science, 14

Church
  at Corinth, 185-86, 193, 205
  at Philippi, 199
  at Rome, 197, 206-7
  at Thessalonica, 181
Confucianism, 5, 14, 15, 210

Death
  contemporary responses to, 1-3, 13-16
  in Buddhism, 4-5, 14-15
  in Christianity generally, 12-13, 15-16
    in the Fourth Gospel, 141-42
    in Hebrews, 153-54, 249-51, 260-63
    in the Johannine Apocalypse, 273
    in the Pauline corpus, 190, 194-97, 198-200
    in the Synoptic Gospels, 118-19
  in Confucianism, 5, 14-15
  in Egyptian thought, 21-29
  in Greco-Roman philosophical thought, 5-7, 14-15, 51-64, 67
  in Hinduism, 3-4, 14-15
  in Israel/Judaism, 7-11, 15, 42-48, 80-85, 87-90
  of Jesus, 99-103, 105-6, 107, 115-16, 118, 120, 123-24, 126-27, 129, 131,

289

Index of Subjects

INDEX OF SUBJECTS

Index of Modern Authors

293

Index of Scripture and
Other Ancient Literature

INDEX OF SCRIPTURE AND OTHER ANCIENT LITERATURE